T0329865

Gangsters to Governors

Gangsters to Governors

The New Bosses of Gambling in America

DAVID CLARY

RUTGERS UNIVERSITY PRESS
NEW BRUNSWICK, CAMDEN, AND NEWARK,
NEW JERSEY, AND LONDON

Library of Congress Cataloging-in-Publication Data

Names: Clary, David, 1974–
Title: Gangsters to governors : the new bosses of gambling in America / David Clary.
Description: New Brunswick : Rutgers University Press, [2017] | Includes bibliographical references and index.
Identifiers: LCCN 2016053268 | ISBN 9780813584546 (hardback) | ISBN 9780813584553 (e-book (epub)) | ISBN 9780813584560 (e-book (web pdf))
Subjects:LCSH:Gambling—Governmentpolicy—UnitedStates—History.|Gambling— Political aspects—United States—History. | State governments—United States— History. | United States—Politics and government. | BISAC: POLITICAL SCIENCE / Public Policy / Economic Policy. | POLITICAL SCIENCE / Government / State & Provincial. | HISTORY / United States / 20th Century. | HISTORY / United States / 21st Century.
Classification: LCC HV6715 .C53 2017 | DDC 338.4/77950973—dc23
LC record available at https://lccn.loc.gov/2016053268

A British Cataloging-in-Publication record for this book is available from the British Library.

"Atlantic City" by Bruce Springsteen. Copyright © 1982 Bruce Springsteen (Global Music Rights). Reprinted by permission. International copyright secured. All rights reserved.

∞ The paper used in this publication meets the requirements of the American National Standard for Information Sciences—Permanence of Paper for Printed Library Materials, ANSI Z39.48–1992.

www.rutgersuniversitypress.org

Manufactured in the United States of America

For my mother and in memory of my father

There's no such thing as a lucky gambler, there are just the winners and the losers. The winners are those who control the game, the professionals who know what they're doing. All the rest are the suckers.

—Meyer Lansky

Contents

Gangsters to Governors

Bad Bet

NEW JERSEY AND THE REVEL
ATLANTIC CITY FIASCO

*Atlantic City is dying. The question is, are we going to allow the same
doctors who put the patient in this condition to treat the patient?*
—New Jersey governor Chris Christie, discussing his plans in 2010 for a state
takeover of the city's casino and entertainment district

On a bright morning in late March 2012, Chris Christie ambled up to a
microphone placed on an outdoor balcony of the nearly complete luxury
casino-resort Revel Atlantic City. The setting of the New Jersey governor's
brief remarks purposefully showed off a commanding view of the spar-
kling ocean. The sleek skyscraper gleamed in the early spring sunshine
and towered above the far northern end of Atlantic City's famous Boardwalk. Other casinos along the edge of the narrow barrier island looked like
instant relics with their hokey themes and schlocky architecture. At Revel,
the only theme would be modern elegance. Sweeping curves of blue glass
and steel above the porte cochere would welcome visitors into a soaring
atrium flooded with natural light—a refreshing contrast to the usual bun-
ker mentality of casinos. When opened, Revel would boast a dozen gourmet eateries and ten saltwater and freshwater pools for guests who wanted
a change of pace from the beach or casino.

The Boardwalk had never seen anything quite like it, and Christie had
seized on the glitzy project as a lifeline for the struggling city. Decades
earlier, New Jersey had authorized casinos and transformed Atlantic City
into the capital of East Coast gambling. However, nearby states steadily

undercut Atlantic City's monopoly until New Jersey found itself surrounded by clusters of newer, more convenient resorts for the region's gamblers. Atlantic City's gross gambling revenue peaked at $5.2 billion in 2006, the same year neighboring Pennsylvania opened its first legal casino. By 2010, the year Christie took office, Atlantic City's casino revenue had plummeted by nearly a third to $3.6 billion and Pennsylvania was on its way to surpassing New Jersey in casino revenue.[1]

The bumptious son of Newark and former US attorney had made it his mission as governor to revive Atlantic City at seemingly any cost. In 2011 the state seized control of the city's tourism district and charted an ambitious five-year rescue plan for Atlantic City. The largest recipient of government largesse was Revel. Beset by financial problems, construction was halted after key backer Morgan Stanley pulled out in 2010. Christie vowed to get the cranes moving again, save 2,600 construction jobs, and create an additional 5,500 positions once the half-finished complex opened.[2] The state awarded a $2.6 million grant—the biggest of Christie's administration at that point—to train employees at Revel.[3] In early 2011, at Christie's urging, the state approved a $261 million package of tax credits and incentives linked to revenue targets that the project ended up missing, but the move attracted new private investment and restarted construction. "The tax credit showed Wall Street that the state of New Jersey was going to stand behind Atlantic City," said Revel CEO Kevin DeSanctis. "It was a huge boost in financing, and I think it would have been very difficult to do without it."[4] DeSanctis successfully secured $1.15 billion in loans from hedge funds to reboot Revel.[5]

Christie seemed thunderstruck when he toured Revel on that bright spring day in 2012 and soaked in what all of that money created. "You look around and this is really one of the most spectacular resorts I've ever seen, and people are going to be wanting to come to Atlantic City, to come here and experience this," he said. With a note of pride at what the state was able to accomplish, he added, "We're sending a signal to not only just the region but to the entire country that Atlantic City is back."[6] Christie expected Revel to attract large-scale conventions, rehabilitate the Boardwalk, and inspire additional investments in Atlantic City. DeSanctis predicted that fourteen thousand people would enter Revel each day.[7]

The $2.4 billion project officially opened during Memorial Day weekend in 2012—the traditional beginning of Atlantic City's all-important summer season. Revel's Ovation Hall booked pop star Beyoncé for a series of high-voltage shows to give the resort a buzzy start, and its nightclubs targeted a younger, more edgy clientele than Atlantic City was typically known for. Yet something about Revel seemed off. Its cavernous interior spaces, endless escalators, and icy chandeliers conveyed more of a feeling of hollowness than grandeur. The expensive furniture in Revel's lounges and waiting areas seemed more like austere museum pieces than places where real people would want to hang out. Las Vegas or even Manhattan—without the casino, of course—would have been a better fit for the forty-seven-story resort than the gritty Boardwalk. Revel's sheen of wealth and artistic pretentions were incongruous with the weedy lots, cracked sidewalks, and boarded-up houses only a few blocks away.

Revel's noisy opening masked the stubborn fact that it glided through summer without making a profit. Then Superstorm Sandy struck the Northeast in late October, a terrible reminder of how quickly the shore's blessing of geography could become a curse. Superstorm Sandy didn't hit Atlantic City nearly as hard as the state's other shore towns, but it did darken Atlantic City's already gloomy financial picture. As the twelfth casino in the cramped city, Revel had joined an overcrowded field clamoring for a shrinking revenue pie. Something would have to give, and it turned out to be Revel.

In early 2013, less than a year after opening, Revel entered bankruptcy protection and managed to wriggle out of it in two months, reporting a staggering $111 million loss in its first year. That summer Revel stirred up media attention with its promise to refund slot machine losses for players, but the desperate gambit was too late to make a difference. Revel filed for bankruptcy again in June 2014 and failed to find a buyer. The project that just two years earlier was heralded by the governor and others as Atlantic City's savior closed in September 2014.[8] A month later a global commercial property company won a bid for Revel at the fire-sale price of $110 million but backed out. An eccentric property investor from Florida named Glenn Straub took ownership in 2015 for $82 million—about 3 percent of what it cost to build Revel. His efforts to rebrand and reopen the resort have fallen into a miasma of court hearings and disputes with the city over property maintenance issues.

Atlantic City's annus horribilis of 2014 saw the closure of three other Atlantic City casinos: the Atlantic Club, the Showboat, and Trump Plaza—ripping out the heart out of the Boardwalk, eliminating more than seven thousand jobs, and placing Atlantic City's future in jeopardy.

The story of Revel's colossal failure illustrates how intertwined the fates of governors and gambling have become. Revenue-dependent states and cities lobby for more casinos, more slot machines, more table games, bigger lottery prizes, and higher betting limits by pitching overly optimistic economic forecasts to voters. In the case of Revel, the consequences of an overreaching governor were the waste of state resources and precious private capital on a doomed project in a declining gambling market. Christie's visions of Revel as a gold mine for the state and a beacon for an Atlantic City turnaround were as evanescent as sandcastles on the shore.

Governors today are under intense pressure to maintain public services without raising taxes, which is why so many are latching onto the "painless tax" of gambling as a quick and easy budget fix. More gambling means governments can rake in tens of billions of dollars in tax revenue from lotteries, casinos, and other forms of wagering each year. When neighboring states ramp up their gambling portfolios, they saturate markets and cannibalize profits as in Atlantic City. Today every state except for Hawaii and Utah has some form of legal gambling. Nationwide, roughly 890,000 gambling machines entice players, more than two hundred thousand retail outlets sell lottery tickets in forty-four states, and about one thousand tribal and commercial casinos stretch from Florida to California.[9] Gambling has an enormous economic footprint: US casinos directly employ 734,000 workers, and the gaming industry supports more than 1.7 million jobs—more than the airline industry.[10] Gambling's total annual economic impact is estimated at $240 billion in a 2014 report—equivalent to the combined budgets of New York and Texas—and contributes $38 billion in tax revenues to all levels of government.[11]

As legalized gambling continues its march across America, governors are in the curious position of managing enterprises that had long been the dominion of gangsters. Their embrace of gambling is a reversal of the traditional view of government that gambling needed to be suppressed for the good of society. The moral arguments of clergymen and social reformers influenced public perceptions for more than a century, nearly extinguishing legal gambling in the United States. However, banning gambling produced the worst of all possible worlds for governments: States received no revenue from a flourishing underground activity, corruption crippled local law enforcement, and, worst of all, crime syndicates asserted control of gambling. Betting poolrooms linked to racetracks, casinos (legal and illegal), and the numbers rackets all fell under the sway of gangsters.

When Nevada became the first state in modern America to legalize most forms of gambling in 1931, official oversight was exceptionally weak. Out-of-state crime syndicates secured a foothold in Las Vegas that lasted for decades. Benjamin "Bugsy" Siegel and his unsavory partners received a gambling license for the lavish Flamingo casino on the fledgling Las Vegas Strip because the state did not require an investigation into the background or the character of applicants. If anything, the gangster was welcomed as an investor. Lester Ben "Benny" Binion picked up a license to operate Binion's Horseshoe in Las Vegas even though he was under indictment for running an illegal gambling racket in Dallas and had been arrested twice on murder charges.

By the time state politicians felt roused enough to confront the threat, organized crime interests had become the masters of Las Vegas and the gambling underworld. It was only when the fight against organized crime became a federal issue that Nevada strengthened its authority, ultimately opening a path to mainstream corporate ownership that loosened the mob's hold on casinos.

Until the 1960s legalized gambling in modern America was limited to Nevada and scattered locations in other states that allowed pari-mutuel betting at racetracks. Two decades ago only Nevada and Atlantic City operated officially sanctioned casinos. As this book shows, one form of gambling led to others being legalized. When states approved pari-mutuel wagering on horse races, it undercut arguments against establishing lotteries. Once governors got a taste of lottery revenue, it set off a stampede for more. State after state lifted bans on gambling and approved dockside casinos, riverboat casinos, big-city casinos, small-stakes casinos in old mining towns, and casino-resort complexes on tribal reservations.

Today state and local governments wield extraordinary powers to direct the expansion of the gambling industry. They have the authority to decide how many commercial casino licenses will be granted, select who will get them, approve where the casinos will be built, spell out what games will be played, and specify the number of slot machines. States also exercise considerable leverage in negotiating agreements with Indian tribes that want to operate gambling halls on their reservations.

On the whole, governments were right to legalize many forms of wagering as a concession to reality and as a tool to fight organized crime. Through their efforts, they transformed gambling from a shadowy element of the underworld into a legitimate business enterprise and a socially acceptable form of entertainment. Governors did this by deftly co-opting the methods of mobsters: State-run lotteries mimic the numbers rackets; government-authorized off-track betting parlors and casino sportsbooks resemble old-fashioned illegal poolrooms; and corporate-owned casinos operate in much the same way as when they were controlled by crime syndicates. By ensuring the integrity of the games, governments encouraged greater participation and more money for themselves.

Some of the old habits of prohibition have persisted in online gambling and sports wagering. In the first few decades of the twentieth century, underworld rivals had fought to control the flow of racing information over telephone and telegraph wires. Congress passed the Wire Act in 1961, which prohibited the interstate transmission of betting information. The ban was expanded and applied to the Internet. In 2011 the Justice Department cracked down on online poker operators, alleging that they were involved in fraud and money laundering. The move dealt a blow to online poker it has never fully recovered from. A handful of states are gingerly entering the Internet gambling arena to mostly disappointing results.

Sports betting is largely illegal in the United States because of a 1992 federal law that has been as ineffective and counterproductive as were previous antigambling measures. Daily fantasy sports companies like DraftKings and FanDuel market their "games of skill" that seem quite like games of chance. The majority of Americans who want to bet on NFL games or play real-money online poker must consort with shady bookies or take their chances with dicey offshore websites. And just like in the past, gangsters benefit from the tide of illegal money.

Legal or not, gambling has always been deeply ingrained in the national character. The exploits of professional gamblers on Mississippi River steamboats, in gold rush mining camps, and in the saloons of the Old West are the stuff of legend; Powerball winners and multimillion-dollar poker champions are the folk heroes of today. Governments wrestled for generations over how to respond to such a popular activity until belatedly deciding that it's far more sensible to legalize, regulate, and tax all forms of gambling than to ban them.

Governors are now the unquestioned masters of gambling, but their enthusiastic embrace of more casinos and richer lotteries is tipping the business out of balance. The question of how government should handle sports wagering and online gambling sets up a fascinating catch-22: Keep the barriers and risk losing ground to organized crime and missing out on revenue, or remove them and put governors in command of yet more forms of betting and accept the likelihood that they will overreach. The hurdles to online gambling and sports wagering in America seem certain to fall someday. State and federal leaders will need to adopt smart, realistic policies on these and other gambling issues to keep up with trends and stay ahead of underworld interests. But how long will they wait?

PART I

Dens of Thieves

GOVERNMENT MUSCLES OUT THE MOB

CHAPTER 1

The Sport of Kings

HORSE RACING AND THE
DARK POWER OF THE WIRE

As has been done with liquor it will be found that the best public policy is to regulate [gambling] and to obtain a revenue for the state.
—Richard A. Canfield, Gilded Age casino proprietor
in New York City and Saratoga Springs

John Morrissey was a poor Irish immigrant, a street thug, and a bare-knuckled boxing champion—an unlikely background for his later life as a high-society horseman, entrepreneur of posh casinos, and member of Congress. Yet somehow he was all of those things, and his influence is felt to this day as the founder of one of the sport's leading venues. For many states, horse racing was the first time in the modern era that they had a piece of the action in gambling, laying the foundation for many more legalized games of chance. Morrissey's criminal past also showed the challenges of overcoming gambling's origins of gangsterism.

Born in 1831, Morrissey endured a hard-knock boyhood in Troy, New York, marked by violence and lawlessness. He taught himself to read and write in an Albany penitentiary while serving a two-month sentence for burglary and assault.[1] Upon release, Morrissey moved to New York City where he earned the nickname "Old Smoke" when he thrashed a fellow hoodlum even while Morrissey's flesh burned from being rolled onto hot coals from an overturned stove.[2]

Such tales of his remarkable strength and stamina would become legend. When he was barely out of his teens, Morrissey traveled to gold rush–era California, where he honed his gambling skills. He fattened his bankroll by fleecing dupes at the tables. Once, a victim of one of his swindles challenged Morrissey to a duel and allowed him to choose his weapon. When Morrissey appeared at the appointed time carrying two meat cleavers, his mortified would-be duelist wisely backed down.[3]

Morrissey channeled his rage into the boxing ring, winning his first professional bout near San Francisco in 1852 and pocketing a $4,000 purse and side bet winnings of $1,000.[4] He returned to the East Coast and defeated champion Yankee Sullivan in a gruesome match lasting thirty-seven rounds, claiming the heavyweight crown. Morrissey retired from the ring undefeated after successfully defending his title against challenger John C. Heenan in Canada.

Throughout his boxing days, Morrissey was a fearsome enforcer for the Tammany Hall political machine in New York. He led the Dead Rabbits gang in the notorious Five Points slum dramatized in Martin Scorsese's film *Gangs of New York*.[5] Morrissey's toughest opponent in the street wars was William "Bill the Butcher" Poole, also an accomplished pugilist and Bowery Boys gang leader who despised immigrants and Roman Catholics. In 1855 the feud boiled over at a saloon when Morrissey pulled out his pistol and Poole brandished his knife. Police broke up the fight, but Morrissey's goons returned later that night and shot Poole, who died two weeks later. No one was convicted, and Morrissey was untouched by the crime.

Morrissey parlayed his fame and political protection into a lucrative career as the city's top gambling impresario. He bought and sold a succession of swanky gambling houses popular with the city's leading politicians and other free-spending sportsmen. Morrissey netted a profit of $1 million in just five years managing the plush casino at 8 Barclay Street in Lower Manhattan before selling it and operating another establishment uptown, further expanding his wealth.[6]

He took his gambling expertise upstate to the bucolic resort town of Saratoga Springs, a summer playground for the wealthy who reveled in the town's soothing mineral springs. Morrissey's gambling house opened in

1861 and enjoyed the patronage of many of the same captains of industry who thronged Morrissey's casinos in Manhattan.

Morrissey sought to capitalize on horse racing's popularity and believed that a first-class racetrack would lend further appeal to Saratoga as a summertime destination. Morrissey and tycoons such as Cornelius Vanderbilt financed a racetrack built about a mile from the center of town. Organized thoroughbred races were conducted on former trotting grounds for a four-day meeting in 1863; the following year, the turfmen purchased land across the street to build Saratoga Race Course. Tellingly, Morrissey's name was not officially listed as an incorporator even though he was the driving force in the track's creation. His raffish background was apparently too much to take for some of the well-bred horsemen.

Saratoga Race Course remains America's oldest active racetrack and is one of the sport's most hallowed sites. Even today, it still retains much of its old-time charm. Asked how to get to Saratoga from New York City, famed sportswriter Red Smith wrote: "You drive north for about 175 miles, turn left on Union Avenue and go back one hundred years."[7]

———

Through the years, thanks to the patronage of the elite and the participation of the many, horse racing won a measure of respectability that helped it survive waves of crackdowns on gambling. Even so, racetracks nearly disappeared from the American landscape when reformers gained the upper hand in the early nineteenth century. Illegal off-track betting and the corrupt system of relaying racing information dominated the scene until an automated system of organizing wagers enabled governments to legalize betting.

Ever since there have been at least two horse owners in the same place, racing and gambling have been intertwined. In 1693 two Virginians bet money and four thousand pounds of tobacco on the speed of their respective sprinters.[8] Smaller bets were more common. The South's rigid social hierarchy barred the lower classes from participating in the races. A Virginia court in 1674 imposed a fine on a tailor for having the temerity to enter his mare in a contest, calling racing "a sport only for Gentlemen."[9] Nonetheless, the colorful spectacles drew crowds consisting of common people and servants who bet informally among themselves.

For the Puritans in New England, racing horses was just one of many activities considered to be unproductive diversions and thus contrary to God's law. The Plymouth Colony in Massachusetts levied fines (or, if unpaid, one hour in the stocks) on anyone caught racing horses on the main street or near meeting houses.[10] Other states thought of racing as a public nuisance and prohibited betting. In Philadelphia, official warnings were roundly ignored; the racing thoroughfare Sassafras Street was dubbed Race Street, a name that persists in Center City.[11]

The expense of raising thoroughbreds motivated horsemen to organize more races and bigger purses to defray costs. That meant building large racetracks that could appeal to the masses as well as the wealthy. In New York, a band of millionaires attempted to overcome antiracing sentiment by organizing associations and constructing luxurious tracks. A leader in the movement was Wall Street financier Leonard W. Jerome. Along with friends William R. Travers and August Belmont, Jerome founded the American Jockey Club in 1894 and set out these high-minded goals: "To promote the improvement of horses, to elevate the public taste in sports of the turf, and to become an authority on racing matters in the country."[12]

The turfmen purchased land in Westchester County and built Jerome Park, a course complete with a giant ballroom, skating rink, and a lavish clubhouse. Membership in the Jockey Club was limited to the wealthy and powerful, who met in the club's downtown Manhattan headquarters to trade racing gossip and make wagers. Jerome Park's first meeting in September 1866 attracted figures such as Gen. Ulysses S. Grant, fresh from his triumph on the battlefields of the Civil War. The track won praise for its clean approach to racing. "Nothing goes on at Jerome Park which the purest-minded person could object to," wrote a New York newspaper. "There is no bribing of jockeys, no 'dosing' of horses with laudanum. Never did the history of racing in any country begin with so fair a page."[13]

John Morrissey's Saratoga was a destination racetrack that appealed to the rich and the lower classes. With Saratoga Race Course proceeds pouring ever more money into Morrissey's pockets, he set out to build a casino in the Spa City that would exceed in grandeur his gilded gambling rooms in Manhattan.

In 1870 Morrissey erected a graceful brick building in the center of town and transformed the surrounding swampland into elegantly landscaped grounds. The furnishings inside were even more elaborate. Morrissey spent more than $100,000 on wall tapestries, linen draperies, and fine-grained walnut furniture with "J. M." monogrammed in gold leaf.[14] Roulette and faro—a popular card game of the time—were offered in the stately drawing rooms on the ground floor; high-stakes gamblers convened in private rooms upstairs. The casino, known then as the Club House, catered exclusively to the out-of-town crowd: no residents or women were allowed in the gambling rooms.[15]

After it was expanded to keep up with demand, a visiting writer compared the gambling palace and Saratoga to the famous Baden-Baden spa resort in Germany. Saratoga visitors would spend the day attending the races or taking in the waters at a fashionable spa and later let off steam around gambling tables in the town's hotels and billiard parlors. Morrissey's gambling house was a favorite spot of the elite of Wall Street. In Saratoga, Morrissey presided as a prince in his "white flannel suit, huge diamond rings, and pin containing brilliants of the first water, and of immense size."[16] Morrissey didn't drink and talked little, but his imposing stature and reputation spoke loudly enough.

Morrissey's alliances with powerful men and his own political standing ensured that his gambling enterprises could proceed even though gambling was technically illegal in Saratoga Springs. An observer noted that Morrissey "is liked in Saratoga because he divides the profits of his sinning with the good people of the village with a generous hand."[17]

In 1866 the Tammany-backed Morrissey won a seat in Congress and held it for two terms. Morrissey's record as a legislator was undistinguished; he reportedly ran a faro bank while he was in Washington. During a floor debate, the ex-boxer's pugnaciousness shone through when he threatened to fight disagreeable House members with his bare hands.

The last years of Morrissey's life were difficult. Although he lost a fortune in bad investments on Wall Street and endured a falling out with Tammany's William "Boss" Tweed, he did win a seat in the New York state Senate after leaving Congress. Morrissey attempted to move back to his hometown of Troy and build a house in the fashionable part of town, but his prospective neighbors were wary of the gambler and bought the property he wanted. The snub infuriated Morrissey, who got even by purchasing a nearby piece of land and building a soap factory that emitted streams of fumes.[18] Wealthy residents bought him out just to shut down the factory.[19]

Morrissey died in 1878 at the age of forty-seven; an estimated twenty thousand people turned out to witness his funeral procession through Troy. Morrissey's Club House ended up in the hands of Richard A. Canfield, a wealthy art collector and casino operator in New York City.[20] Canfield, a man of taste who gorged on fine food and drink and took to wearing a corset to constrain his girth, added to Morrissey's elegant handiwork by installing a first-class restaurant and dining room to lure high-rollers like the Whitneys and the Vanderbilts. The extravagance of the restaurant was matched by Canfield's office at the Club House, which featured a splendid $10,000 Tiffany window and a safe containing $1 million in cash for emergencies.[21]

Canfield's casino interests ran afoul of reformers who were persistent enough to have a chilling effect on gambling in Saratoga. Among them was the famous reporter Nellie Bly, who visited Saratoga in the summer of 1894 to see the resort town for herself. What she found there shocked her sensibilities. "Saratoga is the wickedest spot in the United States," she began her dispatch published in the August 19, 1894, edition of the *New York World*. "Crime is holding a convention there and vice is enjoying a festival such as it never dared approach before." Bly, who had achieved renown for her trip around the world in seventy-two days, was troubled that women and children were feverishly betting amid scenes of decadence at the racetrack.

Weary of being hassled by authorities, Canfield closed the Club House for good after the summer of 1907 and sold it at a loss to the village of Saratoga Springs, which today operates the "Canfield Casino" as a history museum and rents out its gilded rooms for special events.

––––––

The growing fervor for racing after the Civil War challenged racetrack owners to develop a betting system that would set up fair odds and process wagers on a mass scale. At Saratoga, Morrissey had paid himself a flat commission by acting as a broker for high-stakes bettors who wanted to make head-to-head wagers. He had also managed an auction pool in which each horse in a race would be put up to bid, and the highest bidder would collect all of the money in the pool if his or her horse won. Morrissey deducted a percentage for himself from the total amount wagered. According to horse-racing expert Richard Sasuly, the system had several problems: favorite horses typically went to the wealthiest bettors; low-stakes gamblers were usually unable to bet their desired amounts on their horses of choice; and the odds were not calculated.[22]

The auction pool system had its roots when wagering was a private affair between gentlemen. They were usually acquaintances of the owners of the horses and knew how they were trained and bred. Such a primitive method of placing bets couldn't last if the sport hoped to keep up with its broadening appeal. For better or worse, bookmaking emerged as the dominant way to handle wagers.

The first professional who kept a "book" of wagers in America set up shop in Philadelphia in 1866, processing bets on horse races as well as cricket matches and regattas.[23] Soon racetracks reserved space for betting enclosures or rings where bookmakers took bets of all sizes based on odds posted on blackboards or shouted over the heads of the milling crowds. The increased participation created larger purses and higher profits for track operators, who charged bookmakers a fee for the privilege of taking bets on racetrack grounds.

Racing's popularity surged with the openings of Saratoga and Jerome Park. Other big-time tracks popped up across the nation: in 1870, Monmouth Park in Long Branch, New Jersey, and Pimlico in Baltimore, home of the Preakness Stakes; in 1872, the Fair Grounds in New Orleans; and in 1875, Churchill Downs in Louisville, which ran its first Kentucky Derby the same year. Even the nation's business took a back seat to racing fever. On October 24, 1877, Congress adjourned so members could catch a special train bound for the "Great Sweepstakes" at Pimlico. Racing was then by far the nation's most popular spectator sport.[24] Most important, it enjoyed the blessing of government, unlike other forms of gambling.

However, the accelerating pace of expansion and the sport's lack of a central governing authority pushed racing to the breaking point. The number of tracks multiplied into the hundreds, and they ran more races with more horses to maximize gate receipts and bookmaking concessions. Each track devised its own rules and racing calendar, and there was no supervision of breeding.[25] One track in New Jersey promoted a continuous 176-day meeting that included Christmas Day; another in Illinois ran 364 days a year.[26] Inclement weather was no reason to call off a race: records from the 1880s show that meets ran in New Jersey despite a "blinding snow storm" at one track and a dense fog that obscured the horses at another.[27]

At too many tracks, racing was less about the horses and more about the gambling. Many track attendees were there solely to bet and "didn't know a thoroughbred from a jackass," in the vivid words of a horse-racing historian.[28] A New York newspaper estimated that about sixty bookmakers were operating at the Brighton Beach racetrack with a gross handle—the total amount wagered—of more than $1 million per day in 1894.[29]

Stories of famous "plungers," or big bettors, livened up newspaper accounts of horse races. Among the best known was John Warne "Bet-a-Million" Gates, a man who eagerly bet on anything that moved—literally. One time while riding a train, Gates laid a huge bet on which raindrop would reach the bottom of a window first, winning $22,000.[30] "For me there's no fun in betting just a few thousand. I want to lay down enough to hurt the other fellow if he loses and enough to hurt me if I lose," he remarked.[31]

Gates, who made his fortune in barbed wire manufacturing and stock market speculation, loved playing the ponies and spent summers—and loads of money—in Saratoga Springs. One day in 1902 Gates lost nearly $400,000 at the track. That evening, he dined at Canfield's luxurious restaurant and repaired to the Club House's gambling parlors to recoup his losses. By 10:00 p.m., Gates had lost another $150,000 at the faro table where the top limit was $5,000. Gates tracked down Canfield and asked that the limits be doubled. Canfield agreed, replying, "Are you sure that's enough?" Gates then went on an incredible run, betting between $5,000 and $10,000 on each turn of the cards. By 2:00 a.m., Gates was even; by dawn, when he quit, he was $150,000 ahead at the tables but still about $250,000 down overall counting his racetrack losses.[32]

Another notorious gambler of the era was George E. Smith, better known by the nickname "Pittsburg Phil." Smith obsessively studied everything about the races—the jockeys, the trainers, the winning times, the condition of the track, and the quality of horses—and assembled the data into detailed charts to guide his wagering. Smith was soon rich enough to buy his own horses. He believed that one of his purchases, King Cadmus, was severely underrated and ran the bay colt in highly competitive races to hide his true ability.[33] In 1891 King Cadmus's training improved the horse to the point that Smith had the confidence to enter him in a stakes race he felt the horse could win. Pittsburg Phil dispatched his confederates to quietly place big bets on King Cadmus to win the contest at New York's Sheepshead Bay. Smith coolly watched the race through his binoculars as the horses charged around the track into the homestretch. King Cadmus edged out his competitors and netted $143,000 for his owner—the biggest win the sport had ever seen. The former cork cutter from Pennsylvania was a rare example of a gambler who died a wealthy man; his mother commissioned a statue of her son clasping a racing program to adorn the top of his grand mausoleum in a Pittsburgh cemetery.[34]

The huge amounts of money at stake made it extremely tempting for bookmakers to cut corners and cheat to avoid getting cleaned out by the likes of "Pittsburgh Phil." Jockeys were bribed to pull back the reins on a horse during a race and trainers were paid off to manipulate their horses to ensure they would lose.[35] Bookies hired "touts" to roam the grounds, sidle up to bettors, and dispense rumors masquerading as inside information from the stables.[36] The false "tips" were doled out to steer wagerers in a direction that benefited the bookmaker. If a favored horse lost in a fixed race, the bookmaker stood to gain a handsome profit.

In 1894 a group of owners and breeders formed the American Jockey Club in New York to impose order. The club licensed jockeys, trainers, and horses; organized the racing calendar; administered *The American Stud Book*, the official listing of thoroughbreds; and appointed racing officials.[37] Tracks that broke the rules were branded as outlaws, and horse owners were discouraged from racing at such places. The Jockey Club's standards did bring cohesion to a wild sport, but it failed to stop reformers who viewed bookmakers as a pestilence on the people and nearly abolished horse racing in the United States.

———

State after state banned bookmaking and prohibited other forms of gambling as part of a nationwide temperance movement. Many racetracks had no choice but to close because they depended on fees they charged bookmakers who took bets on racetrack grounds. A sport that expanded too quickly contracted almost as fast. By 1908 the number of racetracks in the United States plummeted to 25 from 314 roughly a decade earlier.[38]

In New York, the victory of law professor Charles Evans Hughes over publishing magnate William Randolph Hearst in the 1906 race for governor extended the gains made by reformers. With Hughes's encouragement, the New York legislature approved a bill in 1908 that banned on- and off-track wagering on horse races. Racing and scattered betting continued; a subsequent law spelled out that racetrack owners were subject to fines and imprisonment if wagering occurred on or near their grounds. All tracks in New York—including Belmont and Saratoga—shut down in 1911 and 1912; some never reopened.[39] In 1911 only six states permitted betting at racetracks.[40] With few places left to race in America, thoroughbreds by the thousands were shipped overseas, and many jockeys and trainers moved to friendlier pastures in Europe.[41]

A system of betting imported from France saved horse racing from extinction in the United States. In 1865 Paris perfume shop owner Pierre Oller was unhappy with the odds offered by bookmakers. At his store, bettors bought a ticket for their favorite horse in a particular race; after taking a percentage of the pot for himself, Oller paid winners in proportion to the number of tickets sold.[42] The system, which he called "parimutuel" (or "mutual stake"), allowed bettors to wager against each other and determine the odds based on the amount bet on each horse. It quickly caught on in France and was the only legal form of wagering at the nation's racetracks. Inventors in other countries devised tabulating machines that improved the speed and accuracy of totaling bets.

In the United States, bookmakers correctly sized up the pari-mutuel machines as a mortal threat to their livelihoods. They feared that they would become obsolete middlemen since the bettors themselves would determine odds, not the bookies with their unreliable chalkboards. At Saratoga, Morrissey used the system to handle five-dollar wagers as early as 1872, and it appeared at other courses in the 1870s. Churchill Downs managers purchased several versions of the machines and put them into service in 1878, but they baffled many horse players accustomed to auction pools and bookmakers.[43] The bookies pushed back, and by 1890 they were back on racetrack grounds leveraging their personal relationships with bettors. While the machines gathered dust in deep storage, the climate for legalized gambling darkened and the track itself was in financial peril.

In 1902 Louisville native and tailor Matt J. Winn joined with civic power brokers to buy Churchill Downs for $40,000 in the hope of reversing its decline. Winn, a moon-faced salesman with a flair for publicity and bonhomie, loved the sport and cherished Churchill Downs and its famous twin spires. At age thirteen, he had watched the first Kentucky Derby in

1875 from the seat of his father's grocery wagon, taking in the crowds, color, and enthusiasm from the infield.[44] (Winn lived long enough to witness the seventy-fifth "Run for the Roses" in 1949, never missing one in between.[45]) When it came to business, Winn was no sentimentalist. In the year after Winn and his group took command, Churchill Downs showed a profit for the first time in its history.

Still, even Louisville wasn't immune to the nationwide assault on horse racing. In 1908 the city imposed a ban on bookmaking just before the running of that year's Kentucky Derby.[46] Winn knew that the prohibition would devastate the track: "Without some form of wagering to offer to the public, we might just as well close the gates," he wrote in his memoir, "because the zest in racing is supplied by the fact that a man, first, can back his opinion as to the merits of the horse of his choice, and then watch his horse trying to justify that faith."[47] Winn and his cronies discovered an obscure municipal provision that permitted "French pools" or pari-mutuel wagering. The race was on to harvest as many of the machines as possible before derby day. One rusty machine was uncovered in a Churchill Downs storehouse, another turned up in a pawn shop, and four others were scavenged.[48] Mechanics repaired the battered machines in time for the Kentucky Derby, and Winn went to great lengths to educate bettors about the system.

Winn's long institutional memory paid off. The machines handled more than $67,000 on derby day, five times more than the bets placed with bookmakers the year before.[49] The track kept a percentage of the total as a fee for handling the money, and winners were paid according to odds that all could see. As the ban on bookmaking persisted, the pari-mutuel machines became more popular, especially when the track cut the minimum ticket price from five dollars to the now-standard two dollars. Winn's innovations—including wrangling wealthy owners like August Belmont and Harry Payne Whitney to enter their horses in the Kentucky Derby—raised the race's profile and made the first Saturday in May the most notable date on the racing calendar.[50] By exclusively using pari-mutuel betting, he also showed that tracks could prosper without on-site bookmakers.

However, the manually operated wagering machines were prone to inaccuracies. Johns Hopkins–trained engineer Harry L. Straus was tired of being shortchanged at the track and believed that there had to be a faster, more automated way to calculate odds and payouts. He helped invent the electrically operated "totalisator," a betting system that handled thousands of bets accurately, transmitted the tabulations to a display board, and printed tickets for customers. In 1930, Pimlico in Baltimore became the first US racetrack to install his equipment; Hialeah near Miami and Arlington Park near Chicago followed soon after. The electronic indicators in the infields constantly updated the odds on each horse in a race, noted the order they finished, and displayed payout amounts. Tracks clamored for them once they noticed the surge in betting wherever the devices operated. It certainly helped that the totalisators were practically error-free: in 1940 about $375 million passed through the machines with a combined error of less than $5,000.[51] Straus's breakthrough made him a millionaire and enabled him to buy an estate in Maryland where his thoroughbreds had ample room to roam.

The long-delayed acceptance of pari-mutuel wagering was the key that unlocked the gate to official approval of racetrack gambling. States embraced the system because it automatically computed the odds and payouts, eliminating the nettlesome on-track bookmakers. The move boosted public confidence in the honesty of horse racing, encouraged more wagering and bigger purses, and, above all, promised a reliable revenue stream for governments. Kentucky and Maryland were among the first states to authorize pari-mutuels and take a fixed percentage of the handle. For the first time in modern America, states directly benefited from gambling.

Governments didn't just take the money; they were also becoming partners with the tracks. States set up racing commissions and boards that worked with tracks on racing standards, organized the calendar to avoid overlapping dates, and licensed personnel.[52] During the Great Depression, government involvement accelerated because states were desperate for any source of new revenue. In 1933 alone, ten states approved pari-mutuel wagering, with California the most significant entry into the field. Picturesque Santa Anita Park in Los Angeles County opened in 1934; Bing Crosby was a major investor in the Del Mar Racetrack, the place "where the turf meets the surf" north of San Diego that hosted its first race in 1937; and Hollywood Park welcomed fans in 1938, the year the exploits of Seabiscuit and War Admiral riveted the nation. These celebrity-studded sporting palaces thrived in the glow of their sudden legitimacy.

———

Horse racing was back from the abyss, but this time most of the real action took place away from the track, illegally. Racing fans put down bets at handbooks, which were side businesses in neighborhood spots like cigar stores, barbershops, or saloons. Bettors who were unable to attend a race or who lived too far from a track could place wagers and follow the results in crowded urban "poolrooms." Thousands of these poolrooms—so named because they hosted betting "pools"—were connected by a nationwide network of telephone and telegraph wires that transmitted racing information. News about track conditions, late scratches, and jockey assignments helped gamblers make their decisions. Poolrooms displayed blackboards listing the odds at races at an array of tracks, and wagers were accepted in person or over the phone. An announcer dramatically narrated the race. Smoke and rumors filled the rooms, and betting slips papered the floors. They were low-tech versions of modern-day casino sportsbooks where goggle-eyed wagerers follow the action on multiple screens and odds boards.

States that had gained a foothold in on-track betting were overmatched by the popularity of off-track gambling. There were simply too many handbooks and poolrooms that could afford the price of law enforcement protection. One operator of a Manhattan poolroom paid $100 for rent and handed out $1,200 a month to police and antivice societies. Even after paying other bills, he cleared nearly $8,000 a month during racing season.[53]

With fortunes at stake, battles erupted over who would collect the racing information and control its dissemination across the wires. In the late nineteenth century, Western Union held a monopoly on transmitting racing news. The company dispatched employees to tracks to relay race odds and report on the contests as they occurred. Western Union leased telegraph tickers to horse parlors and bookmakers. The volume of racing-related messages generated big profits for the company, which argued that it had an obligation to carry all messages even though some ended up in illegal poolrooms. Under public pressure, Western Union stopped using their agents to gather racing information in 1904, which crimped the supply of up-to-date track information to poolrooms.

Other companies rushed in to quench the thirst of gamblers. Two of the largest were the Metropolitan News Company of Louisville and the Payne Telegraph Service of Cincinnati. They leased wires from Western Union to spread racing information gathered by their own networks of track correspondents. Chicago gambling kingpin Mont Tennes launched a rival company, purchased the Payne service, and absorbed it into his innocent-sounding General News Bureau in 1910. Tennes ruthlessly positioned it as the dominant player in the race wire, particularly in the Midwest.

Meanwhile, another businessman in Chicago who would one day monopolize horse-racing information was accumulating his own empire. Moses "Moe" Annenberg, a poor Jewish immigrant from Prussia whose family settled in Chicago when he was a boy, entered the city's newspaper circulation war. Newsboys fought on street corners over sales territory, and newspapers hired thugs to thrash newsstands, hijack delivery trucks, dump bundles of rival papers in rivers, and clobber uncooperative agents. Too often, the violence turned deadly: twenty-seven newsagents were killed during Chicago's newspaper wars, which were proving grounds for Prohibition-era gangsters.[54]

Annenberg and his older brother, Max, engaged in these turf battles as employees of the *Chicago Tribune*; they later switched to the *Examiner* when the upstart Hearst paper offered them more money. Moe managed legions of newspaper boys who fought for dominance in the city's South

Side and suburbs. Max had more of an appetite for brawling than Moe, who set off for the more placid city of Milwaukee to launch a newspaper circulation agency. There he reinvested his expanding profits in other businesses and real estate. Annenberg was hired as the publisher of a Milwaukee newspaper later bought by Hearst, which summoned him to New York to direct circulation for the nationwide chain's publications.

Moe Annenberg, a slender man who peered solemnly through small, wire-rimmed glasses propped up on his narrow face, was already a millionaire by his early forties when he purchased the *Daily Racing Form*, a publication that would be his introduction into the world of horse racing. Annenberg, not a gambler and with no particular interest in racing, simply viewed it as a good investment. When Annenberg and his partners took ownership of the *Daily Racing Form* in 1922, the horse-racing industry was still recovering from years of governmental hostility. Still, the underperforming publication was considered a vital source of track information for horse players. Annenberg applied the bare-knuckled business practices learned during his Chicago days to undercut local competitors and expand the publication's reach. He made back his initial investment in his first year of ownership and bought out his partners for $2.25 million, which would end up being a bargain.[55]

When states relaxed their restrictions on gambling at racetracks, it was a boon to the fortunes of the *Daily Racing Form*. The paper provided a detailed preview of every race at every major racetrack in the country, and Annenberg used his personal wealth and clout as a top Hearst executive to muscle out or buy up competing tip sheets. The *Daily Racing Form* was—and remains today—an essential purchase for bettors on and off tracks. It became so successful that Annenberg left his executive post at Hearst to devote his full energies to assembling his own publishing kingdom.

Annenberg acted quickly to add an electronic monopoly of racing information to his printed one. In 1927 he purchased a sizable interest in the General News Bureau from Tennes, the aging Chicago handbook czar whose reign was under siege from a new generation of gangsters led by

Al Capone. Annenberg was playing a dangerous game by getting involved with the race wire. Although sending racing information over the wire was technically legal, the bulk of the wire's customers were illegal poolrooms. Annenberg and his lawyers took solace in that legitimate news organizations also subscribed to the wire. Moe's son, Walter, later explained the rationale: "They told him racing results were news and that he would be collecting and disseminating news. . . . He wasn't gambling. Race results are news."[56]

It was a case of wishful thinking. Running a race wire was far different than managing a newspaper or even the *Daily Racing Form*. Annenberg now had to deal with bookies and poolroom operators—many of them tied to or members of organized crime organizations—involved in an illegal enterprise. The bookmakers who relied on the race wire for their livelihoods paid their subscription fees directly to the Annenberg organization.[57] Annenberg did his best to insulate himself from the sordid realities of the business he chose. He picked James M. Ragen, a hard-nosed ally from the Chicago newspaper wars, to run the operation and eliminate smaller competitors. Small-time operators were either bought out or shoved aside. Blanie Shields, a Kentuckian who serviced about thirty bookies, declined General News Bureau's offer of a buyout. He changed his mind after receiving threatening phone calls to his office and a visit from the wire service's enforcer who promised he would be "bumped off" if he didn't cooperate.[58] Similar examples of intimidation occurred in New Orleans and Philadelphia; even Capone himself was rebuffed when he approached Annenberg about sharing the race wire.[59] The General News Bureau doled out about $150,000 in bribes each year to ensure friendly relations with Chicago politicians.[60]

Annenberg had a falling out with his race wire partners, so he settled with them out of court and renamed his agency the Nationwide News Service. Despite its name, the agency's tentacles spread beyond the United States into Canada, Mexico, and the Caribbean and employed teams of reporters and handicappers at all of the top tracks. Racing information was transmitted to about fifteen thousand bookies across the nation, and the race wire earned Annenberg more than $2 million in profits each year, as did the *Daily Racing Form*.[61] In the 1930s Annenberg's network was the fifth-largest customer of the American Telephone and Telegraph Company, and he paid rental charges of more than $500,000 a year.[62] He defended his business as a convenience for the workingman. "It isn't right to deprive the little people of a chance to be lucky," Moses told his son, Walter. "If people can wager at a racetrack why should they be deprived of the right to do so away from a track? How many people can take time off from their jobs to go to a racetrack?"[63]

Annenberg was amassing power and wealth that rivaled his former employer, William Randolph Hearst. Annenberg could easily afford to expand his publishing empire, purchasing the *Philadelphia Inquirer* in 1936, launching the *Miami Tribune*, and buying up a host of smaller publications. Like Hearst, he used his newspapers as a cudgel for his political beliefs, attacking President Franklin D. Roosevelt and any publishers who supported the New Deal.

As Annenberg's wealth and national profile grew, so did the government's formal investigations into his business dealings. Annenberg's monopolistic race wire operated in a gray legal zone, but authorities failed to build a convincing case against him. What did in Annenberg was the Internal Revenue Service, which tripped up so many big shots of the era. IRS agents unearthed records that they said were evidence of rampant tax evasion. A federal grand jury agreed and indicted Annenberg in 1939 with evading $3.3 million in income taxes, tacking on penalties and interest of $2.3 million—the biggest tax evasion case in American history up to then.[64] The judge was James H. Wilkerson, the same jurist who sentenced Capone to prison for tax evasion in 1931. Annenberg disassociated himself from the Nationwide News Service and entered a guilty plea in the hope that paying a heavy fine would save him from prison. However, Wilkerson handed down a three-year prison sentence, shattering Annenberg and his friends and family.

In his early sixties, the publishing baron reported to his new residence at the federal penitentiary in Lewisburg, Pennsylvania. Annenberg's body was wasting away, and the parole board granted his release to treat an inoperable brain tumor. He died at the Mayo Clinic in 1942. His son, Walter, seized command of the tarnished empire, purged it of any remaining ties to the race wire (though he did hang on to the profitable *Daily Racing Form*), and developed popular magazine titles such as *TV Guide* and *Seventeen*.

Walter Annenberg worked assiduously to rehabilitate his family's image, devoting much of his later life to philanthropy and courting the rich and powerful. Two top journalism schools—at the University of Southern California and the University of Pennsylvania—carry the Annenberg name, as do many other educational and arts centers. Annenberg served as the US ambassador to Great Britain, the plummiest post in the diplomatic corps, and frequently entertained the Nixons, the Fords, and the Reagans at Sunnylands, his tasteful midcentury modern estate in the Southern California desert. The son had done his best to atone for the sins of the father, yet all of the latter-day fabulousness—the Presidential Medal of Freedom, the collection of French Impressionist masterworks—stands on the shoulders of ruthless business tactics and illegal gambling.

———

After Moe Annenberg's exit from the race wire, other players rushed in and battled for primacy. Ragen, Moe Annenberg's old crony, was convicted in the same tax evasion case. While in prison, Ragen relinquished control of what remained of the Annenberg race wire to Arthur "Mickey" McBride, a taxicab operator in Cleveland. Like Ragen and Annenberg, McBride's career began in the crucible of newspaper circulation wars. Ragen reasserted control of the renamed Continental Press Service after leaving prison, and McBride bought a one-third interest in it in the name of his son, Edward.[65] During his time with the wire, the elder McBride founded the Cleveland Browns—one of several NFL franchises founded by heavy gamblers.

In 1945 Ragen was under pressure from Chicago gangsters Tony Accardo, Murray "The Camel" Humphreys, and Jake "Greasy Thumb"

Guzik, who wanted to muscle in on his business. When Ragen refused, the remnants of the Capone organization set up the Trans-American Publishing and News Service. It leveraged a nationwide network of organized crime figures—Bugsy Siegel oversaw the Las Vegas operation, for example—to build the enterprise. The gangsters kept the heat on Ragen, who at great expense surrounded himself with bodyguards at all times. Nevertheless, gunmen ambushed Ragen and severely wounded him while riding in a car in Chicago in 1946. He died a few months later from mercury poisoning that was supposedly orchestrated by rival gangsters.

Crime syndicates folded Trans-American into the Continental Press Service on its way to constructing a race wire monopoly. The rising influence of organized crime in gambling caught the attention of the federal government. An ambitious Democratic senator from Tennessee, Estes Kefauver, convened a committee in 1950 to examine crime syndicates. Kefauver held a special distain for the race wire: "In my opinion, because the wire service keeps alive the illegal gambling empire which in turn bankrolls a variety of other criminal activities in America, Continental Press is America's Public Enemy Number One."[66] Testimony revealed that Continental and its distributors leased twenty-three thousand miles of telegraph circuits from Western Union to supply thousands of bookies with vital racing information. Continental charged subscribers wildly varying rates: a legitimate news organization such as the Associated Press would pay about eighty dollars a month while a big-time bookmaking operation would be charged thousands of dollars a month for the same service.[67]

The committee scrutinized South Florida's S & G Syndicate, founded by five bookies in 1944 who pooled their resources for greater profits. The syndicate consisted of about two hundred local bookmakers whose membership ensured them protection from police harassment. All involved profited handsomely. By its own estimate, S & G grossed $26 million in 1948—the true figure was almost certainly much higher.[68] The dollar figures caught the attention of the Chicago gangsters who ran Continental, which transmitted racing information to S & G via its race wire. Kefauver's committee alleged that the "Chicago-Capone Syndicate" dispatched front man Harry Russell to Florida in 1949 to muscle in on S & G's lucrative business. When S & G's partners resisted, police raided their offices, and Continental shut off the race wire. S & G closed for two weeks; when it reopened, Russell was an S & G partner for a nominal $20,000 investment, the raids ceased, and wire service was restored.[69] Mickey McBride and fellow Continental Press partner Tom Kelly were hauled before Senate committee investigators and professed ignorance of the true power behind the company. Asked why he would install his son as a figurehead in a violent business with underworld ties, McBride shrugged it off and replied: "My boy might get hit by a brick from this building and [be] bumped off. Life is a game of chance."[70]

After additional Senate and Justice Department investigations into organized crime, Congress belatedly approved the Interstate Wire Act of 1961. The far-reaching law, which now also applies to Internet gambling, banned the interstate transmission of wagering information, targeting those "engaged in the business of betting or wagering" rather than the individual bettor.[71] The statute also prohibited the interstate transportation of wagering paraphernalia such as betting slips designed for use in bookmaking and other illegal enterprises.[72] Of course, an exception was made for pari-mutuel equipment and tickets in the two dozen states where on-track betting was legal. Off-track wagering remained illegal in every state except for Nevada, but gambling proponents used the decades-long acceptance of pari-mutuel wagering as their most potent argument for expansion.

―――

Efforts to license off-track betting began almost as soon as states endorsed on-track betting. As early as 1935 University of Chicago urban sociologist Ernest W. Burgess wrote an open letter to the governor to Illinois urging him to support a bill to legalize handbooks in Chicago. Burgess had served on a coroner's jury in a murder case in 1933. The jury subpoenaed witnesses and viewed the scene of the machine-gun shooting, but it became clear to the panel that the crime would be another unsolved murder, like many other gangland killings in Chicago. The jury shifted its attention to the intertwined relationship of crime, politics, and gambling.

The operating director of the Chicago Crime Commission drafted a report that relied on testimony to assert that illegal gambling was prevalent in Chicago. The jury-adopted report went further and pointed out that the state legalized pari-mutuel wagering in 1927 and thus was "now a partner in the gambling business."[73] Then the jury members took the next logical step: "It is rather difficult to understand how the State of Illinois can condone betting by persons in attendance at a horse-race meeting conducted in an enclosure and licensed, and then prosecute persons unable to attend such meetings but nevertheless desirous of betting on the same races when they place their bets with a bookmaker."[74]

The jury's report pointed out that neither the city nor state received any revenue from the thriving bookmaking business, which paid off police for protection. The revenues ended up in the pockets of crime bosses who terrorized the city. It concluded that the city had to decide whether to strictly enforce the existing laws or abandon them in favor of licensing bookmakers. Asked for his reaction to the report, Chicago mayor Edward Kelly said, "If it is legal to bet at the racetracks under state license it should be legal to license handbooks. . . . It would be easier to license them and see that they are run on the square."[75]

Handbooks were far busier than racetracks, according to a 1935 survey by the *Chicago Times*. The city's estimated 1,600 bookmakers received 150,000 patrons each day; in comparison, the six Chicago-area racetracks had an average daily paid attendance of 3,500.[76] The net profit to bookies (and, by extension, organized crime) was estimated at more than $8 million a year—ten times what the state received for pari-mutuel wagering.[77] Burgess argued that legalizing handbooks would deliver the biggest blow to organized crime since repeal of Prohibition.

Kelly sponsored a bill approved by the Illinois legislature to permit the Chicago City Council to license and regulate handbooks in the city. Despite the mayor's support, Gov. Henry Horner vetoed the legislation in 1935 and wrote, "It is a hazardous experiment for a state to legalize a business which is now illegal everywhere in this country."[78] Six years later, Gov. Dwight H. Green rejected a bill that would have allowed statewide licensing and regulation of handbooks. In his veto message, Green said the state had an obligation to enforce existing laws and warned that "widespread gambling devastates the character and enterprise of individuals and communities."[79]

In 1950 another big-city mayor in an important racing state pushed hard for the legalization of off-track betting. New York City mayor William O'Dwyer asked state legislators to regulate and control gambling not only for horse racing but for all public sporting events. O'Dwyer, who gained fame as the prosecutor of Murder, Inc. crime figures before being elected mayor, argued that organized crime reaped huge profits from "the widespread human instinct to gamble."[80] The state's voters had approved parimutuel betting a decade earlier, bringing hundreds of millions of dollars into the treasury. The mayor said it was time to accept reality and admit that the prohibition of off-track gambling was self-defeating. "The state, through regulation and control, should step in and not only obtain large sources of revenue, but also destroy the underworld's last major source of financial support," he wrote.[81]

The governor of New York, Thomas E. Dewey, took only six days to deliver a stinging reply. Dewey, who had also built his public career on high-profile prosecutions of gangsters and had made two unsuccessful runs for the presidency, called O'Dwyer's request "a shocking, immoral and indecent proposal."[82] He thought it improper for the state to generate revenue from the weaknesses of its people. The governor did acknowledge that pari-mutuel wagering brought money into government coffers but noted that such betting was strictly confined to the track. Dewey then advanced the slippery-slope argument in his attack on O'Dwyer: "Obviously if the state puts the imprimatur of approval on the morals and decency of wholesale, universal betting on sports events of every kind, then there would be no logic whatever in refusing also to legalize lotteries, betting pools, dice games, slot machines and public gambling halls with all their attendant evils."[83]

Dewey closed with a blanket condemnation of gambling: "The entire history of legalized gambling in this country and abroad shows that it has brought nothing but poverty, crime and corruption, demoralization of moral and ethical standards, and ultimately a lower living standard and misery for all the people."[84] O'Dwyer's proposal to regulate and control gambling for all sporting events went nowhere—a police corruption scandal forced him to resign as mayor before the year was out, and Dewey stayed on as governor through 1954. For years, New York City officials lobbied lawmakers in Albany to legalize off-track betting without success, even though a 1963 referendum showed that city voters supported it. A legalization proposal by New York mayor Robert F. Wagner Jr. stirred the city's Protestant council to issue a blistering public resolution against the bill, saying it would create "a grave social and moral evil" and seek "to prosper government by prospering a virulent parasite in the body politic."[85] The legislation was stymied.

Horse racing remained popular in the 1960s, and an expanding number of states authorized on-track pari-mutuel wagering. Track attendance reached its peak in the early 1970s, when brilliant thoroughbreds like Triple Crown–winner Secretariat transfixed the nation and inspired heavy wagering.[86] Government approval of on-track betting and the federal government's assault on the race wire failed to put much of a crimp in illegal wagering. In 1972 gambling expert John Scarne surveyed three thousand bettors at several major tracks about their wagering habits. He discovered that for every dollar the horseplayers wagered at the track, they placed seven dollars in illegal bets with bookies.[87]

Governments knew they were missing out on a rich vein of revenue, and chronic budget crises lowered their resistance to gambling as a funding source. After all, New York state had long sanctioned pari-mutuel bets on horse races and bingo games for religious or charitable fundraising purposes, and the state's voters had approved a lottery in 1966, so it was not a great leap in logic to also legalize off-track betting.

In 1970 New York City mayor John Lindsay faced a $300 million budget shortfall, and among the ideas to close the gap was to launch a city-run off-track betting scheme.[88] This time the familiar proposal had the fortuitous backing of New York governor Nelson Rockefeller, who maneuvered it into an aid package for the city and rammed it through the legislature without debate or much regard for the objections of the racing industry. Suddenly New York—the preeminent state for horse-race wagering—became the first state to legalize off-track betting, better known as OTB.

At first OTB was limited to New York City, which set up a public bene-fit corporation to handle the first legal bets in 1971. Not surprisingly, the revenue-sharing structure was heavily weighted in favor of government. In its first twenty months, the New York City Off-Track Betting Corpora-tion handled $569 million in bets and sent about $30 million to the state and city, more than double what was funneled to racetracks.[89] The rac-ing industry complained that whatever they received from OTB fell far short of the declines in track attendance and on-track betting. Bookies also grumbled about a sharp decline in business, but some looked at OTB as a useful entry point for two-dollar bettors. "OTB runs a great kinder-garten," said one Manhattan bookie. "When the kids graduate, I'm their finishing school."[90]

A study of OTB customers prepared for the OTB Corporation under-mined the argument that legalizing off-track betting would exploit the poor. Instead, the report found that the typical OTB customer was above-average in socioeconomic status compared to the population as a whole. Nearly all had betting experience, and three-quarters reported that their total horse betting increased from previous years. Many continued to patronize illegal bookies, but 13 percent said they placed one hundred or more bets a month at OTB branches.[91] Pat Mahony, former executive with the New York Racing Association who directed the state's pari-mutuel operation for years, today views legalizing OTB as the right decision for the state, but one that came with a cost. "This gave people a legal outlet to bet at their convenience and made betting more accessible to New York-ers," he said in an interview with the author. "At the same time, it hurt on-track betting."[92]

A sometimes-unreliable computer system and a telephone betting center connected the OTB branches and made it possible to process the enormous volume of bets. OTB quickly became the city's largest retailer, with one hundred branch offices handling wagers from up to 150,000 bettors each day, the equivalent of opening two new racetracks the size of Aqueduct in Queens.[93] Approval of the "simulcasting" of races further boosted the appeal of remote wagering. An impressive roster of celebrities such as Jackie Gleason and Bob Hope appeared in OTB ads for free, as if they were making public-service announcements. The humorous ads helped soften the raffish reputation of OTB parlors, which spread to Long Island and upstate New York.

In 1978 the federal Interstate Horseracing Act authorized other states with racetracks and casinos to carry simulcast races, which further broadened the base of bettors and undercut illegal off-track bookies. The expansion of remote wagering allowed some tracks to survive ebbing attendance and handle. Some states propped up failing tracks by converting them into "racinos" by adding a casino or slot parlor. Mahony, whose grandfather and father oversaw pari-mutuel wagering at leading tracks from Canada to Florida, has mixed emotions about the trend toward racinos. "Personally, I don't like it," said Mahony, who is not a gambler. "It's completely different from horse-race betting—it's more of challenge and a reward for successful handicappers."[94] But he concedes that the money from casino operations pumps up the purse levels needed to attract high-quality horses and keep tracks open. "Anything to help bring more people into the game, I'm for," he said.[95]

The racing industry has been trapped in a seemingly irreversible downturn. Today about forty states allow pari-mutuel betting, which includes dog racing and jai alai, but they have been steadily seeing less money from it. Overall state revenue from pari-mutuel wagering plummeted from $554 million in 1993 to $150 million in 2010. That translates to an 80 percent drop when adjusted for inflation.[96] The overall betting handle and on-track attendance are declining, horse breeding is down, and racing days are being trimmed. Famous tracks like Bay Meadows in the San

Francisco Bay Area and Hollywood Park have closed. The sport still shines for the Triple Crown events—the Kentucky Derby, Preakness Stakes, and Belmont Stakes—or when a thoroughbred like 2015 Triple Crown–winner American Pharoah captures the public's fancy, but racing's overall prominence is likely to shrink ever further.

As long as horses run around a track, people will gamble on them. Most of the betting will be done at off-track locations. With their floors strewn with betting slips and a menu of races to wager on, the smoke-filled OTB branches and simulcasting rooms in casinos resembled the illegal poolrooms of an earlier era. The major difference, other than the level of technology to calculate odds and transmit bets, was that off-track betting enjoyed the approval of government. "They are the regulators and that's who the public looks to," Mahony said. "You want the perception and the reality that horse racing is aboveboard, beyond reproach. . . . If you don't have betting, you don't have the sport."[97]

CHAPTER 2

Golden Ticket

STATE-RUN LOTTERIES TOPPLE
ILLEGAL NUMBERS RACKETS

All you need is a dollar and a dream.
> —New York Lotto slogan in the 1980s and 1990s

Dreams and their meanings were once part of life's daily rhythm in places like the South Side of Chicago and Harlem in New York. In urban centers, "playing the numbers" was not merely a topic of idle conversation or a simple diversion—it was central to a way of life. When the numbers or "policy" games were at their height in the late nineteenth century and much of the twentieth century, they employed thousands of people as runners, bankers, managers, and distributors who served tens of thousands of bettors every day. Individual bets could be as small as a penny or a nickel to bait the poor, but a player who hit the lottery benefited handsomely. News of a winning ticket that paid off at 600:1 spread like quicksilver across entire neighborhoods.

Few gamblers in history were more conscious of their subconscious than numbers players. Indeed, the pamphlets they consulted to decide what numbers to play were called "dream books." For years dream books were best sellers in cities, particularly in black communities. Publications like *Old Aunt Dinah's Policy Dream Book*, *The Gypsy Witch Dream Book*, and *Aunt Sally's Policy Players Dream Book* were illustrated with apocryphal depictions of exotic fortune tellers and soothsayers from Africa and the Orient. Players avidly thumbed through them in the hope that the folk wisdom would unlock the mysteries contained within their visions. The fictitious authors of the books boasted that their methods of conjuring the numbers were steeped in "ancient traditions and mysterious arts."[1] "To dream of snakes, is a good dream for luck in the lottery, for snakes are curious reptiles, and the sight of them always produces a singular feeling," according to *Old Aunt Dinah's Policy Dream Book*, a pamphlet from the 1850s that promised to convert dreams into winning lottery numbers.[2]

The cheaply printed guides listed words and phrases in alphabetical order with corresponding numbers. For instance, if a person had a dream that involved a harp, *Policy Pete's Dream Book* suggested that he or she should play 570 that day, a vision of a tractor meant 647 was the most suitable number to play, the reliable presence of a sheep translated to 156. The book also listed details from dreams such as a dead horse (419), a dog fight (724), and a house on fire (791). Some were related to extraordinarily detailed personal experiences such as meeting a cross-eyed person (285) and sneezing three times (483). Current events also influenced what numbers were played. When the humorist Will Rogers died in a plane crash in 1935, so many bettors played 7–10–11—the combination of numbers for "William"—that the syndicates that oversaw the games urged their members not to accept bets greater than fifty cents for fear of losing big if that sequence happened to hit.[3]

"Spiritual advisers" offered their services to players who sought additional guidance. At worship services, attendees received "gigs," a combination of three numbers played in some games. "To give numbers is no sin because the people have to live, and to try to win a little money. That is no harm," said one Chicago preacher. "On many occasions God comes to me in a dream. That dream I will play in policy and catch it. Then, I invest the money wisely. That is all there is to it."[4]

Others like Edward Lowe were more blatantly commercial, selling gigs for ten cents to three dollars. Lowe styled himself a professor and "astronumerologist" and claimed he possessed a gift for divination deepened by his close study of the zodiac. His Chicago shop displayed books on numerology and sold anointing substances like "Policy Player's Oil" and the

"Lucky Oil of Mystery."[5] Neighborhood stores promoted special incenses for people to burn at their homes for luck.

To modern eyes, numbers players who consulted dream books and "spiritualists" may seem like gullible followers of the irrational superstitions of a bygone age. Yet they were little different from today's lottery players who regularly play the numbers of their children's birthdates or important anniversaries in the belief that following a meaningful routine will affect the outcome. Numbers, policy, lotteries—by any name, such long-shot schemes have always attracted dreamers. The big change would come in who would profit from those dreams.

————

Lotteries helped build America. In the colonial era, more than 150 lotteries benefited disparate causes such as paving the streets of Newport, Rhode Island; establishing King's College, known today as New York's Columbia University; and constructing a lighthouse in New London, Connecticut.[6] Leading figures of the age embraced them, lending an aura of legitimacy to the proceedings: Benjamin Franklin promoted a lottery to pay for artillery batteries to fortify Philadelphia, and John Hancock helped direct one to rebuild a fire-gutted Faneuil Hall in Boston. Lottery proceeds were essential in setting up the basic building blocks of civic life—libraries, schools, roads, hospitals, and courthouses. Dozens of churches stepped up to receive lottery funds, which muted the usual distain for gambling expressed by ministers.[7]

In early American history, lotteries were usually local affairs overseen by upright citizens who sold tickets to people who directly benefited from the bridge or school that would be built with the proceeds. They were close in spirit to modern-day raffles conducted by a church group or a youth sports league in which money is raised for a worthy cause. A purchaser of a raffle ticket often has a personal connection to the seller, a stake in the organization, or roots in the community. Such drawings for nonprofit groups are seen as fundraisers that offer the incidental chance of winning a prize; they are not intended for those who like to gamble for gambling's sake.

Government-approved lotteries gained popularity in the early years of the Republic: twenty-four states approved lotteries for infrastructure improvements from 1790 to the Civil War for a total of 287 authorizations.[8] States freely granted the petitions of churches to conduct lotteries: Pennsylvania approved sixty lottery licenses for the benefit of a broad range of religious groups between 1790 and 1833.[9] As it is for today's lotteries, education was a popular cause: forty-seven colleges and about three hundred lower schools were lottery beneficiaries from 1790 to the Civil War.[10]

However, fundamental changes in how lotteries were managed and a series of notorious swindles gave rise to a favorable climate for reformers who wanted them prohibited. Lottery organizers transferred management duties to professional companies, which handled the tasks of printing tickets, conducting drawings, and paying out prizes.[11] Lottery managers deducted a fixed percentage of the total amount of money collected, giving them an incentive to sell as many tickets as possible. Enterprising salesmen took note of the public's fervor for lotteries and offered their services to lottery managers to help them offload tickets. The brokers bought blocks of discounted tickets and discovered the riches that could be made as middlemen.

The professional managers promoted ever-larger, more frequent, and longer-lasting lotteries and proceeded to oversell them. In one case the Massachusetts legislature in 1812 authorized a lottery to raise $16,000 to make improvements to Plymouth Beach. After nine years of drawings, a legislative committee found that $886,439.75 worth of tickets had been sold, yet only $9,876.15 had been turned over to the project.[12]

With so much money at stake, the temptation to rig the drawings proved to be irresistible. In 1819 a New York state legislative committee uncovered numerous instances of fixed drawings and exposed the relationships among lottery managers, politicians, and lobbyists. Among its findings was the revelation that a lottery manager orchestrated a drawing to ensure that a $35,000 prize went to a lobbyist (and a former lottery manager himself) in Albany.[13]

Lottery managers and ticket brokers felt little sense of accountability to the communities that were supposedly the beneficiaries of the lotteries. Patrons who bought tickets for out-of-town lotteries did so solely in the hope that they would win a prize; the actual purpose of the lottery made no difference to them. After all, they would never cross the bridge or attend the school that received lottery proceeds.

Many entrepreneurs and quick-buck artists wanted in on the action and raced to open lottery outlets; by 1815 brokers served practically every sizable town in America. In Philadelphia the number of offices grew at an astonishing rate: 3 in 1809, 60 in 1827, then a leap to more than 200 by 1833.[14] In 1832 the *Boston Mercantile Journal* reported that tickets sold in 420 lotteries in eight states amounted to gross revenue of $66 million—roughly double the federal government's total revenue that year.

Among those who saw promise in the lottery business was a young, enterprising Connecticut native named Phineas Taylor Barnum. As a boy he watched his grandfather help manage a lottery to benefit the Fairfield Episcopal Society and advance the novel idea of a lottery with no blank tickets.[15] That meant a holder of a $5.00 losing ticket was guaranteed a minimum of $2.50 in return. (Ticket buyers were furious when they learned that their $2.50 "prize" was subject to a 15 percent fee, payable in sixty days.)

When P. T. Barnum was a teenager, he ran small-stakes lotteries and raffles and learned how to unload tickets with ease. Barnum learned that managers, after deducting the customary 15 percent from the total prizes for themselves, then sold blocks of reduced-price tickets to their agents that yielded a 25 to 30 percent profit for the sellers. Armed with that knowledge, Barnum approached lottery managers in Connecticut and "obtained my tickets directly from them at 'the scheme price.' In my turn I established agents all through the country, and my profits were immense."[16]

By 1830 Barnum claimed he sold $500 to $2,000 worth of tickets per day. His talent for self-promotion was ideally suited to the task. He whipped up

excitement with a torrent of handbills, pamphlets, and newspaper advertisements, and he papered his Bethel, Connecticut, lottery office—referred
to in ads as the "Temple of Fortune"—with gold signs and colorful plac-
ards to entice customers. "Nothing venture, nothing gain. Call without
delay and load your pockets with the shiners, at the old established 'Temple of Fortune' in Bethel," blared one of his ads.[17]

The window for proprietors like Barnum to make easy money wasn't
open for long, however. In 1834, the Connecticut legislature banned lotteries, forcing Barnum to close his "Temple of Fortune" and pursue even more
lucrative ventures. Long after he left the lottery business to find worldwide
fame as a perpetrator of hoaxes and impresario of the three-ring circuses
he billed as "The Greatest Show on Earth," P. T. Barnum remarked, "Hum-
bugs certainly existed long before I attained my majority."[18] Although Barnum didn't coin the phrase "there's a sucker born every minute," he did
indeed live and profit by those words.

States that had authorized and allowed the expansion of lotteries to
such untenable levels were faced with public pressure to shut down the
corruption-plagued system. Instead of regulating lotteries, many states
like Connecticut simply abolished them. Pennsylvania, thanks in part to
the relentless work of the fiercely antigambling Quakers, became the first
state to approve a measure to abolish lotteries in 1833. New York and Massachusetts quickly followed with their own bans, and with punishments
ranging from fines to jail time for repeat offenders. Some states wrote anti-
lottery provisions into their constitutions while others let existing lottery
grants expire without approving new ones. By 1860 thirty of the thirty-
three states had constitutional or statutory prohibitions on lotteries.[19]

The Supreme Court strongly endorsed the bans. In 1850 the justices
unanimously rejected a Virginia plaintiff's argument that he had the right
to sell lottery tickets under a grant approved before the state banned lotteries. Justice Robert C. Grier, who delivered the opinion of the court, wrote
that state grants had time limits and defended Virginia's suppression of
lotteries as sound public policy: "Experience has shown that the common
forms of gambling are comparatively innocuous when placed in contrast

with the widespread pestilence of lotteries. The former are confined to a few persons and places, but the latter infests the whole community; it enters every dwelling; it reaches every class; it preys upon the hard earnings of the poor; it plunders the ignorant and simple."[20]

———

Even though lotteries were almost entirely banned after the Civil War, the Louisiana legislature boldly authorized a private company to run a lottery in 1868, granting it a monopoly for twenty-five years in exchange for an annual $40,000 payment to the state for educational and other charitable purposes. The Louisiana State Lottery Company would become the most notorious lottery in American history; killing it required not only the efforts of the Supreme Court but also the influence of Congress and the president of the United States.

A New York gambling syndicate, the true financial power behind the Louisiana State Lottery Company, kept state legislators plied with bribes and hired armies of lawyers and lobbyists to protect its position. With the energetic businessman Charles T. Howard as its president, the Louisiana State Lottery Company escalated the frequency of drawings and prize amounts and launched aggressive newspaper advertising campaigns to expand its reach far beyond Louisiana.[21] Less than a decade after its incorporation, the company sold tickets in every state and territory in the United States.

A triumphant Howard reportedly boasted, "Give me the monopoly of a wheel in Louisiana and I'll rule the State."[22] It was no exaggeration. The company used its vast resources to manipulate the press, banks, lawmakers, and judges. When the *Democrat* of New Orleans exposed the company's history of bribery and criticized the lottery's low payouts and excessively long odds, the company seized control of the paper and gagged it. The company "had absolute control of the whole State government," wrote a Baton Rouge newspaper, "and now we have the lamentable spectacle of a State, such as ours, at the mercy of a rich, unscrupulous gambling corporation."[23]

The company's money and influence were so far-reaching that it became popularly known as the Octopus or the Serpent. Ticket sales were staggering: an estimated $28 million was collected in 1890 and about 5 million people bought tickets each year.[24] Managers marketed tickets to all income groups: monthly and semimonthly drawings for grand prizes sold tickets priced as high as $40 for a top prize of $600,000; the cheapest tickets were offered at 25¢ for a chance at winning $3,750; and daily drawings (except on Sundays) enticed the poor to "insure" numbers at a fraction of the cost of a regular ticket.[25]

With the company awash in cash and its political position seemingly unassailable, lottery managers felt emboldened to request a renewal of its charter. John A. Morris, scion of a distinguished family involved in horse racing and one of the original backers of the Louisiana State Lottery Company, proposed in 1890 that the company would pay $500,000 each year to the state for twenty-five years starting January 1, 1894, a dramatic rise from the $40,000 annual amount that it had paid for decades.[26] When his proposal met with pockets of resistance in the legislature, Morris unleashed his legions of lobbyists in Baton Rouge and agreed to raise the company's annual payment to $1 million—later boosting it to $1.25 million—an indication of the firm's willingness to pay any price to extend its franchise.

After bitter debate and accusations of fraud and bribery, both chambers passed the bill and included an amendment requiring a public referendum on the lottery. But the governor vetoed the bill even though the company sent him a $100,000 check—ostensibly to reinforce the levees of New Orleans—which he refused.[27] Overriding a veto required a two-thirds vote in the Louisiana legislature, which was achieved in the House but not in the Senate. A senator who had switched sides and voted for the initial lottery bill suddenly fell ill—reportedly after a trip in which he overindulged in the pleasures of New Orleans—and died, leaving the Serpent one vote short of an override. (Upon his death, it was discovered that the senator was wearing a money belt containing $18,000, presumably a bribe for his vote in favor of the lottery bill.)[28] The remaining pro-lottery senators successfully argued that the people should decide whether to keep the lottery alive.

Meanwhile, public disgust at the Serpent was coalescing into an organized movement that found a sympathetic audience in Washington. Groups such as the Louisiana Anti-Lottery League petitioned Congress to act, but bills were introduced in session after session with little success. The antilottery forces settled on a strategy that attacked the company where it was the most vulnerable: the mail system. The Serpent relied on the nation's Post Office Department for its sustenance: more than 90 percent of tickets were sold outside Louisiana and a third of the mail that arrived at the New Orleans Post Office was related to the lottery.[29]

Legislative efforts to sever the lottery's vital lifeline stalled, provoking President Benjamin Harrison to issue a special message to Congress. In his statement dated July 29, 1890, Harrison argued that because the lottery's influence reached far beyond a single state, "severe and effective legislation should be promptly enacted to enable the Post-Office Department to purge the mails of all letters, newspapers, and circulars relating to the business."[30] The president concluded: "The people of all the States are debauched and defrauded."[31]

Harrison's strong stance motivated Congress to approve legislation to ban the mailing of lottery-related materials such as tickets and money orders and publications that carried lottery advertisements or lists of prizes awarded at drawings.[32] The law was put into immediate effect, and an industrious postmaster in New Orleans seized thousands of pieces of mail and collected piles of evidence to use against lottery agents.[33] The Supreme Court upheld the law in 1892, ruling that it did not abridge the First Amendment's freedom of speech or of the press.[34]

With the lottery bloodied on the national level, the company shifted its attention to the 1892 election in Louisiana that would decide the fate of the constitutional amendment to renew its charter. The Anti-Lottery League organized political meetings and reached out to women's groups, clergy, and the press to fight the amendment. The Louisiana Lottery Company claimed it had $6 million to spend on the election, which would also decide the state's next governor.[35]

This time money and influence were not enough to save the Serpent: Louisianans overwhelmingly rejected the lottery amendment 157,422 to 4,225, and antilottery candidate Murphy J. Foster was easily elected governor. The Louisiana legislature approved a bill that banned all lotteries after December 31, 1893.

With time running out in Louisiana and nowhere to go in the United States, anxious lottery managers found a haven in Honduras starting January 1, 1894. Even in exile, the lottery's leaders believed that it could continue to tap into its network of agents in America. The lottery conducted the drawings in Honduras or at sea and began an express delivery service to ship tickets and money into the United States to avert the interference of postal officials.[36]

Antilottery groups, religious leaders, and newspapers expressed frustration that the lottery was still able to operate—albeit in a much diminished state—and lobbied for additional legislation. Congress responded with a law in 1895 that prohibited the transportation of all lottery-related materials in interstate commerce.

By the time the Supreme Court upheld the law in 1903, little remained of the former colossus of Louisiana.[37] It quietly went out of business in 1907. The example set by the Louisiana State Lottery Company was so repellant and the federal government's defeat of lotteries was so complete that it would take nearly sixty years for a state to dare enter the lottery business again.

Illegal policy games were ideally positioned to fill the void created by the demise of the Louisiana State Lottery Company. They were rooted in urban neighborhoods and therefore didn't need to use the mail to process bets or advertise in newspapers. The term "policy" derived from the pre–Civil War lottery practice of allowing players to make a sideline bet that a particular number would be called in a drawing.[38] Lottery managers billed it as a kind of "insurance policy" or a hedge against losing. Policy was popular among the poor because, unlike the fixed price of buying a lottery ticket, there was no minimum bet required to "insure" numbers. It had the added attraction of giving players a feeling of control by allowing them to select their own numbers.

Hundreds of long-established policy shops or "exchanges" in cities like New York and Chicago operated essentially wide open thanks to friendly relations with politicians and police. New Yorker Anthony Comstock, an anti-smut crusader whose billowing mutton chops framed his dour visage, took it upon himself to purge the mails and bookstalls of material he judged to be obscene. He also disapproved of gambling, taking note of the police department's protection of policy shops. A popular lottery office occupied two floors above a hat store on Broadway, and patrons waited in lines that stretched down stairwells and into the street where bribed policemen maintained order. When police felt motivated to conduct a raid, nothing came of it because the district attorney's office failed to prosecute. Any seized money or gambling materials were returned to the managers, and business would soon proceed as normal.[39]

Comstock thundered against "corruption in legislative halls and courts of justice, while officials on every side are tainted with the odious smell of bribery."[40] In 1882 Comstock and his Society for the Suppression of Vice conducted raids and grabbed financial records showing heavy play and big profits. The persistence of the righteous band of reformers did push some lottery offices out of New York, but convictions remained elusive, as was a solution to the larger problems of graft plaguing all levels of city government.

One of the most corrupt "policy kings" was Albert J. "Al" Adams, who controlled most of illegal activity in New York from the 1880s to the turn of the century. Adams forged strong connections to Tammany Hall but was widely considered "the meanest man in New York."[41] Adams, a millionaire several times over, was a notorious miser. His lone extravagance was that he never reused an umbrella because he considered it to be bad luck.[42] He had few friends—even one of his sons threatened to shoot him and served jail time for an assault charge.

The unloved Adams sat atop of an organizational chart with lieutenants in thirty policy districts that arranged for protection and dispatched lawyers whenever problems occurred. The winning numbers were supposedly transmitted from far-off lottery wheels in Kentucky, but in reality the devious policy managers fabricated the twice-daily drawings to manipulate the outcome. A 1900 exposé in the *New York Herald* concluded "the policy kings realize that money must be paid out to keep the public interested, but the winning numbers are purposely arranged so that the amount to be paid out shall be as small as possible."[43]

Adams's wealth and arrogance made him a fat target for the Society for the Prevention of Crime, a group that took its cues from the Reverend Charles H. Parkhurst. From the pulpit, the Presbyterian pastor denounced the policemen and Tammany politicians in cahoots with the gamblers. In an 1892 sermon that was front-page news in New York, Parkhurst rebuked "the mayor and his whole gang of drunken lecherous subordinates" as a "lying, perjured, rum-soaked and libidinous lot."[44] To prove his sensational allegations, Parkhurst hired a private detective to guide him on an undercover tour of the city's low-life dens. During their nighttime prowl, they encountered cops who volunteered directions to the city's hells and dives and offered to alert them if a raid was imminent. The pastor gamely endured brothel entertainments such as can-can dancers and he stonily sipped a beer while watching nude women play a spirited game of leapfrog with the evening's clients.[45]

Parkhurst cited nearly two hundred instances of lawbreaking amid the presence of police and delivered his report to a grand jury. State lawmakers pounced on his findings and uncovered extensive police corruption in which policy shops and other illegal business set aside regular payments to precinct captains for protection against raids. A special investigative committee's damning report in 1895 documented New York Police Department budgets that included line items such as "brothel contributions" and "gambling-house contributions."[46] Such bribes added up to millions of dollars. It was revealed that police positions could be bought at an escalating scale according to rank. An advancement to captain could cost upward of $15,000; an appointment as a humble patrolman carried a $300 price tag.[47] Among those brought in to clean up the department was a young police commissioner named Theodore Roosevelt.

A few years later, Parkhurst Society agents raided Adams's offices and uncovered evidence connecting him to eighty-two policy stations, some masked as barbershops and cigar stores. The previously untouchable Adams was swept up in the reform movement led by William Travers Jerome, the district attorney who hounded Richard A. Canfield and other gambling-house proprietors and pushed them out of Manhattan. Adams was tried and convicted of running an illegal gambling enterprise in 1902. After serving a prison sentence in Sing Sing, Adams returned to the streets of New York a man without an empire and ultimately shot himself in the head with a revolver.

———

With the demise of Adams, policy faded away (though the label persisted) and was reborn in the 1920s as "numbers" gambling that thrived in black neighborhoods like Harlem. Residents blended the daily routines of collections, drawings, and payouts into their lives, making numbers "Harlem's most popular indoor sport."[48] In the most common form of play, a bettor chose a three-digit number from 000 to 999. Although the player had a one in one thousand chance of picking the right sequence, payouts were only 600:1 to account for the operation's ample administrative costs and profit margin. Yet the prospect of turning a ten-cent wager in the morning into a sixty-dollar win later in the day was hard to resist when the whole neighborhood was in on it. The black newspaper *New York Age* warned that the numbers craze "assumed proportions that constitute a distinct menace to the moral and economic life of the race."[49]

The system's elaborate hierarchy involved thousands of employees: shopkeepers took bets at their cigar stores or barbershops; numbers runners working on commission collected the wagers, distributed betting slips, and delivered prize money along their routes; a "pickup man" brought the money and slips to a central office where bankers and bookkeepers calculated payments to employees and winnings; and the office bankers answered to a syndicate consisting of about a dozen members.[50] The syndicate chiefs divided cities into exclusive territories and agreed to help other leaders in times of financial duress. The top operators lavishly bribed elected leaders, political bosses, and police—a Chicago syndicate reportedly paid $400,000 a year to such "downtown" interests.[51] In exchange for protection, the syndicates ensured that the neighborhoods within their spheres of influence would line up behind the preferred candidates come election time.

The corruption went just as deep as it had during the policy days of Al Adams a generation earlier. In Boston a patrolman received five dollars a month from every storefront on his beat that sold numbers, a sergeant netted ten dollars a month, and lieutenants and captains even more.[52] Numbers operators supplemented cash payments with plenty of extra goodies. "Every Christmas and Easter my boss makes up a big bundle of groceries from his store for all the cops he pays off, and I deliver it for him to their houses," said one racketeer. "And then the cop never pays for nothing."[53] Even clean policemen felt little desire to raid numbers games because they were so pervasive. "We all know it's going on," said one Boston police captain. "As long as it is kept quiet, the cop can't complain. We might say, 'For God's sake, don't write them under my nose. Go in the back street.' The police have to see that it doesn't become too open."[54] When raids were deemed necessary for political reasons, the small-time operators were sacrificed and the heavy-hitters were left untouched.

These new "policy kings" lorded over predominately black neighborhoods in cities like New York, Chicago, and Boston. Many of the leaders were black and were viewed by their communities as notable examples of racial uplift. Their connections admitted them into realms previously off-limits to blacks. In Chicago the three Jones brothers, Edward, George, and Mack, led a lucrative syndicate and accumulated enough capital to branch out into other businesses. They bought a building on a main shopping street that had been hostile to black businessmen and converted it into a department store, the only black-owned shop of its kind in the city.[55] When it opened in 1937 the brothers promoted it as an important community event. Thousands gathered outside the "Jones Boys' Store" to catch a glimpse of boxing champion Joe Louis and hear jokes by entertainer Bill "Bojangles" Robinson. A local restaurant owner summed up the pride felt in the achievement: "They may come under the head of racketeers, but as long as they have done something that no other one of our group has done, they should be given a lot of credit and are entitled to the support of our people."[56]

The qualms felt by some about the realities of the numbers racket was balanced by the understanding that it provided employment to thousands of people. With so many people on the tax-free payroll, it was difficult to attack the syndicates for the way they acquired their wealth. "Just suppose they would absolutely stamp out all policy in Chicago—what would all these people do?" asked a housewife who lived in Chicago's South Side.[57] The policy kings knew this well and spread their wealth around the neighborhood to buy loyalty. Some in the neighborhood looked up to them as saviors. "The few pennies that the public loses in policy can hardly be missed by them. Yet it amounts to thousands of dollars a day and goes to make it possible for many a family to survive," said one resident.[58]

To draw the numbers, Chicagoans used "wheels" that were actually barrels or small drums containing seventy-eight numbered balls pulled out one by one while hundreds of people watched with rapt attention. Once all of the winning numbers were announced, a printing press in a back office churned out slips that runners distributed on their routes. The players developed their own lingo: a "saddle" was a combination of two numbers, a "gig" was a combination of three, and a "horse" was a combination of four. All were paid out at increasingly higher odds: a saddle paid 32:1, a gig 200:1, a horse 680:1.[59] For players, having the power to choose their numbers gave them a feeling of control. The most popular gig was 4–11–44, listed in dream books as the "washerwoman's gig" or the "Negro gig" and frequently cited in blues songs. When the heavily played gig hit, as it did twice in two days in Chicago, it set off celebrations and emptied the coffers of policy banks.[60]

In New York, numbers organizers searched for a more efficient way of drawing numbers that would assure bettors that the game was on the level. Their system relied on the daily report of the New York Clearing House. The respected financial institution near Wall Street handled exchanges among the city's banks and issued figures scribbled on a chalkboard every workday morning.[61] The all-important number was a three-digit combination gleaned from the bank clearances total and the Federal Reserve Bank balance. Afternoon newspapers rushed to print the balances so numbers players in Harlem could figure out if they had a winning ticket. The New York Clearing House, chagrined that their legitimate work was used as the backbone for an illegal numbers game, stopped publishing the balances in 1930.[62] Undeterred, policy operators turned to other sources of randomly generated digits such as the daily close of the New York Stock Exchange, the US Treasury balance, or racetrack results.

With their nickel and dime bets, numbers players were unwitting participants in a larger struggle between underworld crime bosses for supremacy. With the repeal of Prohibition in 1933, bootleggers looking for a new line of work took an interest in a different kind of illicit income: the numbers games. Gangster and ex-bootlegger Dutch Schultz muscled in on black bankers in Harlem, prompting a disgruntled resident to complain to the *Amsterdam News*, "You know this is a Negro game in a Negro neighborhood and it has been carried on by Negroes for twelve years without outside groups."[63]

However, Schultz and other organized crime figures were too powerful and dangerous for blacks to ignore; by the mid-1930s they formed alliances with the existing operators or seized control of what became known as the numbers rackets. In Chicago one of the Jones brothers was kidnapped—supposedly by white gangsters—and he moved to Mexico with another brother after a ransom was paid. A Chicago Outfit crew led by Sam Giancana violently asserted control over the remnants of the policy operation. Gunmen convinced reluctant operators to join their syndicate,

and resentful employees and players had little choice but to fall in line.[64]
The crime bosses spent freely to ensure police protection of their new,
wildly profitable enterprise.

————

Organized crime's strengthening grip—not to mention the sight of all that
untaxed numbers money—stirred a smattering of lawmakers to call for
legal lotteries. In the 1930s legislatures in California, Michigan, New Jersey, New York, Ohio, and several other states debated the issue, but not one
proposal made it into law. Although about a dozen states had approved
pari-mutuel wagering and a few others decriminalized bingo to benefit
charitable and religious causes, the stigma against legal lotteries remained
too great to overcome even during the hardships of the Great Depression.

While states gingerly approached the lottery question, Americans were
hooked on an overseas scheme that put a twist on the traditional lottery:
the Irish Sweepstakes. In 1930 the Irish Parliament approved the game to
raise money for the fledgling nation's hospitals. The sweepstakes awarded
prizes based on the results of three major horse races each year in England.
Participants contributed to a pool, and then a drawing assigned horses to a
lucky few who won prize money depending on the race's outcome. Coun-
terfeit tickets were abundant and the odds were long—1 chance in 390,000
of drawing the winning horse to claim the $150,000 grand prize in one of
the sweeps—but the Irish Sweepstakes was a phenomenon nonetheless.[65]
It didn't take long for America to overtake Britain as the nation that contributed the most to the sweepstakes even though the genuine tickets had
to be smuggled in from an ocean away.

Public officials were infuriated by the many millions of dollars stream-
ing from America to foreign lotteries and sweepstakes in flagrant violation
of antilottery laws. In California, Atty. Gen. Stanley Mosk investigated the
influence of the Irish Sweepstakes in his state. Mosk discovered a highly
organized operation that depended on layers of sellers and buyers sending
ticket books and stubs through the mail in plain envelopes. He studied
bank drafts sent to Ireland through Bank of America and found a sharp

increase in traffic whenever the Irish Sweepstakes' closing date neared. In September 1959 hundreds of thousands of dollars in currency was sent to Ireland, leading Mosk to conclude that "on an annual basis the take in California dollars runs into the millions."[66]

One of the most persistent voices in favor of legalizing lotteries was Rep. Paul A. Fino, a New York Republican who agitated for a national lottery in the 1950s and 1960s. Fino considered gambling an "instinctive and universal human trait" that will carry on whether it is legal or illegal, citing as an example the heavy participation in the Irish Sweepstakes.[67] He compared the suppression of gambling to the folly of Prohibition. People still wanted to enjoy a beer or a cocktail—the Volstead Act be damned—and their thirst was satisfied thanks to the efforts of bootleggers. The illegal trafficking of alcohol was immensely profitable for the crime bosses at the expense of government, which was unable to tax it. The repeal of Prohibition put the bootleggers out of business and resumed the flow of alcohol taxes into government treasuries.

Just as bootleggers thrived during Prohibition, the congressman argued, crime syndicates were flourishing under the illegal numbers racket. The way to break them was to stop pushing gambling deeper underground, Fino declared. "A national lottery, under proper Government control and regulation, would not only strike a death blow to the crime syndicates by depriving them of one of their major sources of revenue but, would make the people's gambling dollars work for the public welfare," he wrote in a statement submitted in Congress in 1961.[68]

Fino's proposal never made it out of committee, but the idea that a legal lottery would have the dual benefit of undercutting organized crime and raising revenue gained traction elsewhere. In 1955, after years of trying, New Hampshire lawmakers pushed through a scheme that would add two horse races a year at Rockingham Park racetrack in Salem and use a format similar to the Irish Sweepstakes to determine winners. The bill provoked strong opposition across the state, including from a local newspaper publisher who wrote, "We are not convinced that 'easy money' or the appeal of something for nothing—which is the basis of the sweepstakes idea—is

good either for the individual or the state."[69] The governor backed down
from his initial support and vetoed the bill.

By 1963 New Hampshire, which had legalized pari-mutuel wagering at
racetracks, seemed ready at last to embrace a lottery scheme. The state that
swore by its motto "Live Free or Die" had no sales or income tax, but living free had its limits. The state raised two-thirds of its revenue from "sin"
taxes on alcohol, tobacco, and horse racing.[70] When state aid to education
slowed to a trickle, lawmakers looked for another sin to tax. This time fiscal realities outweighed the arguments about the influence of organized
crime and the lottery's exploitation of the poor. Republican lawmakers
approved a lottery bill and Democratic governor John King announced
his support.

It marked a milestone in the nation's serpentine history of lotteries.
Sixty-eight years after Congress effectively ended the Louisiana State Lottery Company, a government in the United States at last awarded legal
sanction to a lottery. In 1964 the New Hampshire Sweepstakes would
become America's first legal lottery in the twentieth century.

———

Yet the weight of history bogged down New Hampshire's effort from the
outset. The federal laws that killed the Louisiana State Lottery Company
and staved off others from forming remained in effect. One of the most
important laws prohibited interstate transportation of all lottery-related
materials, a problem for a small state like New Hampshire that counted
on the participation of its neighbors for a successful lottery. Advertising
the sweepstakes to stir up public interest was out of the question. In the
1930s the federal government followed the lead of the postal codes and
banned the "broadcasting of, any advertisement of or information concerning any lottery, gift enterprise, or similar scheme."[71] Violators were
subject to a fine of up to $1,000 or a prison sentence of up to a year—or
both—for each offense.

These shackles restrained the sweepstakes to an extreme unimaginable today. Each ticket was three dollars, and they were sold only at the

forty-nine state-operated liquor stores and New Hampshire's two race-tracks. A ticket buyer was required to provide a name and an address on a form and feed it into a machine, which kept the ticket and dispensed a numbered receipt. The convoluted system allowed out-of-state players to participate since they technically would not be taking a lottery ticket across state lines. The governor bought the first ticket (he promised to donate any winnings to charity), and the former head of Boston's FBI office was brought in to oversee the sweepstakes and rebuff potential threats from organized crime. Prizes could not be sent through the US Post Office because they would qualify as mail relating to a lottery, so winners received the money via wire transfer or bank credit.

The winners were tied to the results of two horse races a year at Rockingham Park. The names of the horses nominated to run were put in a small drum and the purchased tickets were placed in much bigger drums. After a horse's name was selected, a ticket was drawn and assigned to the horse. The process continued until all of the horses had corresponding tickets.[72] A holder of one of the drawn tickets anxiously waited for the race to see if he or she won the $100,000 grand prize or a much lesser amount if the horse didn't make the final field.

Unsurprisingly, the cumbersome process produced underwhelming sales. In 1964 the sweepstakes' first year, the gross was $5.7 million, well below the projected $10 million.[73] The gross fell to $3.9 million the following year, with $1.4 million paid in prizes, $1.8 million directed to schools, and operating costs eating up the rest. Sales continued to sink even as a much bigger state in the Northeast considered getting into the lottery business.

New York was having trouble paying for Gov. Nelson Rockefeller's grandiose construction projects, and there was no appetite for a further increase in the state sales tax. Lottery advocates pointed out that the state sanctioned bingo for charitable purposes and pari-mutuel betting at racetracks, so approving a lottery wouldn't be a great stretch. Besides, the New Hampshire experiment had removed the taboo against legalizing lotteries. Lawmakers approved a state lottery amendment and placed it on the ballot for a public referendum.

During the campaign, Rockefeller called it "the most retrogressive taxation you can get" (a few years later, amid another budget crunch, he supported legal off-track betting).[74] Even though lottery proceeds were earmarked for public education, the state Board of Regents unanimously opposed the concept, declaring, "We believe that attempts to support public education by the lottery involve serious moral considerations and, in our opinion, are inconsistent with the goals of education."[75] Nevertheless, 61 percent of voters backed the lottery in November 1966.

New York's lottery organizers tried to avoid New Hampshire's mistakes. Tickets were priced at only one dollar each to encourage wider play; they were sold at thousands of outlets such as hotels and, oddly, bank branches; and drawings were monthly and prizes were bigger. Initially, the changes appeared to pay off. Demand was exceptionally strong when the lottery commenced in June 1967; one bank said it sold two hundred tickets in fifteen minutes.[76] Annual sales forecasts soared to $360 million, of which the state's take would be $200 million.

However, the lottery was bedeviled by the same strictures that thwarted New Hampshire. Soon after the lottery began, Congress expressed alarm that banks were being used as the main conduit for sales. "I do not feel this is an appropriate function for financial institutions, the traditional bastions of thrift and frugality," said one congressman.[77] Congress amended the banking laws to ban federally insured banks from distributing or advertising tickets, a blow to New York lottery commissioners who suddenly had to find new sales outlets.

Customers endured the familiar inconveniences of furnishing a name and address just to purchase a ticket and receiving a numbered receipt instead of the actual ticket to sidestep lottery laws. The drawing process was even more complicated than New Hampshire's and involved the results of previously run horse races in New York. (This was done so the state could avoid paying a 10 percent federal wagering tax.) Collecting prizes was a hassle. To avoid mailing them, lottery officials opened a bank account in the winner's name, then closed the account and mailed a bank draft to the winner.

The ban on broadcasting lottery information forced authorities to install billboards and signs in subways and buses to drum up publicity. One poster read: "Big $100,000 winner every month—plus 3,618,863 little winners," a reference to the state's schoolchildren who would benefit.[78] But even manufacturing the signs had its difficulties. Truckers carrying materials needed to create the billboards had to stay within the state's borders even if the route took the driver hundreds of miles out of the way because it was illegal to transport lottery material across state lines.[79]

It all added up to disaster for New York's lottery. When the results came in, they were nowhere near the state's laughably optimistic projections. Sales in the first full year were $62.4 million, and public education received $34.3 million of that amount, far below the hoped-for $198 million.[80]

Winners of the $100,000 jackpots seemed blasé about their good fortune. "I suppose some people would be thrilled," said Walter Burnley, a semiretired private detective. "But I have money to live on."[81] Another winner, a factory worker, cut short an interview, telling a reporter, "Okay, I've got to get back to work."[82]

While sales in the New Hampshire and New York lotteries kept declining, participation in illegal numbers games surged. The US Treasury Department estimated that the annual take from numbers gambling in New York City was $1.5 billion, according to a 1970 report in the *New York Times*.[83] After payment of prizes, salaries, and protection money, the crime syndicates took a profit of 10 to 15 percent, dwarfing state revenue from the New York Lottery.

In 1972 the Fund for the City of New York studied gambling and estimated that one in four New Yorkers played the numbers racket, with 40 percent saying they took part in it full time or six days a week. The study concluded that the New York legislature should legalize the numbers game with the justification that "the primary objective of any legal form of gambling should be the elimination of its illegal counterpart."[84]

Nearly a decade after New Hampshire's foray into lotteries, it was hard to see how state-run games could ever hope to compete against the numbers rackets. After all, players could pick their own numbers, place bets practically every day, promptly receive prize money, and pay no taxes on winnings. States would have to innovate, challenge hidebound rules, and then blatantly copy the numbers games in order to defeat them.

———

In November 1969 New Jersey voters overwhelmingly supported a lottery referendum to become the third state to authorize a lottery. This time, lawmakers co-opted many of the qualities that made the numbers racket so successful. Tickets were only fifty cents; they were sold at about two thousand locations at places like bars, newsstands, and grocery stores; and drawings were weekly with a twice-a-year shot at a $1 million jackpot.[85] Unlike in New Hampshire and New York, New Jersey did not require bettors to fill out a form with their name and address, and drawings were not tied to outcomes of horse races.

New Jersey's governor purchased the first ticket on December 16, 1970, and 6 million more were sold in the next two weeks.[86] For once, a state's lottery revenue estimates were too pessimistic. The state expected $25 million in sales in the lottery's first full year; instead it grossed more than $137 million, with half of the money steered to education.[87]

The state fearlessly promoted its jackpot winners in a direct challenge to the Federal Communications Commission's prohibitions. The lottery was a bona fide sensation and an irresistible story for the media. The first players to claim the "millionaire drawing" in March 1971, Edward and Kathleen Henry of West Caldwell, chatted about their good fortune on *The Mike Douglas Show* and many other TV and radio outlets. The FCC determined that such interviews were permissible to put on the air if they were human-interest features and not pitches to buy tickets. But to audiences at home, the sight of ordinary folks marveling at their sudden wealth was the most powerful endorsement of lotteries imaginable.

In 1972 a New Jersey-based licensed radio station asked the FCC if it could mention the winning number of the state's weekly drawing during its Thursday night news broadcasts.[88] The FCC replied that it would be a violation. A federal court reversed the commission, ruling that such an announcement enjoyed First Amendment protection as legitimate news. While the issue wended its way through the legal system, Congress carved out an exception for state-authorized lotteries, allowing them to transport tickets and advertise on radio and TV within the state and in adjacent states with legal lotteries. By 1975 about a dozen states had enacted lotteries, and the federal government showed little interest in interfering with their legal efforts to raise revenue.

Freed from the quaint legal constraints that bedeviled the early lotteries, states devised ever more ways to increase their appeal to drive up revenue:

- The Massachusetts Lottery, which held its first drawing in historic Faneuil Hall in Boston in 1972, was the first to sell scratch-off tickets in 1974. The widely available "instant" tickets meant that a player didn't need to wait for a drawing to know if a ticket was a winner or loser.
- The New Jersey Lottery became a true numbers game in 1975 when advancements in computer technology gave players the chance to choose their own numbers. Within a year, "Pick-it" became the state's most popular game and doubled total lottery sales to $158 million.[89]
- In New York, computers linked weekly drawings in a game that the state called Lotto. The odds of correctly picking six numbers were absurdly high, but so were the jackpots that ran well into the millions of dollars.

States rushed to adopt instant scratch-off tickets, pick-your-own numbers games, and multimillion-dollar payouts. These innovations were complemented by aggressive marketing campaigns that encouraged frequent play for the good of the state. When scratch-off tickets made their debut in New York in 1976, the state couldn't print them fast enough to keep up with demand. Nearly 19 million tickets were sold in the first week, a record for any lottery.[90]

By the end of the 1970s fourteen states—all in the Northeast or Midwest—legalized lotteries, with most of them benefiting education

programs. In 1981 Arizona became the first state west of the Mississippi
to operate a lottery, and most states in the West followed in the next few
years. California's entry into the lottery game in 1985 pushed jackpots past
the $100 million mark. Western expansion created a domino effect in the
Rocky Mountain and Great Plains states; by the end of the 1980s thirty-
one states plus the District of Columbia had adopted legal lotteries.

States with much smaller populations than New York banded together
to conduct drawings with equally high jackpots. In 1987 the District of
Columbia, Iowa, Kansas, Oregon, Rhode Island, and West Virginia united
to create the Multi-State Lottery Association, a consortium of state lotteries
that participated in lotto games. Among them was Lotto America, the pre-
cursor to Powerball. As more lotteries joined multistate ventures—Mega
Millions is the other major national player—the odds and jackpots sky-
rocketed. Early Powerball games featured a 1 in 55 million chance of a bettor correctly picking five "white" numbers out of forty-five, plus the "red"
Powerball number out of forty-five. When Powerball raised its ticket price
from one dollar to two dollars in 2012, the odds jumped to 1 in 175 million and the minimum jackpot doubled from $20 million to $40 million.
Powerball, which forty-four states participate in, changed the rules again
in 2015 to increase the number of white numbers to sixty-nine. The chance
of winning the jackpot soared to 1 in 292 million.

The grim mathematical probabilities of hitting the jackpot don't deter
ticket buyers, especially when weeks pass without a grand-prize winner
and the pot multiplies into the hundreds of millions of dollars or even
into the billions, as what happened in January 2016 when the Powerball
jackpot swelled to $1.6 billion. When such an astounding sum is seemingly
there for the taking, it sends jolts of electricity through workplaces and
swells their lottery pools. Ticket buyers who wait in long lines at convenience stores, supermarkets, and gas stations vibrate with giddiness at the
wonder of it all. Lottery players crack dark jokes about the lottery as their
main retirement plan and idly fantasize about how they would spend such
a vast fortune.

Jackpot winners are treated like folk heroes by news organizations and lottery organizers to show the millions of losers that with a different number here or there, it could have just as easily been them. Some of the stories tap directly into the American dream. In 2006 eight workers at a meatpacking plant in Nebraska claimed a $365 million Powerball jackpot, the largest in US history up to then. Among them was a man who had left Vietnam for America and pledged to help family members still in Southeast Asia. Another winner, Alain Maboussou, had fled the civil war in Congo in 1999 and said his share of $15.5 million after taxes would allow him to quit work and go back to school. Maboussou believed the money would create a bright future for his young family. "She's going to be happy for the rest of her life," he said about his three-month-old daughter.[91]

Winning the lottery turned out to be a curse for Abraham Shakespeare, an ex-con who claimed $30 million in the Florida Lottery in 2006. His troubled life included an arrest at age thirteen, reform school, arrests for trespassing and assault, a prison sentence, and another arrest for falling behind on child support. Shakespeare was working as a truck driver's assistant for eight dollars an hour when he won the lottery and elected to take the lump sum of $17 million.[92]

The barely literate man who had never even had a bank account was suddenly hounded with pleas for assistance, to which he wearily responded with stacks of cash. He met a woman named Dorice "Dee Dee" Moore, who ingratiated herself with Shakespeare as his financial manager and steadily wheedled money out him. Shakespeare's family reported him missing in November 2009; two months later investigators found his body buried underneath a concrete slab behind Moore's home. He had been shot twice in the chest with a .38-caliber pistol. Moore, who had a criminal record of her own, was arrested and convicted of first-degree murder in Shakespeare's killing.

The litany of made-for-reality-TV cautionary tales has conditioned winners to be much less conspicuous. In June 2013 an eighty-four-year-old Florida widow claimed what was then the largest undivided lottery jackpot in history: $590 million. Gloria MacKenzie waited more than two weeks after the drawing to cash in her Powerball ticket for a lump sum of $370 million, or about $278 million after taxes.[93] MacKenzie shied away from the usual publicity bonanza: no photos of her posing with an over-sized check, no tearful news conference, no interviews on the *Today* show or *Good Morning America*. Instead she released a written statement asking for privacy and hurried past a clutch of reporters outside Florida's lottery headquarters in Tallahassee. MacKenzie, who wore dark sunglasses and a dazed expression, took no questions and was ushered into her silver Ford Focus by her son and her hastily arranged team of legal and financial advisers.

––––––

With their mind-boggling jackpots, state lotteries captured the imaginations and the dollars of bettors and effectively broke the back of illegal numbers games. Forty-four states and the District of Columbia operate lotteries. (As of 2017 the only states without legal lotteries are Alabama, Alaska, Hawaii, Mississippi, Nevada, and Utah.) State lottery games generated a total of $68.8 billion in sales in fiscal 2012, more than six times the total sales of domestic movie tickets in 2012. More than $19 billion was transferred to public schools or other state programs.[94]

For all of the billions of sales racked up by the lotteries each year, the revenue generated has a surprisingly small impact on state budgets. Twenty-three lotteries are explicitly directed to raise money for education, but they accounted for less than 1 percent of total spending for K–12 public schools in at least five of those states in 2006, according to a *New York Times* review.[95] (New York's portion was the highest at 5.3 percent.) Their hefty administrative, marketing, and prize payout expenses leave about a third of total sales for public programs. For instance, the Ohio Lottery took in $2.16 billion in receipts in 2005, but only 30 percent ($645 million) was channeled to education.[96] Such inefficiency calls to mind the schemes of the 1800s, when so little was raised for the supposed purpose of the lottery.

But in an era of tight budgets and strong antitax sentiment, states zealously protect even a 1 or 2 percent contribution to their education budgets. Underperforming lotteries spur states to pump up their generous advertising budgets and introduce new drawings and scratcher games to encourage more play. In 2010 California governor Arnold Schwarzenegger reversed his state lottery's slide by authorizing bigger prizes and higher-priced tickets such as ten-dollar and twenty-dollar scratch-off tickets.

Unfortunately, such aggressive moves tend to entice the people who can least afford to play. In 2013 the Florida Lottery expanded the menu and increased the price of scratch-off tickets and authorized selling them at self-service kiosks. The lottery also ramped up its advertising in poorer ZIP codes and targeted minority groups, according to an analysis by the *Sun Sentinel*.[97] Scratch-off sales jumped from $2 billion in 2010 to $3.7 billion in 2015, and sales in high-poverty areas rose nearly three times faster than in other areas, the newspaper found. In Miami's poor Little Havana neighborhood, the average household spent $432 on the tickets in 2015, nearly double the amount five years earlier.

Other states are turning to outsourcing to move the revenue needle. In 2013 New Jersey governor Chris Christie privatized much of his state's lottery with the promise that it would ramp up sales far beyond what state operators could accomplish. Northstar New Jersey Lottery Group, the company chosen to run sales and marketing, issued a one-time $120 million payment to the state as part of the fifteen-year contract. The state and the company have squabbled over missed revenue projections.

State governments have conquered the lottery business with governors playing the role of modern-day "policy kings." They also rousted mobsters from their traditional role as titans of the rackets. Organized crime figure Leonard Minuto, who pleaded guilty in 1998 to running a gambling ring on behalf of the Gambino crime family in New York, lamented that that state-run lotteries' frequent drawings, array of games, and astronomical jackpots decimated the once-fruitful numbers rackets.[98] Business got so bad for the longtime Bronx numbers kingpin that he couldn't afford the

$4,000 protection payment due weekly to the Gambino family boss Paul Castellano. (Minuto received mercy and got the payment cut in half.[99])

In federal court testimony in 2006, Minuto pointed out that states keep a much larger share of the take than illegal operators, who accept a 15 percent (tax-free) profit margin. That meant he could offer better odds to customers than the state for picking a three-digit number. "The state pays 500 to 1 and the numbers give 600 to 1," he said at the racketeering trial.[100] Left unspoken was the searing indictment that the states were greedier than the mobsters and had effectively beaten them at their own game.

CHAPTER 3

State of Play

NEVADA BREAKS NEW GROUND
WITH LEGALIZED GAMBLING

Now we can do lawfully what Nevada has always done under cover.
—Reno mayor Edwin E. Roberts after Nevada legalized gambling in 1931

Fittingly, the decision to grant statehood to Nevada was tied to its use-fulness as an election-year bargaining chip. The thinly inhabited terrain first attracted widespread attention with the discovery of the Comstock Lode in 1859, the richest silver deposit in American history. Suddenly the region's rugged mountain ranges were no longer merely seen as obstacles for settlers to climb over en route to California. Virginia City and other mining boomtowns sprung up as word spread of the silver strike. Congress declared Nevada a territory in 1861.

By 1864 the nation was embroiled in the fourth year of the Civil War, and President Abraham Lincoln faced reelection. He permitted the territory to seek statehood for two main reasons: first, an acknowledgment that millions of dollars of precious metals pulled from the Comstock Lode benefited the Union war effort; and second, a political reality that Lincoln needed another state to ratify the Thirteenth Amendment to abolish slavery.[1] The territory's voters approved the Nevada Constitution, and Lincoln proclaimed Nevada a state on October 31, 1864, just in time for it to cast its electoral votes for him in the November 8 election. Nevada's first two senators were Republicans, and its first member of the House voted in favor of the Thirteenth Amendment in 1865 and the Nevada legislature ratified it, more than earning Lincoln's reward of statehood.

During Nevada's early days, saloons and brothels lined the rutted streets of mining towns, and gambling was rampant. William H. Brewer, a visitor to the mining camp of Aurora in 1863, wrote about the town's packed saloons "where lights are bright, amid the hum of many voices and the excitement of gambling. Here men come to make money—make it *quick*—not by slow, honest industry, but by quick strokes—no matter *how*, so long as the law doesn't call it *robbery*."[2] His description of a night on the town in Nevada more than 150 years ago rings true to any visitor to Las Vegas today.

The state's legislature legalized gambling in 1869 and set up a system to collect fees for licenses and enforce rules such as prohibiting gambling in the front rooms of the establishments. By the early 1900s the Progressive-era temperance movement had swept across the country and shut down lotteries, racetracks, and saloons. Reform-minded Nevada approved a law in 1909 that made gambling a felony. A person who possessed a gaming device was subject to $500 fine and six months in jail. Authorities were permitted to destroy such equipment and even gave them clearance to "break open doors" if necessary to seize the devices. Prosecution was scant and bribery of law enforcement officials by saloon operators was commonplace, creating an atmosphere of hypocrisy and corruption.

The 1929 stock market crash and the onset of the Great Depression created favorable conditions for those who wanted to liberalize Nevada's gambling laws and capture new revenue for state and local governments. In 1930 Las Vegas developer Thomas H. Carroll placed a series of advertisements in southern Nevada newspapers that touted legalized gambling as a way to attract wealthy tourists. His prescient vision of Nevada as the "Playground of the United States" relied on making gambling a state industry. It would not only "bring more millions of dollars into Nevada than . . . any other industry we now have," but it would also have the salutary side effect of cutting out underground operators, he argued.[3] Also in 1931 a companion bill reduced the length of residency required for divorce from three

months to just six weeks. As in the gambling legalization debate, supporters argued that the "quickie" divorce bill would attract out-of-state visitors
and their dollars to Nevada. It worked. In 1931 there were 4,745 divorces in
Reno, then a city of fewer than 20,000 people.[4]

Carroll's campaign reflected the changing attitude toward gambling
in the business community and among lawmakers in the capital of Carson City. Newspapers were also softening their stance on gambling. A
1931 article published in the *Nevada State Journal* the day before legislators began what would be a historic session stated "that there is a strong
sentiment, particularly in Southern Nevada, that some state or municipal
revenue should be derived from the games which now run on every hand
with apparent sanction of public sentiment."[5]

First-term assemblyman Phil Tobin, a rancher from northern Nevada
with no links to gambling interests, introduced a gambling legalization bill
on February 13, 1931, that he said would remedy the failures of two decades
of prohibiting gambling. Assembly Bill 98 faced scattered opposition,
mainly from religious groups and women's organizations, but received
wide support in both houses. On March 19, 1931, Gov. Fred Balzar signed
it into law, making Nevada the first state in modern American history to
legalize nearly all forms of gambling—slot machines, casino-style card
games and roulette, sports gambling, and bookmaking. (There was no
provision for a state lottery, a ban that has persisted chiefly because of the
influence of casinos.) Each county organized a five-member board—three
county commissioners, the district attorney, and the sheriff—responsible
for awarding gambling licenses. Cities could also grant licenses for gambling within city limits. Fees were divided among the city, county, and state
even though Nevada itself had no enforcement role, a fatal flaw that would
be exposed years later.

Reaction in the state ran the spectrum from critical to supportive
while out-of-state newspapers adopted a judgmental tone: the *Los Angeles Times* pronounced Nevada "a vicious Babylon," the *Kansas City Star*
called Reno a mixture of "Sodom, Gomorrah and Hell," and the *Chicago Tribune* went so far as to suggest canceling Nevada's statehood.[6] In

Washington, DC, a Methodist conference attacked the law and requested that the federal government intervene—a demand that would be carried out decades later.[7]

For all of the anxiety, legalized gambling in Nevada got off to a quiet start. Nevadans stuck to the old ways of gambling under cover and counties granted few licenses for fear that gambling would spread too fast and provoke the state to repeal the law. The hope that legalizing gambling would somehow immediately launch a major tourism industry was too optimistic for such a thinly populated, remote state. When the act was passed, Nevada's population was ninety thousand; Reno was by the largest city with nearly twenty thousand people, and Las Vegas had barely five thousand residents. The rest of the population was scattered across a forbidding landscape of mountain ranges to the north and the Mojave Desert to the south. In an era before jet travel and interstate highways, these were challenging barriers to overcome just to play a legal hand of poker or feed nickels in a slot machine in a few dank clubs. Nevada would need an injection of carnival-style showmanship for it to find its footing.

———

Reno's enviable location at the foot of the Sierra Nevada near the California border and just north of Lake Tahoe made it well suited to be the state's early gambling center. The town that has long promoted itself as "The Biggest Little City in the World" was big enough to sustain a string of illicit clubs along Commercial Row and Center Street during the 1920s. Visitors from California flooded into Reno on the night gambling became legal in 1931. "They were the strangest sight I've ever seen," said reporter Marion Welliver. "Big fat women had on cheap evening gowns—and they were wearing sneakers. You couldn't shove your way into those places. Those women looked like the wrath of God. They walked the streets all night and slept in the park."[8] About five thousand people flocked to Reno during Easter weekend that year, many of them motivated by reduced travel rates as much as the novelty of placing a legal bet. When told that Al Capone was lurking in California with an eye toward moving into Nevada, Reno's sheriff replied with a straight face, "Al Capone is welcome in Reno as long as he behaves himself."[9]

Despite such bravado—or, more likely, naiveté—Reno was tentative in making the transition from closed-door clubs to wide-open gambling. A stigma clung to gambling because of people like Bill Graham and Jim McKay, proprietors of the Bank Club that counted gangsters like John Dillinger and Charles "Pretty Boy" Floyd among their patrons.[10] Graham and McKay trafficked in bootlegged liquor and prostitution—they owned the Stockade, a brothel in Reno that offered gambling on the side. Their casinos were tough, hard-edged places. At the Bank Club, a guard armed with a shotgun loomed over the faro dealer to maintain order.[11] Graham and McKay profited handsomely from gambling's legalization and had no qualms about using brutal tactics to elbow out competitors. But authorities eventually caught up to them. Graham and McKay faced numerous indictments for running financial scams—a bank cashier who was set to testify against them conveniently disappeared before one of the trials—and were finally convicted of mail fraud and sentenced to prison.

Nevada's great legalization experiment was forward-thinking, but gambling still seemed to be stuck in the past. The state's casinos remained the same dark, intimidating places they had been before 1931, and politicians seemed to be fighting a rearguard action against the new reality. As a result, revenue from gambling licenses came in well below expectations. In 1933, for example, the fees generated only $69,000 for the state and $50,000 for Reno.[12] For legalized gambling to truly blossom, it would need to shed its seedy reputation, build legitimacy, and appeal to a broader customer base. The men who achieved these things in Reno may have looked and acted like bland bank examiners, but they were really revolutionaries who went a long way to changing gambling's image.

———

Raymond I. "Pappy" Smith, an itinerant carnival barker and odd jobber, plied his games of chance in the shadowlands of legality at fairgrounds and seaside attractions. In the 1920s Pappy and his two sons, Raymond A.

and Harold, hustled for customers at Chutes-at-the-Beach, an amusement park in San Francisco crammed with thrill rides like the Big Dip-
per coaster and the Aeroplane Swing. The Smiths were among hundreds
of concessionaires who jostled for pennies and nickels from the fevered
crowds in Ocean Beach. Pappy's booths featured midway mainstays such
as a game that tested a player's ability to knock down pyramids of leather
bottles with a baseball.

The summers at the beach taught the Smiths that hard work and clean
games could make them stand out among their crooked competitors. During the early years of the Great Depression, the Smiths took over a bingo
booth in the resort town of Rio Nido on the Russian River in Sonoma
County. Pappy reasoned that the game's previous operator failed because
he treated his clientele—mostly older women—shabbily. "He didn't treat
his customers as if they were real ladies out to buy enjoyment with their
money," Pappy said. "I did and prospered." The frugal Smiths earned
$4,500 by the end of one summer.[13]

They spent the winter farther inland, in Modesto, where the Smiths set
up a bingo parlor and daringly added a penny roulette game to their reper-
toire. Despite their reputation as aboveboard operators, they pressed their
luck too far. A reform movement in California darkened the state's benign
attitude toward gambling, and prosecutors started to crack down on bingo
and all other games of chance. After unveiling their roulette wheel in 1934,
the Smiths were fined $500 and received a ninety-day suspended sentence
for running an illegal gambling game.[14] "We were weary of building up
businesses only to lose them," Harold Smith wrote in his memoir. "We
didn't want to go jail."[15]

Harold and Pappy Smith had nowhere to go in California, so they
looked across the border to Nevada where practically all forms of gambling had been legalized just a few years earlier. During a trip to Reno,
Harold toured the bleak thoroughfares and came upon a few bingo parlors with scattered clutches of ne'er-do-well customers. Sensing an opportunity, he summoned his father to Reno and they talked to an owner of
one of the storefronts. With sorrow, the man said Reno was a lousy town

to make a living and wanted out. Harold, feeling an "electric tingle" of excitement, persuaded his father to pool their money and buy the shabby place. The Smiths paid $500 to settle the claims against the previous owner and took control with just $1,500 in capital and their gambling equipment scavenged from Modesto.

The dreary hall on Virginia Street was a block east from the cluster of casinos and nightclubs on Center Street—literally on the other side of the railroad tracks. The Smiths dredged up the giant penny roulette wheel that got them in trouble in Modesto and installed it in their shoebox of a casino, which they named Harolds Club after Pappy's son. An early newspaper ad for the casino promised that it wouldn't be business as usual in Reno: "Harolds Club, 236 North Virginia Street. Open at twelve noon. There is a big surprise in store for you."[16]

At first, the Smiths were treated like rubes because of their carnival-barker pasts. The club's first bouncer stole a cashbox from a craps game, and a dealer was fired after letting a crooked player win a $300 bankroll.[17] The local mob dispatched a delegation of councilmen who examined Harolds Club's vertical eight-foot "flasher" wheel. The city imposed a tax on each wheel in Reno, but a corrupt councilman proposed taxing each of the forty-three spaces on the Smith family's wheel. The plan was abandoned, but the intimation was felt. A few days later, the brothers stood firm when a group of hoodlums visited Harolds Club. During the confrontation, Harold secretly cradled a loaded .38 just in case violence erupted. If the Smiths had buckled, it would have sent a message to other racketeers that the family and Harolds Club could be had.

The Smiths dismissed the widely held notion that casinos should be dark, secretive places. Harolds Club cheerfully welcomed all. The club's glass doors and bright lights enticed pedestrians to wander in and place bets of as low as five cents—well under their competitors. Pappy sliced the house take to under 5 percent even though his rivals kept as much as 20 percent.[18] Their slot machines offered more generous payouts then other casinos. Pappy believed that returning a greater percentage of money to gamblers would encourage them to stay longer and play more.

The Smiths tirelessly experimented to find a winning formula on their casino floor, adding "crapless" craps, more progressive slot machines, and the traditional Chinese game fan-tan. But their most novel—and attention-getting—innovation was undoubtedly "mouse roulette." Pappy Smith was intrigued by a casino visitor's idea to use a live mouse instead of the usual spinning white ball in roulette and hired him to run the game at Harolds Club. The mouse was placed in a box on a table with fifty numbered holes and players bet on which hole the mouse would scurry into. A drawer under the table caught the falling mouse, and winners were paid off at the same odds as a normal roulette game. But as Harold himself pointed out, the game was easily rigged.[19] If the mouse approached a section of the board where no one had placed bets, the game operator would make a sudden noise to scare it down one of those holes. The mice also weren't the most reliable of employees, sometimes refusing to scamper down any hole at all.

Although the carnival-style gimmick was suspended after only one week in 1938, the club earned invaluable free publicity. News services transmitted photographs and accounts of "mouse roulette" across the nation, and Harolds Club became the talk of the town. (Even decades later, visitors asked if they could play the game or see the celebrated mouse.) The flamboyant experiment confirmed Pappy Smith's insight that for casinos to truly succeed, they needed to create a fun atmosphere and advertise heavily—two insights that ran counter to conventional casino wisdom.

When Harolds Club began attracting visitors from California, the Smiths launched a vigorous advertising campaign to tout their club as a friendly place to play. They put up twenty-five roadside billboards within five hundred miles of Reno and noticed an immediate uptick in business.[20] Eventually, the nation's highways were dotted with more than two thousand signs emblazoned with the words "Harolds Club or Bust!" and a cartoon of a covered wagon. The folksy billboards became as well known to motorists as the era's poetic Burma-Shave signs, and they even popped up at overseas military bases during World War II—the sign in Casablanca read "10,648 miles to Harolds Club."

Since gambling was legal in Nevada, Pappy Smith reasoned that there should be no shame in advertising his casino as if it were any other legal business. In addition to the billboards, the club aggressively advertised in newspapers. The ads never explicitly referred to gambling, but by then everyone knew what went on there. In its heyday, Harolds Club was the state's single biggest newspaper advertiser.[21]

The Smiths were also believers in the power of word-of-mouth advertising. If a gambler who lost his last dollar approached Pappy Smith with his tale of woe, chances were that if the player's story checked out, he would receive a full refund and even a little extra to pay for the bus fare home. Such generosity had conditions, however. Smith made sure the dissolute player knew that it was a one-time only offer and would record his name and address in a file just in case he or she came back. The loser was instructed never to inform anyone that Harolds Club refunded the money, but it was requested that he or she tell others that the club was an honest place to play.

After World War II, Harolds Club took over building after building on the block, expanding to the point that it became the nation's largest casino. The club opened an exhibit jammed with memorabilia from Nevada's pioneer days and arranged for special family-friendly hours so children and school groups could gawk at the impressive collection of firearms.[22] A three-story-high mural on the outside of the building paid tribute to the state's settlers with a detailed depiction of a wagon train camp.[23]

Business at the rustic, "dime-store" casino remained strong into the 1950s, with more than 1 million passing through Harolds Club each year and as many as nineteen thousand customers on its busiest days.[24] The Smith family's style and décor weren't for all tastes, however. A reporter for *Life* magazine ridiculed the casino in a harsh dispatch in 1954. "Harolds is strictly assembly-line gambling. You can walk in wearing a tattered lumber jacket with the dirt of a farm or a mine on your shoes and feel right at home. There is nothing fancy about Harolds. Indeed Harolds is as garish and as nakedly ugly as an unshaded light blub hanging from the ceiling in a flophouse dormitory," wrote Ernest Havemann, who concluded that he never wanted to go back to Reno.[25] The criticisms he leveled against Harolds Club were precisely the reasons it was popular.

Things weren't running so smoothly behind the scenes, though. Pappy, a teetotaler who refrained from casino gambling, believed Harold's cavorting around town was threatening the family business. Harold drank up to four quarts of whiskey every day and lost piles of money in reckless wagers in rival casinos.[26] Pappy went so far as to draw up legal paperwork to keep Harold's stock in the club out of the hands of competitors by giving Pappy the option to buy him out for $500,000.[27] The provision was never executed and the threat was enough to persuade Harold to stop gambling in other clubs.

In 1962 the Smiths sold the property and buildings to a New York investment firm for about $16 million, but they leased back the casino. Pappy Smith died in 1967, and his despondent son decided not to carry on with his namesake club. "My Pappy and I were partners, and when I lost my Daddy, I couldn't run Harolds Club," Harold Smith lamented.[28] The Smith family exited the casino business for good in 1970 when Harolds Club was purchased by another important player in the history of gambling in Nevada, Howard Hughes.

———

Like the Smiths, Bill Harrah became rich by appealing to the common man. They shared similar origins in seaside carnivals in California, rose together in the casino business as next-door neighbors on Reno's Virginia Street, and managed to steer clear of underworld influence. They were shrewd promoters in an industry that had preferred to operate in private. They had done as much as anybody to make gambling a legitimate business and worked well with government leaders. But long after the Smith family and Harolds Club faded from memory, Harrah's name and influence persisted and lives on to this day.

William Fisk Harrah was born and raised in Southern California where his father ran a successful law practice and invested in real estate across the burgeoning region. John Harrah also dabbled in politics, serving as mayor

of Venice before the city of Los Angeles annexed the beach community
in 1926. The Harrah family's fortunes changed overnight with the stock
market crash in 1929. Real estate values plummeted and John Harrah was
stuck with mortgages that far exceeded property values. He lost everything
except for the family residence and a lease on a building on the Venice pier,
a busy amusement area with rides, carnival games, and hot dog stands.

At the dawn of the Great Depression, Bill Harrah was studying engineering at UCLA but proved to be an indifferent student and was caught
cheating on a chemistry exam. Without a clear direction, Harrah agreed to
help his father scratch out a living on the pier. John Harrah was intrigued
by a fellow concessionaire in his building who was making a few bucks
off a scheme called the Circle Game, which was similar to bingo. Players
bought playing cards from a dealer and tried to aim a marble down a ramp
to hit a number and suit that matched their cards. Winners received a car-
ton of cigarettes worth $1.25.

The Harrahs started their own version of the game and struggled to
earn $100 a week. Bill Harrah wasn't pleased with how his father ran the
business and bought it from him for $500. Bill immediately put his stamp
on the Circle Game, firing the shills his father had insisted were necessary
to ensure the house advantage. Bill also attended to the needs of his customers, installing comfortable stools and putting up drapes to add visual
appeal to the drafty storeroom.[29]

Profits spiked once word spread that the game was run on the square.
Without the shills steering the outcomes, players stood a better chance
of winning. But the Harrahs and other bingo operators on the pier operated at the pleasure of local government. Authorities conducted periodic
sweeps in mid-1930s, shuttering bingo games in Venice and other seaside
spots in Southern California. When policemen tried to close down the
Circle Game, John Harrah crafted a lawyerly argument that it was not a
game of chance because skillful players could maneuver the marble to
their advantage. His legal and political connections won a reprieve for the
Circle Game, making it the only such game in town. The Circle Game's
thirty stools were occupied twelve hours a day with crowds waiting their

turn to play. Bill Harrah estimated that they made $25,000 in the three months they had the bingo business to themselves.[30]

When the political climate improved, Bill Harrah bought out other bingo competitors and operated them the same way he ran the Circle Game. But when the winds of reform blew yet again, licenses were pulled and games were shut down without warning or explanation. "And that happened over and over, and it just got where it was—that's when I started thinkin' of other places," Harrah said in an echo of the Smith family's frustration with California's on-again, off-again interference in their business.[31]

Harrah and a few friends from school took a road trip to Reno, where gambling had been legal for several years. They devoured hearty dinners, gambled at the Bank Club's craps table, and drank at bars that didn't close. As Harrah walked by the city's teeming bingo parlors, he had the nagging feeling that he came to Reno too late to capitalize on legal gambling. A month after his return to Los Angeles, Harrah received a letter from a failed bingo operator asking if he would be interested in buying a closed bingo parlor in Reno. Harrah jumped at the opportunity and scooped it up at a bargain price.

But there was a big problem: it was in a terrible location. In 1937, Center Street was several blocks away from the city's gambling corridor. Harrah managed to keep the bingo parlor open for several weeks before going bust. The failure taught him the lesson that location is everything in the gambling business.

He recovered by securing leases in properties along Reno's two-block gambling district. As an outsider to Reno's folkways, Harrah rejiggered his games to see what would work. He undercut his competitors using tactics honed on the Venice pier. A leading bingo operator sold two cards for a nickel; Harrah's new spot on Commercial Row sold cards two for a nickel and also six for a dime on the theory that players will often spend the dime given that choice.[32]

Like the Smith family, Harrah had his own brush with Reno's underworld. A dollar slot machine and liquor went missing from Harrah's Blackout Bar. Harrah called the police, who discovered that a bartender and a tough guy at a casino across the street worked together to pull off the heist. Even though he recovered his slot machine, Harrah insisted on pressing charges. The manager of the rival casino visited Harrah and suggested that he should just let it go, darkly hinting that he needed to play ball to fit in. Harrah stood firm, and the goons were convicted and sent to prison. He reflected later that it was only time he faced intimidation and added that he never again felt worried about his safety.[33]

Harrah's ascent in Nevada's gambling fraternity was helped along by his innate political savvy. "Throughout his career, Harrah would work behind the scenes with city government and with the state legislature; prompting, pushing, probably occasionally bribing his way ahead," wrote Harrah biographer Leon Mandel.[34] Although the shy Harrah was certainly no glad-hander, he felt enough at ease to go directly to the sheriff or the mayor for pressing business reasons.

Money rolled in, and Harrah calculated that the time was right to graduate from bingo to a full-service casino. In 1946 he opened Harrah's Club on Virginia Street—the same street as Harolds Club. Pappy Smith and Harrah competed for property as well as customers. Smith annexed Harrah's bingo parlor next door to Harolds Club when Harrah's lease expired. Harrah had no choice but to back down to the more powerful man and politely listen to the elder Smith's rambling speeches about his right-wing politics and the virtues of the John Birch Society.

Harrah took some cues from Smith's skill at promotion and unveiled an advertising campaign that referred to "gaming" to ease the stigma attached to the word "gambling." Harrah benefited from spillover from the crowds Harolds Club attracted to Reno. Harrah applied his thoughtful eye for design to the casino's bars and even its carpet to create an elegant atmosphere that distinguished it from the down-home appeal of Harolds Club and other joints in town. "We want nearly everybody," Harrah said of his ideal customers. "We don't want the ones who are dirty and noisy."[35]

Harrah, a tall, bespectacled man with a ramrod-straight posture, set a tone of perfectionism that every employee was expected to follow. Attendants constantly roamed the casino to pick up trash, polish the slot machines, and empty ashtrays.[36] Harrah demanded explanations from his staff whenever he noticed burned-out light bulbs or dust along a railing on an escalator.[37] Harrah installed one-way glass beneath an upstairs office that allowed him to monitor activity on the casino floor.[38] His "eye in the sky" innovation would become commonplace in the industry to keep tabs on gamblers as well as his employees. He hired managers who enforced his passion for order and cleanliness, making Harrah a brand name for brisk, reliable service.

That obsessiveness extended to Harrah's lifelong interest in cars. In an oral history recorded near the end of his life, the normally reticent Harrah talked for hours about his love for collecting antique automobiles. Harrah attended races and rallies around the world and opened a museum in the Reno area to showcase his extensive car collection, which numbered 1,400 vehicles and was considered among the world's finest.[39] Harrah's rows of rare Bugattis and Duesenbergs were as immaculate as his casino properties. The same could not be said for his personal life. The fastidious man with a banker's countenance had a tempestuous romantic life, marrying seven times—twice to the same woman. When he felt lonely between marriages, Harrah consorted with prostitutes in businesslike meetings in anonymous motel rooms.[40] Harrah offered a typically understated explanation for his many trips down the aisle: "I like being married, and so [when] I found somebody I cared for, why, I would get married."[41]

By the 1950s Harrah and the Smiths were anomalies in Nevada because they were clean operators with direct control of their properties. They did not need the money of nefarious out-of-town investors if they wanted to add a restaurant or showroom to their Reno casinos or, in Harrah's case, build casinos and hotels elsewhere in Nevada such as Lake Tahoe. Weak government oversight of gambling in Nevada created problems that became more apparent when the state's center of gravity shifted south to Las Vegas.

———

Las Vegas was barely a speck on the map when Nevada legalized gambling in 1931. It was founded in 1905 as a railroad way station between Salt

Lake City and Los Angeles, and the population grew to little more than a few thousand people well into the 1920s. Las Vegas was so obscure that a magazine writer pointed out to his readers that the Nevada town was "not to be confused with the New Mexican town of the same name," which was then a railroad depot.[42]

Soon after legalization, the editor of the *Las Vegas Evening Review-Journal* warned that the city should impose severe restrictions on the number of casinos. "We are unalterably opposed to the granting of any further city licenses at this time, and from a careful survey of the community we are prepared to state that the sentiment of a great majority of residents is in absolute accord," he wrote.[43] The city council followed that advice and limited the number of licenses to six clustered downtown.

The sputtering Depression-era economy squelched aspiring entrepreneurs. The first recipients of a gambling license from Clark County under the 1931 act were Mayme Virginia Stocker and Joe H. Morgan, hardly the stereotypical hotel-casino magnates.[44] The humble owners of the modest Northern Club on Fremont Street served soft drinks and phosphates in the waning days of Prohibition. The owners struggled mightily to come up with the $1,410 due each quarter to pay for their license and eventually pulled out of the gambling game.

In the early 1930s Las Vegans were more excited about the construction of the Boulder Dam than the legalization of gambling. The staggering scope of the federal government's undertaking—the amount of concrete used to build the dam could pave a highway from San Francisco to New York City—required thousands of workers. Las Vegas, still a tiny desert outpost, swelled with job seekers who wanted to be part of the project going up just thirty miles away. Las Vegas styled itself as the "Gateway City" to the Black Canyon of the Colorado River, a convenient stopping-off point for tourists to witness the dam's construction.[45]

The dam, dedicated by President Franklin D. Roosevelt in 1935 and today known as the Hoover Dam, had a profound effect on the region. The engineering marvel harnessed the mighty but flood-prone Colorado River to serve human needs. The dam formed Lake Mead, which conserved water essential for agricultural and household use. The water and hydro-electric power made possible the explosive growth of cities like Los Angeles, Phoenix, and, of course, Las Vegas. A memorial to the roughly one hundred workers who perished during the project's construction bears the evocative inscription, "They died to make the desert bloom."

––––––

The Boulder Dam kicked off a boom that inspired some would-be casino magnates to push outside of the city limits of Las Vegas. Tony Cornero, a Prohibition-era bootlegger, opened a swanky casino/nightclub called the Meadows in 1931. He and his brothers were the first to break out of the downtown casino core, choosing a spot where Fremont Street turns into Boulder Highway leading to Boulder City.[46] With his rum-running background, Cornero had no reservations about serving fine imported liquors at his establishment.[47] In a town then more suited to blue jeans and cowboy boots, patrons were expected to dress up to attend the club's stage shows. His ambitions ran aground in the Depression economy, and he traded the desert for the ocean to run the infamous casino SS *Rex* that operated illegally off the Southern California coast.

The real focus of casino expansion would not be Boulder Highway but Los Angeles Highway, also known as Highway 91. Prescient hotel-casino entrepreneurs understood that the success of Las Vegas would hinge on its appeal to Southern Californians. For an Angeleno to drive hundreds of miles to a remote desert location, something special needed to be at the end of the road. The novelty of legalized gambling would certainly be an important draw, but that alone would not be enough to motivate the masses to trek deep into the Mojave Desert. Hotel amenities, restaurants, and showroom entertainment had to keep tourists occupied and, more important, distinctive enough for them to come back.

Los Angeles hotel magnate Thomas Hull was one of those early developers who knew what travelers wanted. Hull was the managing director of a chain of hotels in Fresno, Sacramento, and Los Angeles (one of them the landmark Hollywood Roosevelt), and ran two California motels under the "El Rancho" name in the 1930s. Las Vegas businessmen approached Hull about building a resort there, but he surprised them by choosing a tract of land outside city limits on Highway 91. The cheap, undeveloped lot was three miles from the two-block concentration of casinos on downtown's Fremont Street. Hull envisioned transforming the parcel of sand and sagebrush into a full-service resort. (As a true Angeleno, one of the site's attractions for Hull was that it would offer abundant parking.[48])

Hull hired architect Wayne McAllister to use his Spanish-style designs for the El Rancho motels as a template for the new Nevada property. Hull appreciated McAllister's experience as the designer of the thriving Agua Caliente resort in Tijuana and encouraged him to include similar architectural grace notes to El Rancho Vegas.[49] Its opening on April 3, 1941, signified the birth of the Strip. El Rancho Vegas was a full-fledged resort that distinguished itself from the highway's shabby roadhouses, motor courts, and gas stations. A distinctive roadside windmill tower and a neon sign welcomed visitors into the rambling resort where they would find a steakhouse, lounge, casino, and guest cottages. A swimming pool beckoned as an oasis for parched tourists, and stables for horseback riding stayed true to the ranch-style motif.

As Hull had hoped, the innovations appealed to tourists and Hollywood stars alike. But his timing was a bit off. America's entry into World War II brought on gasoline rationing, which put severe restrictions on unnecessary travel. Chronic management problems dogged the hotel, and Hull sold it. Yet it was his insight that the city's future would consist of a strip of resorts along Highway 91 that inspired others to follow his example. R. E. Griffith, a Texan who owned a chain of movie theaters in the Southwest, built the Last Frontier resort in late 1942 about a mile south of El Rancho Vegas on Highway 91. Griffith and his team of interior designers might have gone a little overboard with the frontier theme—cow horns decorated every guest room, and lighting fixtures in the bars were the shape of wagon wheels—but the resort's Old West ambience was a hit with tourists.[50] The dream of creating a desert oasis for adults was edging closer to reality. But who would pay for it?

CHAPTER 4

Mob Scene

CRIME SYNDICATES OVERWHELM
AUTHORITIES IN NEVADA

What you see here is nothing. . . . In ten years, this'll be the biggest gambling center in the world.

—Bugsy Siegel, on Las Vegas in 1947

In the 1940s Las Vegas was a city on the make. America's entry into World War II brought waves of military personnel to newly built airfields and training sites in the Mojave Desert. Legalized gambling and the city's red-light districts made Las Vegas a hot spot for troops to cut loose while on leave. The nearby Boulder Dam generated the power and water supply that would make possible the region's growth. Highway improvements and widespread automobile ownership turned Las Vegas into an easy weekend getaway for Southern Californians.

One of those Angelenos who saw potential in Las Vegas was W. R. "Billy" Wilkerson, a publicist and publisher of the *Hollywood Reporter*. Wilkerson, a natty dresser with a carefully waxed mustache and refined European-style tastes, hobnobbed with the stars at his sophisticated restaurants and nightclubs on the Sunset Strip such as Ciro's, La Rue's, and Café Trocadero. The comings and goings of celebrities at the glamorous clubs were breathlessly documented in his trade newspaper, cementing Wilkerson as a Hollywood player in the 1930s and 1940s.

Wilkerson's outward success masked a severe gambling addiction. Wilkerson haunted the Hollywood Park and Santa Anita racetracks in the afternoons and played high-stakes private poker games in the evenings.

He embarked on excursions into Mexico to Tijuana's Agua Caliente, where a racetrack and a full-service casino beckoned. Las Vegas was but a short plane ride away for a day trip or weekend jaunt. If the tables turned against him, Wilkerson would summon an aide to visit a Los Angeles bank and board the next flight to Las Vegas toting an attaché case filled with cash.[1]

Wilkerson's ruinous gambling addiction consumed his nightclub and publishing profits. In the first six months of 1944, he lost nearly $1 million gambling and nearly went bankrupt.[2] Bills went unpaid, IOUs piled up, and Wilkerson needed personal loans just to stay afloat. Joe Schenck, chairman of 20th Century Fox and a Wilkerson confidant, listened to Wilkerson confess his failings during a dinner meeting at the movie mogul's mansion. Schenck suggested that Wilkerson should simply build his own casino on the theory that it's better to be "on the other side of the table if you are going to suffer those kinds of losses."[3]

Wilkerson hated the harsh desert climate and the casinos' rustic Old West motifs, but he believed that Las Vegas was poised to become the capital of American gambling. In his mind, what was needed there was a spectacular resort that wouldn't be out of place in Monte Carlo—a casino so lush that his glittery friends from Beverly Hills would happily drive hundreds of miles through a barren landscape to play and stay. In February 1945 Wilkerson quietly bought a thirty-three-acre piece of property on Highway 91 far from the center of town.[4] The dusty lot, purchased for $84,000, would be Wilkerson's canvas for his grand plan to build a sumptuous playground for high-flying gamblers. Wilkerson chose the remote location to ensure his resort would stand apart from the city's less impressive casinos.

Wilkerson asked the architects and designers who had worked on his Hollywood projects to sketch the resort of his dreams. A luxury hotel, showroom, nine-hole golf course, full-service health club, and a top-of-the-line restaurant were part of Wilkerson's plans for the sprawling complex. Air conditioning would provide relief on days of stifling triple-digit temperatures; tropical landscaping and a pool with a mighty waterfall would create the illusion of a desert oasis. He reasoned that gambling would be the main reason for people to visit Las Vegas, but the grandeur of the resort's other attractions would compel them to stay longer.

Wilkerson knew how to build successful nightclubs and restaurants, but he had no experience running a casino. He turned to Moe Sedway, Gus Greenbaum, and Israel "Ice Pick Willie" Alderman, the hard-boiled gangsters who operated the El Cortez hotel and casino on Fremont Street in downtown Las Vegas. They were longtime associates of Meyer Lansky, the organized crime figure known as the banker for the mob. As fixtures in the legal and illegal gambling worlds, they agreed to manage Wilkerson's casino in exchange for a percentage of the profits and a silent partnership.

Wilkerson's high aspirations were driving up projected costs to impossibly high levels, so he scaled down his vision and scrambled to secure loans to begin construction in late 1945. He was short $400,000 and foolishly tried to make up the difference at the gambling tables, losing $200,000 in a month.[5] Building materials in postwar America were scarce and expensive, blowing another hole in Wilkerson's budget. Construction was halted, and Wilkerson desperately needed new investors to get it going again.

Sedway, who had steadily tightened his grip on the resort, asked Lansky about making a major investment in the project. Lansky had his doubts about the city's potential as a gambling hub, but Sedway persuaded him to approve the funding in early 1946. Soon after, a mysterious businessman from the East Coast named G. Harry Rothberg approached Wilkerson at the construction site. Rothberg, a bootlegger during Prohibition, said he represented a New York company that wanted to invest. In exchange for $1 million in funding, Rothberg said the syndicate would own two-thirds of the project with Wilkerson claiming the other third.[6] Wilkerson would be allowed to manage the resort and retain ownership of the land.

Wilkerson had little choice but to agree, and the deal soured for him almost as soon as it was signed. He was pushed aside and lost creative control over the hotel's construction and design. On August 5, 1946, the Clark County Liquor and Licensing Board took up an application from the blandly named Nevada Project, Inc., for "a retail liquor and gaming license."[7] The board delayed action until its next meeting on August 14, when the county sheriff reintroduced the application as the only item on the meeting's agenda. The board granted the license without debate even though the licensee was Benjamin "Bugsy" Siegel, a close Lansky associate and mob triggerman. Siegel's project would open later that year as the Flamingo Hotel and Casino on what would become one of the world's most famous streets—the Las Vegas Strip. But that someone with Siegel's criminal background could waltz in and receive approval to build a casino backed by mob money exposed a fatal weakness in the system that would have long-lasting effects on Las Vegas, the state of Nevada, and gambling in America.

————

During the war years Siegel made his presence felt in Las Vegas after establishing a beachhead in Southern California's illegal gambling circles. Despite his fearsome reputation as a contract killer, Siegel disarmed Holly-wood celebrities with his good looks and sharp attire. He swanned around town with starlets and high-society women and regularly turned up in newspaper gossip columns. He fed his insatiable appetites at the Sunset Strip's nightclubs—some of them owned by Wilkerson—and cozied up to Hollywood royalty.[8] Siegel befriended movie stars like George Raft, an actor best known for his portrayal of underworld characters. Raft intro-duced the charismatic gangster to studio executives such as Jack Warner and stars like Gary Cooper, Clark Gable, and Jean Harlow. The connec-tions benefited both sides: the film community got to consort with a bona fide hoodlum who was handsome enough that he could have been in pic-tures himself while Siegel received a sprinkling of stardust that bolstered his aspirations for respectability.

Siegel's longest and most consequential relationship of his life in crime was with Lansky. Their ties went back to Manhattan's Lower East Side in the late 1910s, when it was a roiling stew of upstart immigrant groups fighting for supremacy. Siegel was the son of Jews who escaped the Rus-sian pogroms; Lansky, born Maier Suchowljansky in modern-day Belarus, arrived in America with his family when he was a child. They met as adolescents running around in a Jewish street gang that fought the Irish and formed an uneasy alliance with the Italians, led by a young Salvatore Lucania, better known later as Charles "Lucky" Luciano, the architect of the modern Mafia in America.

Although Siegel and Lansky were from similar backgrounds, their personalities were poles apart. As a teen Siegel was a hothead and quick to violence—characteristics that followed him into adulthood. His volatility would often get him in trouble, but Siegel's fearlessness earned him the respect of rival gangs and made him an invaluable asset to "Lansky and Siegel's mob." "While we tried to figure out what the best move was, Bugsy was already shooting. When it came to action, there was no one better. I've seen him charge ten men single-handed and they would all turn and run. I never knew a man who had more guts," Lansky recollected in his later years.[9] Siegel's wildness earned him the nickname "Bugsy" for being "bugs" or "crazy as a bedbug," as Lansky put it.[10] Siegel despised the nickname, and no one other than Lansky dared say it in his presence.

If Siegel was the brawn of the outfit, Lansky was unquestionably its brains. He was quieter, more deliberative. As a youngster, Lansky observed illegal craps games on Delancey Street and meticulously analyzed numbers schemes to understand every detail of how they worked. He trained himself to calculate odds in his head and constantly recalibrate them as the games progressed.[11] Lansky took note of the shills who would reel in unsuspecting suckers by allowing them a few early wins and then fleecing them when the stakes were raised. He harbored no sympathy for simpleminded bettors ensnared in such an obvious trap. "If you think ahead and carefully plan whatever you are going to do, whatever activity it is, then you can win. It's the fools who rush in unprepared, who try to get rich because they're greedy—they are life's suckers," he said.[12]

Lansky, nicknamed "Little Man" and someone who would never be mistaken for a matinee idol like Siegel, was hooked on gambling from an early age but wisely concluded that it was always better to own a game of chance than to play under someone else's rules. Gambling sharpened his preternatural skill at coldly sizing up a situation for his maximum benefit, and it proved to be essential to his renown as the "mob's accountant." Yet there were limits to how far he could rise in the Mafia's organizational chart because he wasn't of Italian descent and thus was ineligible to be a "made" man. The Mafia, also known as Cosa Nostra or "Our Thing," imported the codes of clannishness and insularity from their Sicilian forebears.[13]

Lansky, Luciano, and other gangsters of the 1920s and 1930s accrued wealth and power during America's ill-fated experiment with Prohibition. They organized a liquor distribution network across multiple states and cities to control the flow of illegal alcohol into the United States. Such bootlegging alliances were early indications that regional syndicates could divide territory among crime "families" and work together in a loose confederation.[14] Luciano, founder of one of New York's notorious "Five Families," established the Commission to coordinate decision making. The Commission was something of "an underworld Supreme Court, whose primary function was to prevent warfare while recognizing the sovereignty of the individual groups," wrote Mafia chronicler Selwyn Raab.[15]

Lansky and his confederates opened their own speakeasies outfitted with gambling tables and slot machines. The syndicate's illegal bookmaking business extended to urban "horse parlors" that simulated the excitement of the racetrack and offered the added attraction of serving high-quality bootleg scotch to bettors. Lower-income gamblers were targeted through Lansky's influence on the numbers racket that had originated in Harlem. To keep these disparate businesses humming, Lansky arranged for payoffs and constructed an elaborate financial maze to keep the mountains of cash outside the grasp of the Internal Revenue Service. On their tax returns, Lansky and Siegel professed to be partners in a "car rental agency" that eked out a meager profit.[16]

By the late 1930s Lansky's gambling empire extended from New York to Florida and overseas into Cuba, where his expertise helped military strongman Fulgencio Batista boost the island's gambling revenues. Lansky cleaned up Havana's two casinos associated with the city's ailing racetrack by clearing out the fixers and straightening out the crooked bookmaking operation.[17] The noticeable improvements won Lansky the regime's respect. Lansky and his cronies guaranteed Batista between $3 million and $5 million in annual kickbacks and a cut of gambling profits in return for a monopoly on casinos at Havana's luxurious Hotel Nacional and elsewhere in Cuba.[18] Lansky's prosperous foothold in Cuba provided a safe harbor for him to conduct high-level syndicate meetings where he could freely attend to his far-flung business interests. With Lansky's help, the island evolved into a Caribbean version of Las Vegas that appealed to sun-seeking American tourists and "sportsmen," the era's genteel term for gamblers. (The fruitful relationship between Lansky and Batista thrived for decades until revolutionaries led by Fidel Castro ousted Batista on January 1, 1959, bringing an end to wide-open gambling in Cuba.)

After overseeing Mafia gambling operations in Los Angeles, Siegel arrived in Las Vegas in 1941 as part of the syndicate's bid to dominate the race wire service in the West. Siegel and Sedway, aligned with the crime syndicate–controlled Trans-American service, ruthlessly shoved the rival Continental Press Service out of horse racing parlors. The fees Siegel collected from his control of the flow of out-of-state track results to poolrooms in Arizona, California, and Nevada further fattened his wallet—he supposedly cleared more than $25,000 a month.[19]

While Siegel was consolidating control of the wire service, hoteliers such as Thomas Hull and R. E. Griffith were making a splash with their Las Vegas resorts. Siegel wanted to mimic the success of El Rancho Vegas and the Last Frontier, despite Lansky's early dismissal of Las Vegas as "a horrible place" where cars overheated on desert roads. Hull rebuffed Siegel's offer to purchase his El Rancho Vegas casino-hotel in 1943. Two years later Siegel seized the chance to take over the El Cortez on Fremont Street. Siegel phoned Lansky and asked him for money. Lansky overcame his misgivings about Las Vegas and agreed to invest $60,000, or a 10 percent stake.[20] Siegel aligned with an array of other casino operators and bookies to purchase the hotel in December 1945. Their timing was ideal. They flipped the property just six months later, clearing a $166,000 profit, thanks to the city's postwar real estate boom.[21]

With the windfall, the investors scouted for bigger opportunities. It was then when it became clear that Wilkerson's ambitions exceeded his budget for the grand resort the LA nightclub impresario was building about a mile south of the Last Frontier on Los Angeles Highway. El Cortez operators and Lansky affiliates Sedway and Greenbaum had already struck a deal with Wilkerson to run his casino in exchange for a cut of the profits. But Wilkerson's cash flow problems had halted construction, and he needed a fresh infusion of funds to get it restarted. Siegel and his El Cortez partners bought a 66 percent controlling interest in Wilkerson's Flamingo hotel, and Siegel supplanted Wilkerson as the project's director.[22]

Siegel wanted it built by Christmas 1946 and beseeched his builders and designers to achieve his lavish vision for the Flamingo. Siegel arranged for the Phoenix-based Del E. Webb Construction Company to decamp to Las Vegas and get the job done as quickly as possible. Webb, a real estate developer and co-owner of the New York Yankees, considered Siegel "a remarkable character" who was "tough, cold, and terrifying when he wanted to be—but at other times a very easy fellow to be around."[23] (Webb's corporation grew into a major force in Las Vegas gambling, owning the Sahara on the Strip and The Mint downtown.)

Siegel's mood blackened as the project's expenses mounted. The postwar scarcity of building materials for civilian use and Siegel's uncompromising attitude—he insisted that each room needed its own sewer line at a total cost of more than $1 million—created overruns that spiraled into the millions of dollars.[24] East Coast crime bosses covered the added expenses but not without questioning Siegel's fitness to manage the enterprise.

Despite Siegel's sordid background, he and his underworld investors had little trouble securing approval for the all-important gambling license from a Clark County board in August 1946. Siegel and his mob backers also needed to obtain a license from the Nevada Tax Commission—a rule enacted in 1945—primarily to allow the state to collect taxes on gambling. However, just like the local boards, the commission wasn't required to assess the character of applicants or conduct background checks. The commission had just one employee dedicated to gambling issues, which made thorough investigations impossible. Some on the commission brushed aside Siegel's history of illegal gambling and killings in the larger interest of economic development. According to Robbins Cahill, a member of the Nevada Tax Commission, many in Las Vegas were excited about the Flamingo despite Siegel's involvement in it. "The only attitude I ever got out of the town at the time was, 'Hooray! He's going to bring money into the town,'" Cahill said.[25]

With the bureaucratic hurdles cleared and the construction problems settled, the resort attained Siegel's desire to replicate the lush Beverly Hills Hotel on a desert highway. The "Fabulous Flamingo" was indeed a full-fledged resort that boasted a health club, gym, golf course, tennis courts, and stables. Exotic plants were shipped in from Los Angeles to accent the hotel's verdant gardens, creating the illusion of an oasis.[26] Lounge chairs and tables with colorful umbrellas ringed the pool court on landscaped grounds to evoke the glamour of Miami Beach. A three-story waterfall splashed near the entry of the air-conditioned hotel. Inside, a riot of pink leather upholstery and green wallpaper and carpet signaled to visitors that by stepping into the Flamingo, they had taken temporary leave of the harsh desert.[27]

However, Siegel's mismanagement of the Flamingo was a pressing item on the agenda of a key meeting of underworld figures hosted by Lansky at Havana's Hotel Nacional in December 1946. They were shocked to learn from Lansky that the Flamingo's estimated cost had soared to $6 million.[28] They blamed Siegel for frittering away their millions of dollars in contributions and bowing to the excessive interior decorations demanded by his unstable mistress, Virginia Hill. Some even accused Siegel of skimming construction money and stashing it in a secret Swiss bank account. Lansky reportedly defended his old friend and appealed to the group for patience, but it was clear that Siegel was on notice. According to mob lore, Luciano supposedly cornered Lansky at a Christmas Eve party in Havana and warned him that unless Siegel made a great success of the hotel, Luciano would have to order Siegel's execution.[29]

The Flamingo's opening night on December 26, 1946, was a debacle. Bad weather kept away many Hollywood celebrities. (Wilkerson, fearing for his life, secretly stayed at a plush hotel in Paris during the opening weeks. He sold out his remaining interest in the Flamingo at a loss.) Although the casino and showroom were ready, the hotel rooms were not finished. Once the Flamingo's expensive opening night gala was complete, guests departed and checked in at the nearby El Rancho Vegas or the Last Frontier and spent most of their money at those resorts.[30] In its first weeks the Flamingo lost hundreds of thousands of dollars, leading Siegel to close the Flamingo until the guest rooms were ready.

The Flamingo reopened in March 1947, and Siegel plunged all of his energy into creating a Hollywood ending for the hotel. Siegel regularly roamed the casino with his two bodyguards, stopping at the bar to buy drinks for patrons and even sitting in for a blackjack dealer and assuring players that the Flamingo ran its games honestly. Siegel cut an impressive figure with his silk ties and expensive suits tailored to his lean frame. Indeed, he was as much of an attraction as the showroom entertainment. The author Erskine Caldwell noted after a chance encounter with Siegel at the Flamingo: "Bartenders, cocktail girls, busboys, porters, and even hard-drinking barstool customers recognized Bugsy either with lingering glances of awe or with unconcealed signs of apprehension."[31] An undercurrent of menace was always present. When a player unwisely insisted on calling Siegel "Bugsy," bodyguards yanked the offender out of his seat and hauled him into the street.[32]

The Flamingo managed to squeeze out a profit a few months later, but Siegel wouldn't live long enough to see it become a success. On the night of June 20, 1947, Siegel stayed at the Beverly Hills home of Hill, who was out of town. Siegel was sitting on a sofa reading a newspaper after dinner when a gunman sprayed the room with bullets, killing him. The murder was never solved.

Later that night Greenbaum and another Lansky associate marched into the Flamingo and informed Sedway that there had been a change in ownership.[33] The staff was instructed to proceed as if nothing had happened, even though Siegel's murder was front-page news. Under the new management, Siegel's losses were erased in the first year, and the Flamingo racked up a $4 million profit.[34] With Siegel's wasteful spending a thing of the past, East Coast mobsters finally received a healthy return on their investment.

The popular but exaggerated perception of Siegel as the "inventor of the Las Vegas Strip" and "the father of modern Las Vegas" has been fueled by decades of mob movies and best-selling books. He was hardly the first man to peer into the desert and envision a gambling mecca: two other resorts—the Rancho Las Vegas and the Last Frontier—preceded the Flamingo on the Los Angeles Highway. Siegel wasn't an able manager like Bill Harrah or a casino innovator like "Pappy" Smith in Reno. The Flamingo wasn't even his idea, and after his murder, it flourished without him.

Although movies like Warren Beatty's *Bugsy* may have overstated Siegel's place in Las Vegas and gambling history, it is still important. Siegel's role in the creation myth of Las Vegas has a strange power; his violent coda only adds to his mystique. The Flamingo—though razed and rebuilt under several rounds of corporate ownership—is one of the few remaining brand names from postwar Las Vegas on the Strip. On the resort's grounds, a monument to Siegel details his exploits. Oddly, it sits in a quiet, flower-filled courtyard facing the Flamingo's Garden Chapel. (The hotel's Bugsy's Cabaret, home to the X Burlesque topless revue, seems altogether a more fitting tribute to Siegel.) Siegel's most lasting contribution was as the leader of a parade of mob figures, crime syndicate money, and others with unsavory pasts who made Las Vegas their place in the sun.

———

Nevada's ineffectual oversight of gambling licenses made it easy for organized crime interests to infiltrate the state. In the early days local governments and sheriffs collected fees and handed out the licenses as if they were processing real estate documents or birth certificates. They lacked the capacity and the authority to conduct a serious examination of the nefarious interests who wanted in on the burgeoning gambling marketplace.

In 1945 the state designated the Nevada Tax Commission to collect taxes on gambling, shifting control from local authorities. That year Nevada assessed a 1 percent tax on the gross receipts of licensees and doubled the rate to 2 percent in 1947, officially giving state government a direct financial interest in gambling. However, the commission had no investigative or law enforcement authority, yet it was the agency primarily responsible for awarding or revoking gambling licenses. They also weren't required to ask where the money came from.

The Desert Inn's path to construction followed a pattern similar to its neighbor on the Los Angeles Highway, the Flamingo, in that out-of-town crime syndicates cashed in as silent partners. Wilbur Clark, a back-slapping businessman with a lifelong passion for gambling, was involved in illegal casinos in Southern California, including the SS *Rex* off the coast of Santa Monica. Like Harrah, the Smith family, and other Golden State gambling operators, Clark grew weary of harassment by California authorities and pivoted to Nevada. By the mid-1940s Clark owned a majority share of the El Rancho Vegas and bought several smaller casinos in town. In 1946 Clark sold his casinos and hoped to use the windfall to achieve his dream of building a palatial resort on the quiet stretch of Highway 91.

When construction began in 1947, it soon became clear that Clark's ambitions far exceeded his means, similar to Wilkerson and the Flamingo. Work stalled on the Desert Inn, and Clark searched for additional financing. He turned to Morris "Moe" Barney Dalitz, a wily operator who lived in the gray area between legitimate and illegal businesses. Dalitz, born into a Jewish family in Boston, began his career in his father's laundry business in Ann Arbor, Michigan, and the Detroit area, where he befriended labor boss Jimmy Hoffa. During Prohibition, Dalitz mastered the logistics of transporting Canadian whiskey across the Great Lakes and into Michigan and Ohio. Dalitz arranged liquor deals with crime figures such as Lansky—who would become a lifelong friend—and members of Cleveland's Mayfield Road Gang. When a 1950s Senate investigative committee asked Dalitz about his rum-running days, he replied, "If you people wouldn't have drunk it, I wouldn't have bootlegged it."[35]

After the end of Prohibition in 1933, Dalitz invested his bootlegging
money in his laundries and bought stakes in other legitimate businesses
such as the Detroit Steel Company. He also opened a chain of illegal road-
house casinos stretching across the region. "How was I to know those
gambling joints were illegal?" Dalitz supposedly remarked to a friend.
"There were so many judges and politicians at them, I figured they had to
be all right."[36]

Dalitz's casino expertise, underworld connections, and real-world business skills made him an ideal person to make a mark in Las Vegas. For Dalitz,
Clark's unfinished casino was the perfect gateway into the city's maturing
gambling industry. Dalitz led a group of Cleveland associates—all of whom
had reputed mob ties—who offered Clark $1.3 million to finish construc-
tion in exchange for a 74 percent interest in the Desert Inn.[37] Dalitz in turn
received backing from his old friend Hoffa, who secured loans from the
Teamsters Central States Pension Fund, which would become a frequently
tapped treasury for financing casino construction.

State officials, jittery about the recent murder of Siegel, noticed the
source of the Desert Inn's construction money and investigated the Cleveland group. Cahill, a member of the Nevada Tax Commission, and his
associates went to Ohio for a week and talked to newspaper reporters,
union officials, and attorneys to find out more about Dalitz and his crew.[38]
Although they clearly had backgrounds in bootlegging and illegal gambling, none of them had faced significant criminal charges. The investigators searched in vain for someone who could confirm their suspicions and
connect the Desert Inn investors directly to the Mafia. The attorney for
the investors disarmingly provided copies of their income tax statements
to the officials to show that they had nothing to hide. Cahill returned to
Las Vegas, wrote a report on his findings, and the gambling license was
approved.

Dalitz sank millions more into the resort to bring it up to the Flamingo's standard of splendor. When Wilbur Clark's Desert Inn opened in
1950, it was an immediate sensation, nearly recouping the initial investment in the first year. The resort's Painted Desert Showroom featured

top-notch entertainment, the world-class golf course drew wealthy visitors, and guests reveled in the figure-eight swimming pool and outdoor fountain. Crowds mingled in the rooftop Sky Room lounge from midnight until dawn, when all eyes would turn to the horizon to witness a mushroom cloud billow from one of the periodic atomic bomb tests at the nearby Nevada Test Site.[39]

Although Clark's name was on the marquee, he was little more than a figurehead. Dalitz was unquestionably the behind-the-scenes power broker who controlled how the money was spent and hand-picked the men who ran the casino. The avuncular Clark didn't seem to mind playing the role of gracious host for visiting dignitaries at the Desert Inn. Clark curried favor with politicians by sending them gifts and extending his hospitality. In 1953 Clark wrote a letter to former president Harry S. Truman, reminding him that they had met in the White House years before and had a mutual friend. Clark enclosed a one-hundred-dollar check for Truman's unbuilt presidential library in Missouri and invited him to the Desert Inn whenever he was in town.[40] Clark hosted Lyndon B. Johnson at the Desert Inn while he was a senator, and Vice President Richard Nixon received an engraved certificate of membership in the Desert Inn Country Club.[41] Clark especially ingratiated himself with the Kennedys, gushing to Sen. John F. Kennedy in a 1957 letter that he would be at the party's service for the 1960 presidential campaign.[42] Clark showered gifts on Jacqueline Kennedy, such as a portable TV set and a necklace charm.[43]

Dalitz's wisdom in keeping Clark around as the casino's front man was a sharp contrast to Siegel's rashness in dumping Wilkerson from the Flamingo. Clark's clean reputation and skill at glad-handing were invaluable in making the Desert Inn a nonthreatening destination for tourists and VIPs alike. The rumors of the Desert Inn being under the sway of the "Cleveland Mob" persisted over the years, but Dalitz was never convicted of any crime. Dalitz expanded his casino interests in Las Vegas (including the Stardust) and became a well-respected corporate citizen, contributing money to civic causes including Sunrise Hospital, which was built with Teamsters funds. In 1976 the American Cancer Society honored him

with a special humanitarian award at an MGM Grand soiree hosted by
Bob Hope. "I think the years have borne it out, that Moe Dalitz has done
more for the city of Las Vegas, and done more to build the city of Las Vegas
than any single man connected with the industry," said Cahill, the Nevada
gambling regulator, in the early 1970s. "I think it was a very fortunate day
for Las Vegas when Moe Dalitz and the rest of them came in."[44]

––––––

In the early days of gambling in Las Vegas, serious charges such as murder or burglary did not automatically disqualify applicants for gambling
licenses. Nearly all forms of gambling were legal in Nevada, so applicants'
arrests for running illegal casinos or rackets in other states were discounted. If such charges popped up during a hearing, state officials reasoned that they showed that the operators knew how to run casinos and
welcomed their expertise and investment.

That was the case for Lester Ben "Benny" Binion. The Texas native
traded horses and punched cattle as a youth and fell under the spell of
road gamblers. The grade-school dropout did some bootlegging during
Prohibition and pulled himself out of poverty by running an illegal numbers racket and high-stakes craps games in Dallas that attracted the likes of
oil tycoons H. L. Hunt, Howard Hughes, and Clint Murchison Sr.[45]

Binion's cowboy charm belied a steely edge. Illegal gambling in Texas
in the 1930s was literally a cutthroat business. Competitors fought with
fists and shotguns to expand their piece of the action. He always carried
at least one gun and kept a shotgun in his car—and didn't hesitate to
use them. Binion's rap sheet included two murder charges in the 1930s.
For the first charge, he received a two-year suspended sentence; for the
other, Binion was acquitted on self-defense grounds. Binion and his associates were also suspected in the killing of gambling competitor Sam Murray in 1938, but Binion avoided indictment and the case was not prosecuted. Later in life Binion expressed no remorse for the things he did to
survive: "I don't have to hire nobody to do none of my dirty work. That

sounds a little bit like braggin', but if they don't think that I can do it, well, just let 'em come on."[46]

Binion applied a lighter touch when it came to stroking politicians and police to protect his dice and card games in hotel suites in downtown Dallas. When the city government felt a budget crunch, the authorities would "raid" Binion's suites without disturbing a single gambling chip. Binion paid "fines" to the city of up to $600,000 a year, an indication of the huge sums Binion was raking in during the Texas oil boom.[47]

In 1946 a reform-minded city administration took command in Dallas and forced Binion to pull up stakes and move to Las Vegas where he could ply his trade in peace. Upon his arrival in Nevada, he was impressed with the El Rancho Vegas and the Last Frontier, enjoyed the town's fine food and entertainment, and judged the opening of the Flamingo as "the biggest whoop-de-do I ever seen."[48] Binion bought an interest in a run-down place called the Las Vegas Club and made a modest success of it.

Binion felt he was ready to build his own casino and run it his way, but he needed a gambling license when the city was still in shock from Siegel's murder. That the crime bosses allegedly took precautions to ensure that the hit on Siegel occurred far from Las Vegas didn't ease the town's anxiety about the gangster's slaying. Newspaper reporters pieced together the depth of Siegel's ties to gangsters and traced the true source of the money that built the "Fabulous Flamingo." The killing made it clear to regulators that they were involved in a dangerous game they were ill-prepared to play. "I really think that was the big element that kicked off the state control," said Cahill, the longtime Nevada Tax Commission member and later chairman of the Gambling Control Board. "People began really finding out that they'd probably gotten a little more than they'd bargained for. They'd gotten a big, beautiful place, but also, there were problems that probably [were] going to start."[49]

When Binion appeared before the commission, he regaled them with tales of his lawless exploits in Texas. When Cahill questioned him about his murder charges and history of violence, Binion confirmed that the stories were true and embellished them with graphic details. He discussed the 1936 slaying of Ben Frieden, a competitor in the Dallas gambling rackets, in which he drove out to meet him and shot him three times in the chest. "Binion had this very engaging style, and he had the Tax Commission in stitches, just laughing at his killing a man," recounted Cahill. "He said it was self-defense, that the man reached into the glove box, and he thought he had a gun. 'So I shot him,' Binion said. Then he was asked if it were true that he had killed another man and Binion said, 'Yeah, but he was just a nigger I caught stealing some whiskey.'"[50]

Judging from the jocular mood, Cahill sensed that the other commissioners didn't share his qualms about Binion's background, ethics, or his crudeness. The license was granted. Binion opened the Westerner gambling saloon and later purchased the El Dorado Club, renaming it Binion's Horseshoe. It was the first casino in downtown's "Glitter Gulch" with a carpet, installed at a cost of $18,000. Binion offered the highest limits in Las Vegas, accepting wagers as high as $500 for craps bets when most casinos had a maximum limit of $50.[51] Binion earned the reputation as the man to see for high-stakes action.

In 1949 Binion brought together Nick "The Greek" Dandalos and Johnny Moss for a no-limit, winner-take-all poker marathon that has passed into gambling legend. Dandalos arrived in Las Vegas with an enormous bankroll that matched his status as one of the world's top professional gamblers. He sought a high-stakes poker game against a single opponent. Binion agreed to the request and summoned his old friend Moss from Dallas to be Dandalos's opponent. Moss immediately flew to Las Vegas even though he was nearing the end of an intense poker game in Texas and hadn't slept in three days.

The game in the lobby of Binion's casino lasted five months, with breaks every few days to give the players a chance to sleep, although Dandalos spent much of his free time at the craps tables.[52] Their audience grew week by week until several hundred spectators regularly crowded around the table to witness the biggest game any of them had ever seen. Dandalos and Moss played five-card stud and draw as well as variations of lowball. After months of up and down play—Dandalos electrified the crowd when he won a $520,000 pot by calling Moss's bluff and winning with a jack in the hole—Moss finally gained the upper hand.[53] When Dandalos lost his last pot, he shook hands with his opponent and softly said, "Mr. Moss, I have to let you go."[54] Moss won an estimated $2 million to $4 million, although the real amount Nick "The Greek" gambled away in Binion's casino has never been revealed.

The contest was a publicity coup for Binion and his casino. Up until then card games of such magnitude were whispered about in private back rooms or hotel suites like the ones Binion used to run in Dallas. The Moss–Dandalos spectacle demonstrated the public's interest in watching high-stakes poker players. Two decades later Binion's Horseshoe invited elite pros to face off in the World Series of Poker. (Moss won the first World Series of Poker in 1970 and triumphed in three of the first five tournaments.)

The contestants popularized a variant of poker known as Texas Hold'em and battled for top prizes that soared well into the millions in later years. The event attracted national television coverage, with Binion playing the role of colorful cowboy front man attired in a Western-cut suit, open-collared shirt with gold buttons, and a Stetson on his head. Binion especially enjoyed posing with his "million-dollar horseshoe"—a nine-foot-tall display containing one hundred $10,000 bills—that became a priceless tourist magnet for the casino.

Even Cahill, the strait-laced Nevada gambling regulator, acknowledged that Binion was an expert casino operator who didn't swindle its customers, but he always persistently questioned Binion whenever he appeared for a renewal. Binion found that he couldn't completely outrun his checkered past in Texas when a prosecutor presented Binion's sketchy tax returns to the IRS. He was convicted of federal and state tax evasion in 1953 and was forced to sell the Horseshoe. Upon his release from prison in 1957, Binion was unable to secure a gambling license, but he and his family repurchased the casino. Binion's immediate family took on management duties, but Binion stayed on as the casino's guiding force. Binion didn't need a title or a formal office anyway; he ran his affairs from a table permanently reserved for him in the Horseshoe's restaurant, which served beef raised from his Montana ranch.[55] Up until the end of his life nothing of note happened at his old-fashioned carpet joint that he didn't know about. When Binion died on Christmas Day 1989, a friend aptly summed up Binion's wild life: "He was either the gentlest bad guy or the baddest good guy you'd ever seen."[56]

In the early 1970s Cahill reflected on his tussles with Binion and sounded a note of concern for what Las Vegas had become: "His background was such that you just couldn't separate it and justify yourself to the people, or anybody else, or to the FBI, or to crime people that were trying to help us in keeping things under control, because you left yourself open to the argument, 'Well, if a man with a background like this can get a license, who can't? Who can you keep out?'"[57]

CHAPTER 5

Enemy Within

GOVERNMENT FIGHTS BACK
AGAINST MOB INFLUENCE

Gambling produces nothing and adds nothing to the economy or society of our nation. America will be in a bad way if we ever have to resort to taxing crime and immorality for the purpose of raising revenue to operate our institutions.

—Sen. Estes Kefauver, 1951

By the early 1950s the mob's foothold in Las Vegas and elsewhere attracted the attention of the federal government, which believed crime bosses were funneling their gambling gains into its other illegal enterprises. Many in Washington believed that local law enforcement agencies were not capable of addressing a problem of such national importance. Sen. Estes Kefauver, a liberal Democrat from Tennessee, took the lead through his chairmanship of the Senate Special Committee to Investigate Organized Crime in Interstate Commerce in 1950 and 1951.

The lean, bespectacled senator exhibited incredible stamina in his drive to ferret out the truth about what he believed to be a nationwide crime syndicate. He traveled 52,380 miles to preside at ninety-two days of hearings in fourteen cities, bringing a prosecutor's zeal to his anticrime crusade. In Miami and Chicago, he blasted illegal bookmakers and the race wire services as tools of organized crime and accused local sheriffs of accepting protection money. "Everywhere we went we found the disillusioning facts: there were some constables, policemen, and detectives who took their $10 bribes to protect gamblers and other malefactors," Kefauver wrote. "It is no wonder that hoodlums and 'sharp' businessmen have come to think they can buy anybody."[1] His stance clashed with FBI Director J. Edgar Hoover's testimony to the committee in which he insisted that illegal gambling could be controlled by local authorities. If the state and city prohibitions were enforced, "organized gambling could be eliminated within forty-eight hours in any community in this land," Hoover told the Kefauver Committee.[2]

The mob's infiltration of gambling and law enforcement drew his panel to Las Vegas, where the committee held a hearing November 15, 1950, in a second-floor courtroom in the Las Vegas Post Office and Courthouse only blocks away from the Fremont Street gambling district. (The building now houses the National Museum of Organized Crime and Law Enforcement—better known as the Mob Museum—which opened in 2012.)

Kefauver's sober tone matched the seriousness of his quest. He summoned casino owners and local officials before his panel and grimly quizzed them about their relationship with or knowledge about the Mafia, a term he helped popularize. (Hoover had denied the existence of a national crime organization and refused to use the word "Mafia" in public or private communications, preferring the more generic "hoodlums.")[3]

Among the witnesses called that day were public officials who owned stakes in casinos. The most prominent among them was Clifford Jones, Nevada's lieutenant governor who helped build the Thunderbird Hotel on the Strip in 1948. Jones maintained his partnership in the casino as well as interests in the Golden Nugget and the Pioneer Club while holding political office. Kefauver pointed out that Jones's $5,000 investment in the Pioneer Club yielded him about $14,000 per year.[4] Another witness, William Moore, was a partner in the Last Frontier even though he reviewed gambling license applications as a member of the Nevada Tax Commission. Moore said he earned between $75,000 and $84,000 from his partnership in 1949.[5] Although such holdings were legal, Kefauver fretted about the commingling of casino money and politics. (Kefauver's

premonition was correct: A scandal involving Jones and the Thunderbird
erupted a few years later.)

The committee questioned Jones about the state's lax scrutiny of the
seedy backgrounds of the businessmen who applied for gambling licenses.
The lieutenant governor shrugged it off, replying that the "people who
came here when the state started to grow, they weren't particularly Sunday
school teachers or preachers or anything like that. They were gamblers."[6]

Moore also had no qualms with licensing people who ran gambling
enterprises in states where it was illegal, mentioning a 1949 "grandfather
clause" in Nevada law that allowed people of such backgrounds to hold
on to their licenses. Otherwise, "how was he going to learn the business?"
Moore asked the committee. "Are you going to throw out a man with a
$3,500,000 investment?" referring to the Nevada Tax Commission's deci-
sion to license Sanford Adler for the Cal Neva casino in Lake Tahoe despite
his arrest record.[7] Under pointed questioning, Moore denied using his
influence to arrange the Last Frontier's extremely favorable subscription
rate for the mob-controlled Continental Press wire service. Moore admitted that the casino paid only $200 a month for race wire results; when a
senator informed him that other customers paid as much as $24,000
a month, the huge gap didn't surprise Moore.[8]

What Kefauver learned in Las Vegas confirmed his suspicions. The committee condemned the idea that gambling could be legalized and regulated
nationwide. "The history of legalized gambling in Nevada and in other
parts of the country gives no assurance that mobsters and racketeers can
be converted into responsible businessmen through the simple process of
obtaining State and local licenses for their gambling enterprises," according to the committee's report.[9] Kefauver charged that many of the state's
casino operators had ties to crime organizations outside Nevada, justify-
ing the Senate's duty to investigate illicit interstate commerce. It wouldn't
be the last time the federal government asserted its right to intercede in
Nevada's affairs.

As the committee rolled across the country, its lurid revelations of
official misconduct transfixed the public in much in the same way the

Watergate hearings did a generation later. In January 1951 Kefauver agreed to a request by a New Orleans television station to broadcast the committee's proceedings in the city. The telecast mesmerized local residents who watched as their sitting mayor discussed gangster Frank Costello's early history with organized gambling in the city. The committee's momentum accelerated as city after city telecast the hearings, which were among the first news events to capture a mass television audience.

When the panel arrived in New York City on March 12, 1951, demand among viewers was so high that the city's utility added a generator to supply an adequate level of electricity to power so many TV sets.[10] National TV networks carried the hearings, which brought tales of organized crime into Americans' living rooms. Those who didn't have TVs followed the suspense inside restaurants and barrooms that carried the broadcast.

Costello, who took over as Luciano crime family boss after the imprisonment of Lucky Luciano, was the committee's star witness. The panel collected wiretaps on Costello that showed his influence over the region's racetracks and linked him to gangsters nationwide. Unlike other mobsters, Costello waived his right to take the Fifth Amendment while being questioned. However, he insisted that his face not be televised. The committee and the TV networks agreed to show only his hands, so viewers at home watched his nervous fingers fidget with his glasses and crumple a handkerchief while he croaked out evasive answers to uncomfortable questions.[11] Costello looked and acted like a guilty man. He refused to testify at subsequent hearings, and the Senate cited him for contempt, for which he spent a little more than a year in prison.

Evidence of his ties to Las Vegas casinos emerged in 1957 when he survived an assassination attempt in Manhattan. Investigators dug into his jacket pocket at the hospital and found a series of numbers written on slip of paper. They were directly related to slot revenue and other financial details of the newly opened Tropicana in Las Vegas in which Costello had a secret investment. The paper was signed by a mobster at the hotel who had worked for Costello at his casinos in Louisiana.

Costello and company made for compelling TV. Nearly everyone in the New York metro area who had a television tuned in: 70 percent of TVs were on during the hearings, and 86 percent of the viewers watched the dogged Kefauver and his fellow senators shine a light on the shadowy gangsters and crooked politicians.[12] As many as 30 million people watched the proceedings—a stunning total for the new medium. The television extravaganza instantly transformed Kefauver into a politician of national stature. The Yale Law School graduate gamely donned his trademark coonskin cap and embarked on a spirited run for the Democratic presidential nomination in 1952, losing to Adlai Stevenson. In 1956 Kefauver settled for a slot as Stevenson's running mate, an election the Democrats lost in a landslide to President Dwight Eisenhower.

The committee's effect in the corridors of Congress proved to be as ephemeral as Kefauver's presidential aspirations. The panel concluded that the Mafia was a centralized organization that had nationwide control of gambling, narcotics, prostitution, and the ports. "The Mafia is the direct descendant of a criminal organization of the same name originating in the island of Sicily," according to the committee's final report.[13] It found major syndicates in two cities—New York's "Costello-Adonis-Lansky" group and Chicago's "Accardo-Guzik-Fischetti" cartel—with tentacles in other regions. Despite the alarming tone of the report, it yielded little concrete change in Congress, deepening the sense among many that government was powerless to confront the threat.[14]

Some critics accused Kefauver of political opportunism and believed that the committee found little hard evidence to justify its sweeping claims. Rufus King, a legislative counsel, called the panel's findings about the Mafia as a national ethnic conspiracy a "romantic myth."[15] The mob wasn't a top-down corporation like IBM or General Motors but rather a loose grouping of local crime associations with spheres of influence in their own regions. Some towns like Las Vegas were considered "open cities," which meant multiple syndicates or families could operate there. At times the committee's work suffered from sloppiness. For example, the panel asserted that gambling formed the backbone of organized crime's finances by generating $20 billion each year—an undocumented figure that was pure guesswork.[16] "We had no real idea," admitted a committee staffer.[17] Misunderstanding the true nature of the problem reduced the chances of effectively confronting it.

Despite the committee's shortcomings, it did awaken the public's conscience to organized crime and change the attitudes of some public officials. A series of blockbuster articles in the *Las Vegas Sun* alleged that Meyer Lansky and his brother, Jake, and another mobster had clandestine financial interests in the Thunderbird, the same casino that the lieutenant governor had a piece of. Other politicos were alleged to have financial ties with underworld casino owners. The newspaper also claimed that Jones was trying to influence the 1954 governor's race by steering his casino moneymen to contribute to a candidate who supposedly would be friendlier to their interests than the sitting governor, Charles H. Russell.[18]

The political corruption allegations were never corroborated, but they tilted the race to the underdog, Russell, who swiftly persuaded lawmakers to set up the three-member Nevada Gaming Control Board within the Nevada Tax Commission in 1955. Russell appointed FBI veteran William Sinnott and longtime gambling regulator Robbins Cahill to the board and permitted them to hire professional investigators. (In the same session the legislature boosted the state's gambling tax, which helped pay for the board's activities.) The board worked closely with the FBI to check into the records of applicants and unravel the complicated financial networks behind the major casinos. If "undesirables" were linked to a casino, the board had the authority to revoke its license.

The state government put a ninety-day moratorium on new gambling licenses and rejected movie star George Raft's attempt to buy a piece of the Flamingo because of his associations with gangsters. The board recommended suspending the Thunderbird's license amid the controversy about the casino's secret financial interests. Jones was forced to relinquish his holdings. The Nevada Supreme Court overturned the suspension, ruling on narrow grounds that the extent of the Lansky brothers' involvement with the resort solely consisted of a loan to finish construction. However, the court upheld the commission's authority to investigate and revoke licenses when necessary. In a speech in Las Vegas, Kefauver seemed pleased at the state's stiffening controls. "Nevada has established stronger safeguards through state and local governments to prohibit criminal activities in the gaming industry. I am delighted at this progress and I have no fault to find with it," he said.[19]

Democrat Grant Sawyer edged out Russell in the 1958 governor's race, pledging to burnish Nevada's reputation by advancing a "hang tough" policy toward organized crime's influence on gambling. In 1959 the state fine-tuned its regulations again with the Gaming Control Act, establishing a five-member Nevada Gaming Commission. It had the ability to approve, decline, or revoke gambling licenses and to collect taxes. Commissioners could not hold elective office and were forbidden to have a direct financial interest in gambling activities—a response to the conflicts of interest that surfaced in the Thunderbird case.[20] The progressive-minded governor chose a few former FBI men as commissioners.

One of the most intriguing innovations came in 1960 with the creation of the "Black Book," officially known as the List of Excluded Persons. The idea mimicked the FBI's Most Wanted List by compiling mug shots and background sketches of people with notorious reputations or reputed ties to organized crime. The few dozen names on the list were banned for life from every licensed gambling establishment in the state. Every casino had a copy of the book, and they were expected to eject the unsavory individuals. If it didn't, the casino would be subject to a revocation of its gambling license.[21] The Black Book had more of a symbolic than a practical effect, though. Its questionable constitutionality was upheld in the courts, and it was modified over the years to add legal protections for the people on the list.[22] At the very least, it earned positive publicity for the state for doing something and added another chapter in the mob mythology of Las Vegas.

The new regulations bolstered the scrutiny of new applicants for gambling licenses, but they could only go so far. "That was, in a way, almost like closing the barn door after the horse had finally slipped into the corral because the people who had come in that immediate postwar period, there wasn't really much you could do with them at that point; you couldn't throw them out, by virtue of you created a new law or a new policy. So we just sort of lived with them," said Edward A. Olsen, a veteran journalist and former chairman of the Nevada Gaming Control Board.[23]

———

In other states, local crime commissions picked up where the Kefauver Committee left off. In 1957 the Massachusetts Crime Commission wrapped up four years of investigating mobsters, gamblers, and corrupt public officials with the conclusion: "Organized crime has evolved into a state of society that amounts to lawlessness."[24] Gambling operators complained to the commission about police and politicians asking for so much protection money that "illegal gambling is police business instead of bookie business."[25]

Starting that same year, Sen. John McClellan, a Democrat from Arkansas, chaired a committee to investigate labor racketeering. McClellan hired Robert F. Kennedy, a young but experienced congressional investigator, as the panel's chief counsel. The most aggressive son of the famous political dynasty widened his scope to include organized crime. The day after Kennedy quizzed a witness about the existence of the Mafia, police stumbled upon a national summit of crime families in the upstate New York hamlet of Apalachin. Limousines and flashy cars with out-of-state plates drew attention to the meeting, and some gangsters fled into the surrounding woods to avoid the raid. Kennedy requested files on the attendees and was stunned when he learned how little the FBI knew about them.[26] (The Apalachin summit forced Hoover to privately admit that organized crime indeed had national reach.) Kennedy accumulated knowledge from those hearings that convinced him that the dimes and dollars wagered every day by innocent Americans on numbers games or with bookies ended up in the pockets of organized crime.

Kennedy ascended to attorney general upon the election of his brother as president in 1960 and from there continued his assault on organized crime. The Kennedy administration pressed Congress to approve the Wire Act in 1961 banning the interstate transmission of betting information—a reaction to previous investigations into the mob-controlled race wire. Kennedy told Congress that the statute was necessary "because profits from illegal gambling are huge and they are the primary source of the funds which finance organized crime."[27] The following year Kennedy successfully pushed to strengthen the decade-old Johnson Act, which limited the interstate transportation of slot machines. Kennedy expanded the definition of prohibited "gambling devices" to include roulette wheels and other common casino games. The Justice Department assumed enforcement duties, allowing Kennedy a freer hand to bust rackets.

One of his chief targets was Jimmy Hoffa, who became president of the International Brotherhood of Teamsters in 1958. They were so different in background and manner that it was almost cartoonish. Kennedy enjoyed the advantages of his family's wealth and education and knew when to deploy his righteous anger and when to flash his barbed wit. Hoffa had little formal education, spoke and thought with the subtlety of one of his Teamster trucks ramming down an interstate, and had his hair cut almost to the scalp on the sides and like a bristle on top. Both men, though, had reputations for ruthlessness.

They first clashed during the McClellan Committee hearings, with Kennedy calling the Teamsters "the most powerful institution in the country, aside from the United States government itself."[28] Kennedy tried to pin down Hoffa on his purported relationships with gangsters and his intimidation of union dissidents. Hoffa parried the questions with practiced evasiveness and a winking defiance. They had a visceral dislike of each other: Kennedy saw "absolute evilness" in the hard-shelled union leader, and Hoffa openly dismissed the moralistic Kennedy as a shrill political grandstander.[29]

Kennedy accused Hoffa of treating the union's Central States Pension Fund as his personal bank with which to reward allies and wield influence. Between 1959 and 1961 the fund granted sixty loans totaling more than $90 million, mostly for real estate development projects.[30] In 1962 nearly a quarter of the fund's disbursements were awarded to companies in Nevada, mainly casinos.[31] During that time Hoffa invested in Las Vegas casinos such as the Stardust and the Desert Inn through gangster-turned-businessman Moe Dalitz. Pension money also flowed to golf courses and noncasino real estate. A $1 million loan was disbursed from the Teamsters in 1959 to the Desert Inn group, which used it to finance construction of Sunrise Hospital in Las Vegas.[32]

The pension fund's use as a personal piggy bank worked out well for the mob interests who operated the casinos and for Teamsters officials. Hoffa and his union confederates received kickbacks in exchange for approving the loans for the mob, which skimmed huge amounts of cash from casino counting rooms. Traditional banks were unwilling to approve loans for casinos, so Hoffa's funds were welcome infusions of money that allowed the mobsters to complete or expand their resorts. Nevada law also required licensing for each stockholder in a casino, effectively ruling out publicly traded companies. The cozy arrangement further entrenched organized crime's presence in Las Vegas.

Kennedy followed Hoffa's money trail and saw that much of it led to Las Vegas, which he believed to be a den of organized crime. Skimming—earnings pocketed by casinos before they could be officially counted and taxed—in particular concerned Kennedy, and he had no confidence in local law enforcement's ability to deal with it. "Only through a nationwide network can we fight the widespread penetration by criminals into our economy," Kennedy argued in his book *The Enemy Within*.[33] Kennedy's Justice Department indicted 116 mafiosi and important associates, by far the most aggressive federal crackdown on organized crime up to that point.[34]

In 1961 Kennedy contacted Nevada's attorney general and requested that sixty-five federal agents be deputized for a planned raid on the state's biggest casinos. When Sawyer heard about the plan, the Nevada governor flew to Washington the next day to express his outrage in person with the Kennedys. The strike force was ultimately called off, with both sides agreeing to cooperate on rooting out organized crime, but a shaken

Sawyer returned to Nevada knowing that the federal government seemed poised to bring down an important state industry. "As a personal matter, I was particularly offended, because I got the impression that Bobby looked upon me as someone who had just stepped out from behind a crap table; and he seemed to imply that I was connected with the mob, which really burned me up," Sawyer said.[35] His stormy relationship with Kennedy never improved.

The IRS opened an office in Las Vegas with dozens of agents, and the FBI bulked up its Nevada staff to mount a full-scale investigation of gambling in Nevada. The FBI contacted the local telephone company and leased about twenty-five private phone lines in the name of a phony business, the Henderson Novelty Company.[36] The lines ran into the Sands, the Dunes, the Stardust, the Fremont, and a few other casinos. Agents placed surveillance devices in the homes and offices of casino executives, investors, and gaming officials.[37] As with the FBI's other wiretapping schemes, the main purpose seemed to be to accumulate secret files that could be used as leverage against the subjects deemed by Hoover to be undercutting American ideals.

Nevada officials were incensed when they learned of the illegal bugging operation. Sawyer believed that Hoover's lawlessness made him a "terrible threat not just to Nevada, but to America in general," and he sharply criticized Robert Kennedy for his hardball tactics.[38] "Anyone who would use and manipulate a federal agency the way he was attempting to was dangerous, and I put him in the same category as J. Edgar Hoover," Sawyer said in an interview long after he left office.[39] In fact, Hoover and Kennedy had a complicated relationship and often worked at cross purposes while serving their own distinct agendas.[40] The FBI and Justice Department competed more than they cooperated.

One of the hidden microphones was discovered in 1963 in the office of Carl Cohen, who had a 10 percent stake in the Sands, which was famous worldwide as home base for the Rat Pack.[41] The stylish hotel served as the backdrop for the 1960 heist film *Ocean's 11* starring Frank Sinatra, Dean Martin, Sammy Davis Jr., Joey Bishop, and Peter Lawford, who performed to sold-out audiences at the Copa Room. Their easy rapport and bad-boy charm showed the country that in Las Vegas—"A Place in the Sun," as the resort's giant roadside neon sign blared—inhibitions could be tossed aside. The Rat Pack's ingredients for a good time—women, gambling, booze—were all available in abundant supply in Las Vegas. Their paragon of cool fellowship formed the template for generations of testosterone-fueled bachelor parties and carefree "boys-only" weekends in Vegas.

But the famous names on the casino's marquee belied the resort's perennial tangles with state regulators. Allegations of mob influence and skimming of casino revenue persisted into the 1960s. Two of the hotel's original investors linked to mob figures were denied gambling licenses, and Sinatra himself was forced to sell his 9 percent stake in 1963 because of his association with Chicago mob boss Sam Giancana.[42]

The Sinatra–Giancana relationship inspired a key test of state resolve. Giancana disappeared while under subpoena by a Chicago grand jury in 1963, and it turned out that he was secretly staying at Lake Tahoe's Cal Neva, where Sinatra was the seasonal resort's majority owner and principal gaming licensee. Giancana was a well-known gangster and a member of the Black Book, spurring a Gaming Control Board investigation. The scenic resort on the California–Nevada border was a haven for the Hollywood and Rat Pack crowd in the early 1960s. Tunnels built during the Prohibition era to smuggle booze were adapted for moving celebrities around the resort out of public view.[43] During his ownership, Sinatra constructed a showroom and helicopter pad to further cater to his famous—and infamous—clientele.

Gaming Control Board agents interviewed witnesses to a physical altercation at Cal Neva involving Giancana that was reportedly broken up by Sinatra but became public enough to make the Chicago papers. The board quietly issued subpoenas to people who wouldn't talk. Edward A. Olsen, chairman of the Gaming Control Board, had taken part in an interview with Sinatra in Las Vegas, but the advancing probe raised more questions. Olsen turned down an invitation from Sinatra to come up to Cal Neva to see a dinner show and meet with him personally. Through a Sinatra representative, Olsen offered to host the meeting in his Carson City office on a Sunday over Labor Day weekend to minimize publicity.

An infuriated Sinatra called Olsen directly and complained about the board's subpoenas. Olsen said if Sinatra refused to meet with the board again, he too would receive a subpoena. "You just try and find me," Sinatra replied in a menacing tone. "And if you do, you can look for a big, fat surprise . . . a big, fat, fucking surprise. You remember that. Now listen to me, Ed. . . . Don't fuck with me. Don't fuck with me. Just don't fuck with me."[44] Olsen suggested to Sinatra that it might be for the best if he departed the Nevada gambling scene, to which Sinatra replied, "I might just do that . . . and when I do, I'm going to tell the world what a bunch of fucking idiots run things in this state."[45]

Governor Sawyer encouraged Olsen to pursue Sinatra as if he were any other license holder, telling him not to be intimidated by his threats. The investigation proceeded, much to Sinatra's displeasure. A Gaming Control Board auditor who observed the procedures in the casino's counting room reported that he found two hundred-dollar bills in the crook of his arm, placed there by a Cal Neva official. The casino official explained away the "gift" as compensation for the agent having to work on a Saturday night, but the money was not accepted.[46] The ham-handed effort to buy influence was reported to the board. Olsen drew up a detailed complaint to revoke Sinatra's license on the grounds that he associated with undesirable characters and ran an unsuitable operation. Rather than contest the revocation, Sinatra decided to withdraw from the gambling industry in Nevada, saying that his investments were "too diversified" and that it would be in his best interest to focus on the entertainment business.[47]

The Sinatra–Giancana case demonstrated how far Nevada gaming regulation had come. In the past, regulators would have overlooked such an incident for fear of upsetting an important casino investor. Bribes and political connections would have ensured that business would continue without interruption. This time the state stared down a wealthy superstar and forced him to surrender his interests in the Sands and the Cal Neva. A few months after the Sinatra incident, Olsen said he bumped into Sammy Davis Jr. after watching him perform at the Sands and the entertainer praised the state for taking action against his old friend. "That little son of a bitch, he's needed this for years. I've been working with him for sixteen years, and nobody's ever had the guts to stand up to him!" Davis said, according to Olsen.[48]

Improvements on the regulatory front were overshadowed by more revelations of federal government interference in Nevada's affairs. As the 1966 governor's race heated up, an FBI agent in charge in Las Vegas testified in federal court that the FBI had secretly installed microphones in the executive office suite of Ruby Kolod, the co-owner of the Desert Inn and the Stardust. An outraged Sawyer accused the FBI of breaking Nevada wiretapping laws and called upon the state's attorney general and district attorneys to prosecute violators, even though the eavesdropping program had ceased in 1963.[49]

A scathing report issued by the Nevada Gaming Commission dated September 1, 1966, showed how toxic relations between Nevada and the federal government had become. Although Robert Kennedy was no longer attorney general, resentment over his actions lingered. The commissioners brought up Kennedy's desire to raid the state's casinos and accused the Justice Department of leaking unfavorable stories about Nevada to the press. The commissioners pointed to a *Chicago Sun-Times* report in 1966 charging that millions of dollars had been skimmed off Las Vegas casino revenues. The untaxed money found its way into organized crime activities across the nation, according to the newspaper's story.[50] The commission called these stories obvious plants to distract from the eavesdropping controversy and conducted its own investigation, interviewing thirty-two witnesses under oath.[51] All of the federal witnesses declined to testify, the report noted. No substantial skimming operation was discovered after all.

Hoover remained an unmovable force at the FBI after the Kennedy administration, but that didn't stop the commission for calling out the bureau for its "morally reprehensible program of domestic espionage upon the citizens of this State."[52] The commissioners complained that no federal agency had ever turned over hard evidence to back up their accusations of tax evasion due to skimming. The illegally obtained records gathered by the FBI's microphones were unusable in court.

In the 1966 governor's race, Sawyer's bitter standoff with the federal government contrasted with the softer tone of his Republican challenger, Paul Laxalt, who promised to ease relations with the federal government and said he would try to meet privately with Hoover if elected. He criticized Sawyer's "war policy with the FBI" as recklessly placing the industry in peril. "We must prove to people across the nation that we are an honest state, operating aboveboard and out in the open," Laxalt said.[53] Nevada voters, reluctant to hand Sawyer a third term after years of antagonism, opted for Laxalt in November. Later that month the arrival in Las Vegas of a ghostly figure aboard a train signaled a new day for gambling in Nevada.

CHAPTER 6

Vegas, Inc.

CORPORATE AMERICA TAKES COMMAND IN SIN CITY

We build places for folks who don't think of themselves as gamblers.
—Steve Wynn

Howard Robard Hughes Jr. was never one to leave anything to chance, especially as he slid ever deeper into flights of madness and paranoia. The famous industrialist's tumultuous life cycled through many remarkable acts: scandalous filmmaker and Hollywood studio chief, record-setting aviator, bold businessman, and, finally, reclusive tycoon. The Houston native's wealth derived from taking control of the family's Hughes Tool Company as a young man. His aspirations extended far beyond mastering drill bits. Hughes founded an aircraft company that won billions in government contracts and was an early investor in the commercial airline business. A court battle over the control of Trans World Airlines ended with Hughes relinquishing his majority ownership in 1966 and selling his roughly 6.6 million shares of stock, which was paid to him in a single check for the astounding amount of $546,549,171.

As one of the richest men in the world, Hughes could afford to indulge his obsession for secrecy and power. Once a handsome man who dated the likes of Ava Gardner and Katharine Hepburn, Hughes's lifelong fear of germs degenerated into an extreme form of an obsessive-compulsive disorder that reduced him to a hermit unwilling to make genuine human contact. No known photograph had been taken of him since the early

1950s, and tales of his bizarre personal habits—his refusal to cut his hair or nails, his insistence on having his rooms sealed with masking tape and black curtains to keep out dust and pollen—became legend.

Since Hughes wasn't fit to attend meetings, he hired a retinue of highly paid intermediaries to conduct his byzantine business dealings. Hughes's closest adviser was Robert Maheu, a well-connected former FBI agent. Maheu worked for Hughes from 1954 to 1970 and yet not once saw him face to face: Hughes preferred to communicate through handwritten memoranda on yellow ruled paper.[1] (Any papers were required to be wrapped in Kleenex before being handed to Hughes.[2]) Maheu was Hughes's fixer, the ultimate operator who satisfied all of Hughes's demands, no matter how absurd.

In July 1966 Hughes suddenly decided that he wanted to move from Los Angeles to Boston, most likely to be closer to a physician in Massachusetts who happened to be a top official at Hughes's namesake medical institute. Hughes insisted on traveling by train, so Maheu haggled with the presidents of three railroads and arranged for a private, well-secured train to transport the party across the country. It was the first time Hughes had ventured outside in more than four years. Maheu had also reserved an entire floor of the Ritz-Carlton in Boston for Hughes, but reporters learned who was aboard the mystery train and staked out the front of the hotel. Aides managed to smuggle Hughes through the Ritz-Carlton's service entrance, but the cover was blown. Newspapers spread rumors that Hughes was seriously ill and watched for any sign of movement.

The trip out east and his seclusion at the luxury hotel had cost $250,000, but Hughes was unhappy and already plotting his next move.[3] He considered flying to Montreal or the Bahamas, so Maheu kept a fully fueled chartered plane ready to go whenever Hughes made up his mind. Hughes shifted his eye to Nevada and mentioned Lake Tahoe as a possibility. Finally, he decided on Las Vegas, a place he frequently visited and briefly resided in the 1950s. In those days Hughes basked in the town's ready supply of gambling and women. An aide would approach a woman of Hughes's choosing and demand that she sign a disclaimer form before joining the ever-wary Hughes at his table.[4]

By the 1960s Hughes's days of cruising Las Vegas at night and mixing with people in public places like casinos were long gone. Nevada's main attraction for Hughes was its favorable tax structure, especially compared to California's. Just as in Boston, Maheu had the task of finding a Las Vegas Strip hotel willing to let Hughes book an entire top floor. Maheu persuaded the managers of the Desert Inn to allow Hughes to occupy its top floor for no more than ten days.[5] The floor contained the hotel's biggest penthouse suites typically reserved for the casino's top gamblers, so managers were understandably reluctant to have a well-known recluse and nongambling Mormon aides stay there for long.

Preparations for yet another cross-country train trip in November 1966 had all the hallmarks of a CIA operation, guided by subterfuge and maximum security. A Hughes decoy was hired to exit the Ritz-Carlton and leave in a limousine, which the press dutifully followed while the real Hughes slipped away. The special train carrying Hughes encountered a problem in Utah that would have delayed his arrival in Las Vegas until late morning or early afternoon—unacceptable for a man who wanted to move about like a ghost. Maheu worked his contacts and paid $18,000 to rent an engine that towed Hughes's railcars toward Las Vegas.[6]

At four o'clock in the morning on November 27, 1966, the train pulled up at a quiet crossing just outside city limits to ensure the secret transfer of Hughes from the railcar to a van bound for the Desert Inn. A fleet of limos arrived at the hotel's entrance as a distraction while Hughes was hustled into his blacked-out penthouse. His staff decamped on the floor below.

Within a few days the Las Vegas press discovered the identity of the city's newest arrival. Unlike in Boston, the Las Vegas media saw Hughes as a figure to be celebrated rather than hunted. One of the town's most powerful figures, *Las Vegas Sun* publisher Hank Greenspun, all but rolled out the welcome wagon for Hughes. In a front-page column on December 2, Greenspun wrote, "Nevada has an opportunity to gain as a permanent resident this man who stands foremost among all giants of industry, finance and humanity. He alone is bigger than any other single Nevada industry or combination of all."[7] Greenspun implored the community to respect Hughes's wish for privacy to make him feel at ease in Las Vegas.

Meanwhile, the Desert Inn's owners were concerned that Hughes was starting to feel a bit too comfortable in Las Vegas. When the agreed-upon ten-day reservation elapsed, hotel management wanted Hughes and his men gone. The holidays were approaching, and the suites needed to be turned over to the out-of-town high-rollers who made New Year's Eve one of the city's biggest nights. Hotel co-owner Ruby Kolod, convicted of federal conspiracy charges in an extortion case but free on bail during the appeals process, warned Maheu to leave or else they would be tossed out. When Maheu informed his boss about the threat, Hughes responded acidly, "It's your problem. You work it out."[8]

Maheu turned to his old acquaintance Jimmy Hoffa for help. The Teamsters president and Moe Dalitz, the Desert Inn's majority owner, were friends from their days in Detroit, and Maheu knew Hoffa had engineered a loan through the Teamsters Central States Pension Fund that was essential in the construction of the Desert Inn. Hoffa agreed to intercede with the hotel's owners on Maheu's behalf and won a reprieve for Hughes to say through New Year's Day. However, Maheu also knew that he couldn't count on indefinite extensions and suggested to Hughes that he should offer to buy the hotel to avoid eviction.

Maheu called on fellow FBI veteran Ed Morgan and Chicago crime syndicate representative Johnny Roselli for assistance in negotiating the purchase of something that wasn't for sale. (Maheu and Roselli's ties went back to the early 1960s when they met to discuss a CIA plot to assassinate Cuban leader Fidel Castro.) The Desert Inn talks were immensely frustrating for all involved because once a tentative deal was struck, Hughes asked Maheu to press for a lower price and impose new conditions. After months of bargaining, they settled on a price of $13.2 million with nearly half paid in cash. (Morgan and Roselli shared a generous $150,000 legal fee.)[9] Importantly, Dalitz and his crew were allowed to stay on as casino managers.

The sale of the Desert Inn in early 1967 was just the beginning of Hughes's unprecedented casino spending spree. Up until then casinos were shunned by the mainstream banking system and had to rely on unorthodox funding sources such as the Teamsters pension fund and crime syndicates. The mob's growing influence in Las Vegas led to scandals and federal government scrutiny, but Hughes's pile of untainted money showed that corporate ownership could be a viable alternative. Once seen as a haven for mobsters, casinos would become a magnet for legitimate businessmen and Fortune 500 companies, thanks to the indispensable efforts of government.

————

Hughes's purchase of the mob-controlled Desert Inn was universally cheered by state and local politicians. Nevada's new governor, Paul Laxalt, was an early champion of Hughes as someone who could change the perception of gambling in the state. To curry favor with the morbidly reclusive Hughes, Laxalt insisted that Nevada regulators waive the customary requirements that an applicant for a gambling license must supply detailed personal and financial information and appear in person at the hearings. No photograph of Hughes was provided, and his fingerprints were not taken.[10] For his part, Hughes pledged to finance a new medical school for the state just days before the Nevada Gaming Control Board and Nevada Gaming Commission took up his application for a license, which received swift approval by both panels.[11] Hughes took control of the Desert Inn on April 1, 1967.

Hughes orchestrated his empire from the hotel's top floor, which he never left during his four years in Las Vegas. Hughes was a king who was a prisoner in his own palace, isolated from the real world. His coterie of aides and nurses worked out of a makeshift office near Hughes's bedroom, and they arranged their schedules so someone would always be on duty to handle Hughes's requests. The floor was sealed off to outsiders: an armed guard watched over a private elevator at all hours, and the fire escape doors were locked. Heavy drapes covered the windows all day and all night. Hughes's extreme germaphobia precluded any face-to-face meetings, so he communicated principally through rambling memos or all-hours telephone calls. Hughes's dependence on drugs apparently hastened his mental breakdown. He reportedly collected his urine in jars and stored them for some unknown purpose.

Hughes and his crew found themselves in the unlikely position of running a major Las Vegas casino, something they were ill-prepared to do. "None of us knew snake eyes from box cars," said Raymond Holliday, one of Hughes's top lieutenants. "We didn't know a thing about [gambling] and nobody here was interested in learning."[12] Maheu, the top adviser to Hughes and his point man in negotiating the purchase of the Desert Inn, also had no experience running a casino. He asked Dalitz, the hotel's former majority owner, for his expertise, which he agreed to share without taking a salary. Dalitz, who earned the respect of the underworld as a bootlegger and illegal casino operator in the Midwest and also felt at home in the city's mainstream circles, believed that Hughes was an asset to Las Vegas. "I felt that it was a good thing for Las Vegas when they moved in here and I was glad to be on their team, so to speak," Dalitz said.[13]

Dalitz had operational control of the casino, but he still had to put up with Hughes's nonsense. According to an anecdote related by a Meyer Lansky ally, gangster Joseph "Doc" Stacher, Hughes's requests frustrated the chef at the Desert Inn's gourmet restaurant. "The chef nearly walked out several times because Howard Hughes wanted Campbell's canned chicken soup served to him twice a day," Stacher said. "Hughes sent notes down to the kitchen complaining that the soup hadn't been prepared exactly the way he wanted it. It was to be heated to a precise temperature and one or two bits of things added. Moe had to plead with his chef to take no notice—the man upstairs was crazy."[14]

Dalitz persevered and became an invaluable adviser to the neophyte casino operators and encouraged them to invest in other Strip properties. Hughes targeted the nearby Sands, which opened in 1952 and was best known for hosting top-flight entertainers like the Rat Pack in its Copa Room. Like many casinos, the Sands had installed a clean front man who masked the casino's true financial backers: Stacher along with other longtime associates such as Lansky.

Just as with Hughes's purchase of the Desert Inn, the state and city's machinery engineered a quick sale of the Sands in mid-1967. For $14.6 million, Hughes owned not only the hotel but also the surrounding 183 acres of prime Las Vegas Strip property.[15] With their latest acquisition, Hughes's advisers demonstrated that they were serious in making Las Vegas their permanent base of operations. Thanks to Hughes's crafty accountants, the move to Nevada amounted to an enormous tax break. Hughes faced a gigantic tax bill for his $547 million windfall from his forced sale of TWA stock, so he invested in new business opportunities instead.[16] The state had no income tax (personal or corporate) or gift tax, which was enormously attractive to Hughes.

Hughes won crucial allies in the city's power structure, especially the prominent banker E. Parry Thomas and Greenspun, who handled countless phone calls from Hughes's team that Greenspun's local TV station didn't broadcast enough old movies at odd hours to the recluse's liking. "The man wanted the station open all night long, and he wanted certain pictures to be shown," said Greenspun, who suggested to Hughes's team that he should just buy the station "and run it any damn way you please."[17] Greenspun sold him the CBS affiliate KLAS-TV for $3.6 million in 1967.

Hughes's pathological need for absolute control propelled his manic drive to swallow up real estate in Las Vegas, a town that was then small enough for a lone rich man to dominate. Large tracts of land were there for the taking. Hughes bought an estate that formerly belonged to a Las Vegas casino executive and purchased a ranch owned by a woman who married into the Krupp arms family—Hughes would never visit either property. The hermit tycoon bought patches of parcels on and off the Strip (including the North Las Vegas Air Terminal) and picked up two more casinos—the Western-themed casino Frontier, formerly known as the Last Frontier, for $14 million and the more modest Castaways for $3 million—within a year of his arrival at the Desert Inn.[18] And still he wanted more.

When his team detected murmurs of antitrust objections among lawyers and lawmakers in the state capital of Carson City, Hughes personally phoned Governor Laxalt to smooth over any concerns. Hughes's rare act of reaching out to someone outside his tight circle of advisers pleased Laxalt and confirmed his belief that Hughes's intentions were noble. "His presence has added a degree of credibility to the state that it would have taken years of advertising to secure," Laxalt told *Newsweek* magazine in 1968. "Let's face it, Nevada has an image problem—the typical feeling is that sin is rampant here. . . . Anything this man does, from the gaming industry all the way down the line, will be good for Nevada."[19] It didn't hurt that Hughes contributed to Laxalt's campaigns and that the governor and Maheu were friendly tennis partners.

Laxalt's view that Hughes brought instant respectability to a beleaguered state prevailed even as the industrialist floated pie-in-the-sky projects like building a desert airport big enough to serve as a supersonic transport facility for the entire West Coast and adding a $150 million resort to the Sands.[20] (Neither project ever materialized, but Hughes had a history of making the improbable possible.) Greenspun traveled to Carson City to press regulators to grant two more gambling licenses to Hughes for his latest pending casino purchases, the Stardust (where Dalitz was the principal owner) and the small-time Silver Slipper casino. Greenspun, who got his start in Las Vegas as a publicist for Bugsy Siegel's Flamingo, said that he had always wanted Nevada to be a clean, decent place; now, with Hughes and his investments, such a goal was suddenly within grasp. He called Hughes "a modest, self-effacing person whose contributions to the betterment of mankind are unmatched by any group or man in contemporary history," fulsome sentiments no doubt colored by the millions Greenspun had received from Hughes for his role in various business dealings.[21]

Hughes needed all of the political and public relations muscle he could muster to secure the licenses, even promising to move the Houston-based Hughes Tool Company to Las Vegas. The addition of the Stardust and the Silver Slipper in 1968 swelled Hughes's gambling portfolio to six properties and vaulted him over Bill Harrah as the state's largest casino operator. More than a quarter of all gaming revenue in Clark County derived from his casinos; more than a third of rooms on the Strip were in Hughes-owned hotels.[22] All of this was accomplished in just two years. "He was, in effect, the King of Vegas," Maheu wrote. "And as his surrogate, I wore the crown."[23]

However, the Department of Justice's intent to file an antitrust lawsuit against Hughes forced him to withdraw his purchase of the Stardust. He later picked up the Landmark Hotel and Casino when the political climate shifted to Hughes's favor. The hotel, which bore a pale resemblance to Seattle's Space Needle, was his final casino purchase in Las Vegas. The Landmark had the misfortune of opening at the same time as the much more attractive International Hotel in 1969, and it was a consistent money loser for Hughes.

Instead of actively managing the hotels he already had, Hughes pushed for more acquisitions and dwelled on pointless issues fueled by his paranoia. In the spring of 1968 he wrote a six-page memorandum to Maheu about his concerns about the Desert Inn's popular annual Easter egg hunt, fearing that a riot could break out and overwhelm the hotel's security staff. He believed that his enemies would delight in the bad publicity. "I am not eager to have a repetition, in the Desert Inn, of what happened at Juvenile Hall when the ever-lovin' little darlings tore the place apart," he wrote.[24] Maheu quietly moved the event out of the Desert Inn.

With Hughes's staff preoccupied with satisfying the boss's trivial whims, the business suffered. For someone whose fortune seemed limitless, Hughes's spending spiraled out of control. Too much money was being spent on a patchwork of projects that weren't generating significant income. At the beginning of 1967 Hughes's company had more than $600 million in the bank. By the end of 1968 that figure had dwindled to $339 million, meaning that Hughes had burned through his savings at a rate of more than $350,000 per day.[25] The wild spree calls to mind the scene in *Citizen Kane* when another enigmatic rich man, Charles Foster Kane, ran a money-losing newspaper and calmly replied to his worried financial adviser: "At the rate of a million dollars a year, I'll have to close this place—in sixty years." But if Hughes kept up his torrid pace, he would run out of money in just a few years.

Overall, Hughes's casinos were bad investments: the Castaways, the Landmark, and the Frontier were perennial losers; the Desert Inn and the Sands managed modest profits compared to their expenses.[26] Maheu detected a coldness in Hughes' communications, as if he felt disenchanted with Las Vegas. On November 25, 1970—the night before Thanksgiving and nearly four years to the day when Hughes secretly arrived in Nevada aboard a train—aides strapped Hughes to a stretcher and spirited him out of the Desert Inn to a van that whisked him to Nellis Air Force Base. There a private jet stood by to fly him to the Bahamas, a notable tax shelter. When word leaked that the tycoon had departed Las Vegas—perhaps for good—the media spread rumors about the reasons for Hughes's disappearance, even speculating that he could have been kidnapped. Maheu went so far as to dispatch an emissary to see FBI Director J. Edgar Hoover and request his intercession.[27]

It turned out to be an inside job. Hughes's aides who attended to his day-to-day needs had driven a wedge between Maheu and Hughes. Maheu, who had been so instrumental in managing the complicated logistics of Hughes's affairs, was purposefully left out of the loop on Hughes's latest move. In fact, the new claimants to the crown briskly informed Maheu that he was fired. The battle over who would control the Hughes business empire involved Nevada's governor and other high-ranking state officials as intermediaries. Ultimately it was decided that Maheu was out.

Hughes spent his remaining years hopscotching around the globe to hotel penthouses while fighting off a spate of lawsuits and rumors about his state of mind. The confusion over who was really in charge spurred Nevada regulators to request a personal conference with Hughes. In 1973 Hughes reluctantly agreed to meet face to face with Nevada governor Mike O'Callaghan and the head of the Nevada Gaming Control Board. The meeting took place at two o'clock in the morning in Hughes's suite at a luxury hotel in London. Hughes appeared in a bathrobe and slippers, but he didn't appear to be as disheveled or incoherent as the state officials expected.[28] They agreed to the frail tycoon's wish to officially designate new representatives for his Las Vegas holdings.

The rail-thin Hughes died at age seventy during a flight from Acapulco, Mexico, to his hometown of Houston in 1976. His company, renamed the

Summa Corporation, liquidated its hotel and casino holdings in the 1980s. Today his name is most closely associated with the Howard Hughes Medical Institute, one of the richest foundations of its kind in the world. In the Las Vegas area, Hughes's lasting legacy is the master-planned community of Summerlin, built on tens of thousands of acres that he bought.

Hughes's bizarre four-year reign as the top casino operator in Las Vegas left behind a decidedly mixed legacy. For all of his early brilliance in the fields of motion pictures and aviation, he contributed no new innovations to the casino business. He did not build any casinos, the ones he bought were poorly run, and he had no interest in developing new attractions for his guests. Hughes never set foot in any of his properties other than the Desert Inn and not once did he visit any casino floor during his time in Las Vegas. Hughes's extreme isolation from other people and his exorbitant wealth granted him the freedom to pursue his fantasies, no matter how far-fetched.

And yet the very fact that a string of casinos transferred from mob ownership to the untainted Hughes had a profound impact on Las Vegas and pointed the way to a new era of respectability in gambling. Politicians were among Hughes's biggest cheerleaders because they knew Hughes didn't need to tap into sketchy pension funds or crime syndicate sources to fund his purchases. He could simply write check after check and instantly achieve what prosecutors had failed to do for decades—dislodge mob interests from controlling casinos. Hughes's piles of clean money went a long way toward improving the image of Las Vegas when the city desperately needed it. His casino investments totaled more than $50 million and coincided with the state's loosening of casino ownership rules, a milestone that encouraged well-respected, publicly traded companies such as Hilton and Holiday Inn to enter the once-taboo world of gambling.

————

Hughes neatly crystallized his worldview in a memo to Maheu written during his empire-building days in Las Vegas: "You just remember that every man—I can buy—I, Howard Hughes, can buy any man in the world, or I can destroy him."[29] Hughes indeed seemed like he could bend entire industries, politicians, and the press to his will, but one casino veteran was unfazed by Hughes's power and money: Bill Harrah.

When Hughes wanted to broaden his reach in Nevada, he pressed Maheu to approach Harrah about buying his casinos in Lake Tahoe and Reno. Unlike Hughes, Harrah spent his life as a gambling operator and constantly tinkered with his properties to maximize revenue. Harrah managed to avoid entanglements with organized crime and enjoyed good relations with the state's powerbrokers. "If more gambling houses were in the hands of men like him, one is told over and over, then the future of Nevada gambling would be completely safe," journalist Wallace Turner wrote about Harrah in a 1965 book. "In short, Bill Harrah is what they wish they had everywhere in Nevada."[30]

By then Las Vegas had far surpassed Reno as Nevada's gambling hub partly because of Reno's "redline," an agreement among casino proprietors that gambling should stay within a confined area of downtown. The Reno City Council formally approved the zone despite concerns that it benefited the city far less than casino operators like Harrah who wanted to restrict competition.[31] The tight urban spaces meant that most casinos lacked adjoining hotels, unlike in Las Vegas, where there was plenty of land to build rambling resorts.[32] Anyone who wanted to build a casino outside the boundary had to receive special permission from the city council. Those who didn't win approval went elsewhere and many did.

In the 1950s Harrah expanded his casino holdings beyond Reno to Lake Tahoe, a sleepy but scenic locale straddling Nevada and California. Harrah's casinos aimed squarely at California's growing middle-class market, promoting free or heavily discounted bus trips from San Francisco, Sacramento, and Oakland. Harrah even maintained a private fleet of snowplows to keep the roads clear in the winter.[33] Fleets of chartered buses crisscrossed California's valleys and mountains each day to visit tiny Stateline, Nevada, for a free cocktail and meal, and a chance to win some money in one of Harrah's places. "A weekly or monthly trip to Tahoe has become part of the way of life for countless Californians and Oregonians," according to a 1962 *Harper's Magazine* profile of Harrah.[34]

Harrah's mastery of operational detail seemingly made him a good match for a controlling person like Hughes, who dispatched Maheu to approach Harrah about selling his properties. Maheu and Harrah engaged in a series of late-night meetings and phone calls, but Harrah was more interested in the intrigue than in actually making a deal. "I said, 'If you want to pay me double what it's worth, I'll consider it, but it's no bargains around here,'" Harrah recalled.[35] Maheu's tone of pessimism about the fruitless offers and counteroffers in his dealings with Harrah frustrated Hughes. "Please don't give me any further report on this subject unless Harrah indicates he wants to sell. You know, Bob, sometimes I think you have an idea that I am about 12 years on this world instead of 62," Hughes wrote in early 1968. "Why would you permit me to invest nine months of my time thinking about this deal, writing messages about it, etc., if it is so God dammed bad?"[36] Hughes did end up buying Reno's Harolds Club, which by then was in far worse shape than Harrah's casinos.

While Hughes and Harrah were jockeying for primacy in Nevada, state lawmakers were considering a bill to allow corporate ownership of casinos. They were influenced by a Nevada legislature–commissioned study in 1966 that concluded casinos had to secure larger investments to expand their properties if they were to survive.[37] That would require them to broaden their financial base beyond Teamsters loans and secret underworld partners. After years of debate, lawmakers in 1969 approved a bill allowing publicly traded corporations to own casinos without the onerous requirement of licensing each stockholder. (Major shareholders still needed to go through the process.) The Corporate Gaming Act applied conventional business operations to the opaque world of gambling. Securities and Exchange Commission disclosure and filing requirements, proxy rules, shareholder meetings, and quarterly statements would be part of the new vocabulary of the industry.[38] Transparent accounting practices and improved security systems promised to ease the worries of investors who associated casinos with skimming.

Harrah had initially opposed the act because he feared a loss of control and excessive public scrutiny, but he backed down when he understood that going public could ease the financial strains from his pricey divorces and expensive taste in cars. Harrah's initial stock offering in 1971 attracted investors from Northern California who were familiar with the lure of his casinos and hoped to get some of their money back via the market. Harrah hosted annual shareholder meetings that were a swirl of cocktail parties and gambling binges. Money raised from going public allowed Harrah to expand and update his casinos, driving up profits even more. Private planes replaced chartered buses as the preferred way to transport Harrah's top customers, and his casinos were flush enough to drop more than $1,000 a week on call girls for the biggest spenders.[39] Harrah filled his showrooms with stars like Sammy Davis Jr. and John Denver, pampering them with Rolls-Royces to pick them up at the airport and providing luxury accommodations during their stay.

Harrah's entry into the stock market was part of a larger change in how gambling was perceived in the business world. When Harrah's executives first met with investment bankers on Wall Street, "those people looked as us like we had to be carrying machine guns under our coats. We were ashamed of what the industry's image was in the East. But we were goddamn proud of what we at Harrah's were," said company president Lloyd Dyer.[40] Once Harrah's was listed on a public stock exchange, it was like any other publicly traded company required to open its books for all to see. The move demystified the business of gambling and encouraged other casino-oriented companies to embrace public stock ownership.

Casinos became standard elements of portfolios of hotel chains better known for catering to vacationing middle-class families. The Flamingo Hilton and Las Vegas Hilton brought in nearly one-third of the chain's profits by the early 1980s, inspiring Hilton's purchase of the Sahara in Reno.[41] Ramada Inn spent about $70 million to buy the formerly mob-controlled Tropicana in 1979, and Hyatt's most profitable hotel was the Four Queens in downtown Las Vegas. After Harrah's death in 1978 the company was sold to Holiday Inn. By 1982 Holiday Inn was the world leader in casino space, with 201,000 square feet and slot machines with 6,273.[42]

The rising importance of slot machines was fitting in an era of mechanized corporate control. Slots with brand names like Wheel of Fortune are
relentlessly efficient at extracting money from gamblers and maximizing
profit for their corporate bosses. In 1970 there were 35,170 slots in Nevada;
a decade later the number spiked to 80,960 and nearly doubled again in
the next ten years.[43] During the Rat Pack heyday in Las Vegas, table games
made up the majority of the revenue, and slots were put in as an after-
thought for the wives. But by the 1980s slot win grew at double the rate
of table games and passed them by as the leading revenue source. In 1984
slots were 53 percent of Nevada's total gaming revenue; the share rose to
67 percent by 2004.[44]

———

And yet the residue of Nevada's mob-tainted past persisted. Skimming and
questionable casino financing didn't end with the Corporate Gaming Act;
it would take years for Las Vegas to flush out bad actors and tainted investment money. Visionary hotelier Jay Sarno relied on Hoffa's millions in
Teamsters loans for his well-regarded projects in Atlanta and Dallas and
then for his large-scale hotel-casinos in Las Vegas: Caesars Palace (opened
in 1966) and Circus Circus (opened in 1968). Sarno's vision stood apart
from the commonplace bland, boxy casino buildings. He conceived of
supersized casino-hotels that formed the template for the Strip's megaresorts. He wanted visitors to feel as if they had been somehow whooshed
from the forbidding Nevada desert to the grandeur of the Roman Empire
or the whimsy of a never-ending circus. Caesars Palace and Disneyland
obviously cater to vastly different audiences, but both create immersive
themed experiences for audiences seeking an escape. Like Walt Disney,
Sarno's eye for design and attention to architectural detail produced
imaginary worlds that seemed larger than life.

For Caesars Palace, Italian marble and stone were shipped in by the
ton. Gleaming statues of emperors, elaborate Roman-style fountains, and
rows of columns impressed visitors unlikely to ever see the real thing. The
casino's grandly named Circus Maximus theater housed top-flight talent

like Frank Sinatra and Barbra Streisand. Guests dined in splendor at the Bacchanal Room, where waitresses dressed like Roman goddesses poured wine and rubbed the shoulders of male patrons. Translating his fantasias into reality was eye-wateringly expensive. Luckily for Sarno, access to money wasn't an issue. Between 1965 and 1972, Caesars Palace received more than $20 million in loans from the Teamsters pension fund, which had total assets of $400 million in the late 1960s.[45]

Circus Circus was one of the first Las Vegas attractions geared to families, although there were slot machines and gaming tables humming amid the trapeze artists and clowns. Ever the innovator, Sarno insisted on figuring out a way to make an elephant fly. A pink-painted pachyderm with pink steel boots attached to a monorail appeared to fly when set in motion against a dark backdrop. The spectacle didn't last long because the elephant feared heights and dropped manure on the crowds below while riding under the big top.[46] Unlike Caesars, Circus Circus was a money loser for Sarno. Hard-core gamblers didn't like the distractions of the midway-style carnival games, and the three-ring circus atmosphere turned off the childless. It opened without a hotel, which made it easy for visitors to stop in to gawk at the acrobats and do their gambling elsewhere. As Hunter S. Thompson wrote in his drug-fueled gonzo classic *Fear and Loathing in Las Vegas*, "The Circus-Circus is what the whole hep world would be doing on Saturday night if the Nazis had won the war."[47]

Meanwhile, federal authorities investigated the financing of the casinos, believing that Sarno was a front for mob interests who would have been unable to secure a gambling license on their own. Teamsters money poured into Circus Circus. In 1971 the pension fund bought the land under Circus Circus, leased it back to the casino, and granted it a $15.5 million loan.[48] Another $10 million in Teamsters loans came into Circus Circus over the next three years. Allegations of skimming dogged the resort for years. Carl Wesley Thomas, listed in Nevada's Black Book and a convicted Las Vegas skimmer, testified in court that Teamsters attorney Allen Dorfman ordered him to preside over a skimming operation at Circus Circus. "It was my understanding that a fee had to be paid for the loans, and I was to do the skimming [to pay the fee]," Thomas said in testimony that helped reduce his prison sentence.[49]

Sarno didn't help appearances by indulging in his extreme appetites. The balding, rotund executive indulged in food, women, and especially gambling, allegedly losing $2.7 million between 1969 and 1971 and another million soon after that.[50] Sarno and his partners sold Caesars to the publicly traded restaurant chain Lum's in 1969 for more than double what it cost them to build it. The Florida-based corporation sold off its food business and renamed itself Caesars World, plowing money into the resort's fitful expansions. Sarno leased and sold Circus Circus to a partnership that managed to make it profitable. He failed to launch his vision for another over-the-top casino he tabbed the "Grandissimo" and died from a heart attack in his suite at Caesars in 1984, but Sarno's influence on the design of themed casino resorts endures.

Another front man, Allen R. Glick, received a Teamsters pension fund loan of nearly $63 million to buy the Stardust and Fremont casinos in 1974.[51] Glick, a young, untainted businessman, did not actually apply for the loan nor did he furnish a financial statement to the Teamsters. Nevada regulators were suspicious that the modest real estate salesman from San Diego orchestrated the moves by himself. It was later revealed that gangsters pushed Glick to hire Frank "Lefty" Rosenthal, a convicted illegal bookie and friend of Chicago Outfit enforcer Anthony "Tony the Ant" Spilotro, as the overseer of the corporation's casinos. (Spilotro also allegedly owned a store in Circus Circus.) Rosenthal had tangled with authorities for years. In 1961 he testified before a congressional subcommittee and invoked his Fifth Amendment right not to incriminate himself, including refusing to answer whether he was left-handed.[52] (The lead characters in Martin Scorsese's 1995 film *Casino* were based on Spilotro and Rosenthal.)

At first Glick seemed to float above it all in a bubble of newfound wealth that bought him an expensive remodel of a historic home in La Jolla and a private plane that ferried him between San Diego and his Las Vegas office at the Stardust.[53] But Glick was shaken by the unsolved murder of an investor in his projects and the Nevada Gaming Control Board's order that Rosenthal's nefarious ties made him unfit to run casinos. In effect, Rosenthal was installed to skim casino money for the Midwest mob. A 1976 raid uncovered evidence of a massive skimming operation totaling $7 million from the slot machines in Glick's casinos.[54] Glick faced a host of lawsuits and had to sell his casinos, but he avoided prosecution by becoming a cooperating witness against the gangsters who did have knowledge of the skim. Rosenthal also was not indicted because he supposedly provided information in exchange for immunity.[55] The out-of-town gangsters who profited from the skim were successfully prosecuted years after the raid. Another skimming scheme involving the Tropicana also resulted in a series of convictions.

Rosenthal never obtained a gambling license and was barred from even working as an entertainment director in a casino, but it wasn't pressure from state regulators that ultimately drove him out of Nevada. In 1982 Rosenthal's Cadillac exploded in the parking lot of a Tony Roma's barbecue restaurant on East Sahara Avenue. He escaped, and no one was ever prosecuted, but Rosenthal got the message and spent most his later years as a handicapper in Florida. By then Hoffa had disappeared and the federal government finally got its arms around the Teamsters Central States Pension Fund by regulating pension trustees and prohibiting them from making casino loans.[56]

In its final report issued in 1976, a federal commission charged with reviewing gambling policy concluded that organized crime's "influence has declined considerably and consistently during the past 10 years. In comparison with the situation 15 years ago, the presence of organized crime in Nevada today is negligible."[57] Although perhaps a bit too optimistic, the commission was right to say that gangsters were on the run in Nevada. By 1980 the twenty biggest publicly held casinos in Nevada generated nearly half of the state's gross gambling revenue and employed about 50 percent of workers in the industry.[58] These corporations drove Nevada's growth, which in turn benefited government. In 1985 statewide gambling revenues were $3.2 billion—nearly $1 billion more than the total generated just five years before—and the state received $177.2 million in taxes.[59]

———

A major figure in Las Vegas history who cashed in during the era of corporate control of casinos was Kirk Kerkorian, the Fresno-born son of
Armenian immigrants. As a young man, Kerkorian was a wiry but tough
amateur boxer, a daring wartime ferry pilot with the Royal Air Force, and a
nervy gambler at the casino table and in the boardroom. The eighth-grade
dropout became a self-made millionaire in the air-charter business and
invested in real estate in Las Vegas, a place he had visited since the 1940s.
Among his purchases were the struggling Flamingo and its land just across
the Strip. That land was later leased to the group that built Caesars Palace.
In 1967, much to the chagrin of Hughes, Kerkorian announced a bold
move to build the world's largest hotel-casino just off the Strip on Paradise
Road near the Las Vegas Convention Center. Kerkorian hired a veteran Las
Vegas hotelier to run his International Hotel and used the Flamingo as a
training ground for thousands of employees.

The rise of a rival casino titan angered Howard Hughes, who looked for
any way to derail the construction of Kerkorian's hotel. Hughes ordered his
aides to tell Kerkorian that his planned high-rise would sink into the soil if
underground nuclear testing resumed in Nevada.[60] Then Hughes threatened
to enlarge the Sands and make it the biggest hotel in the world. The publicity-
shy Kerkorian ignored such idle warnings and proceeded with his plans.

Although he was an established businessman, Kerkorian had difficulty
lining up financing for the $80 million International Hotel. His usual
source of financing for big projects, Bank of America, refused his loan
application. Kerkorian's men speculated that the hand of Hughes, a fellow
Bank of America customer, was behind the loan denial.[61] Kerkorian set up
a company called International Leisure Corp. that had the potential to go
public if the state changed the law to allow corporations to own casinos.

Meanwhile, Kerkorian and his advisers visited bank after bank with no
success. "I wore out two pair of shoes, pounding the pavement, looking for
financing," said Fred Benninger, a top Kerkorian lieutenant. "People don't
believe that Las Vegas has ever changed from the old days. Most of those
Eastern money people have never been to Las Vegas."[62] Finally, Kerkorian

secured a $30 million loan from a Nevada bank by putting up sixty-three acres of land as collateral, clearing the way to break ground on the thirty-story, 1,512-room International in 1968.[63]

However, the loan was only about half of what Kerkorian needed to borrow to complete the project. By early 1969 Nevada law had changed to permit corporations to own casinos, allowing Kerkorian's International Leisure to sell enough stock to raise $26.5 million to finish the job. The shares of common stock that opened at $5 a share in February jumped to $50 in over-the-counter trading in June, just before the resort opened with a string of high-grossing concerts by Barbra Streisand.[64] The hotel boasted the world's biggest casino, a 1,600-seat showroom, a theater, a "youth hotel" that kept kids busy while their parents gambled, and a giant pool that supposedly was the largest man-made body of water in that part of the state except for Lake Mead.[65]

The value of Kerkorian's International Leisure stock swelled to $180 million the year after going public.[66] The soaring value of the shares dismayed Hughes, who rightly saw that publicly traded corporations involved in casinos were equipped to compete with one of the richest men in the world. Teamsters loans and mob money were no longer necessary to prop up casinos. (It also no doubt galled Hughes, the famed aviator and airline magnate, that his upstart rival was also the largest shareholder in Western Airlines.)

International Leisure's rising stock price and the International Hotel's instant success—it boasted revenues of nearly $6 million in its first month and become famous as the Las Vegas home of Elvis Presley, who performed 837 consecutive sold-out concerts there—gave Kerkorian great freedom in plotting his next move.[67] Kerkorian shuttled across the country and crossed oceans aboard his $4 million private DC-9 to meet bankers and arrange deals. By late 1969 Kerkorian outmaneuvered the Bronfman family and bought a controlling interest in the fabled but embattled Metro-Goldwyn-Mayer (MGM) film studio.

Soon after, Kerkorian received a harsh lesson in the downside of running publicly held companies. The Securities and Exchange Commission cited the Flamingo's mob-tainted past as reason for barring Kerkorian's much-needed bid for a secondary stock offering for International Leisure.[68] A recession torpedoed the stock price, and he borrowed heavily from European banks to stay afloat. The value of his holdings plunged from about $500 million in 1969 to $79 million a year later—a paper loss of more than $400 million.[69] In 1971 Kerkorian eased his debts by selling the International and the Flamingo at deep discounts to the Hilton hotel chain, which renamed the properties the Las Vegas Hilton and the Flamingo Hilton. "Sometimes you lose, but that's the nature of the game. There's always another game and another chance to win," Kerkorian said.[70]

Overextended yet undeterred, Kerkorian pushed the MGM board to approve the construction of the MGM Grand Hotel and Casino in Las Vegas, which would be even bigger than the International. The idea was part of a broader plan to diversify the company by extending the brand into the leisure market. Kerkorian owned the bulk of the land on the Strip where the hotel would be built; his sixteen-acre site near the Flamingo included the shuttered Bonanza Hotel and Casino. The other parcel was owned by a group that included Moe Dalitz, the longtime Las Vegas casino operator and former gangster. Kerkorian had to address uncomfortable questions about the nature of Dalitz's role in the project. "I don't see anything wrong with buying a piece of vacant property from these people. What's wrong with Moe?" Kerkorian said in a rare interview with a reporter.[71] Kerkorian denied any involvement with organized crime; for instance, he said he had no dealings with Flamingo investor Meyer Lansky when Kerkorian bought that casino in 1967.

MGM shareholders overwhelmingly approved the arrangement in December 1971, brushing aside the concerns about Dalitz and the accusations that Kerkorian stood to personally benefit from the sweetheart $5 million property sale. Kerkorian's experience with the International Hotel made it easy for him to line up the necessary licenses and variances to accelerate construction on his new project. Groundbreaking on the MGM Grand began in April 1972, and it opened in December 1973 as what was then the largest hotel in the world. Designers stuffed the towering 2,084-room resort with nostalgic touches recalling films from MGM's golden days, and Dean Martin brought his trademark old-school Vegas cool for the grand-opening ceremony. Typically reluctant to be in the public eye, Kerkorian didn't attend the celebrity-studded opening-night events. Kerkorian's focus was always on the next big deal. "It's just that I don't try to get all the meat off the bone. When I get a good figure, I just move something. Too many people try to hit the peak price and they hold on until it is too late," he told *Fortune* magazine.[72]

The MGM Grand was a hit with high-rollers and modest gamblers alike, and Kerkorian ballooned his stake in MGM to more than 50 percent. In 1980 a fire engulfed the MGM Grand, killing eighty-seven people in the worst disaster in the state's history. Kerkorian rebuilt the hotel in less than a year and sold it to Bally Manufacturing Corporation in 1986. In a sweet historical irony, Kerkorian a year later purchased the Desert Inn and the Sands from the Summa Corporation, the company that continued on after the death of Howard Hughes.

Kerkorian was a restless dealmaker, ultimately buying and selling MGM multiple times and making high-flying investments in airlines and automakers—not to mention four trips down the aisle—but he never forgot about the city that made him. For the third time, the billionaire constructed the world's largest hotel, a new MGM Grand south of Bally's on the Strip. The 5,005-room resort opened in 1993 and sat on the site of the Kerkorian-owned Marina Hotel and the Tropicana Country Club. The complex's green-tinted exterior and yellow brick road inside evoked the Emerald City of MGM's *The Wizard of Oz*, and MGM's "Leo the Lion" mascot inspired the ostentatious main entrance that forced visitors to walk through a pastiche of a resting lion. (MGM hastily replaced it when it realized that entering the mouth of a lion was considered bad luck in Asian cultures, steering wary gamblers away from the casino.) The complex also boasted an amusement park, part of the city's ill-judged effort in the 1990s to make Las Vegas a family-oriented destination. The MGM scrapped the park when the tourism pitch shifted to the more fitting philosophy of "whatever happens in Vegas, stays in Vegas." Despite the missteps, the MGM Grand has for decades been a keystone of the Strip.[73]

Among Kerkorian's flashiest deals was the successful unsolicited purchase in 2000 of Mirage Resorts, a casino empire assembled by a man
who also thought on a grand scale but whose personality was the opposite of Kerkorian's. Where Kerkorian was a phantom presence at his own
resorts—his name never appeared on one—the rival he bought out had
no such trouble with self-promotion, hamming it up with celebrities in
TV commercials and sitting ringside at boxing matches. The hyperkinetic
force of Steve Wynn refashioned the Strip into a dazzling Disneyland for
adults and symbolized the new, friendly corporate face of gambling.

————

Wynn, son of a bingo parlor operator on the East Coast, took over the
family business at twenty-one when his father died. In 1967 the University
of Pennsylvania graduate parlayed $45,000 in bingo profits into a 3 percent
slice of the Frontier as an entrée into the world of Las Vegas casinos. The
outgoing Wynn befriended Las Vegas powerbroker E. Parry Thomas, head
of Valley Bank of Nevada—long the only source of legitimate funds for the
region's casinos and the intermediary for Teamsters loans—and helped
him purchase a parcel of land adjacent to Caesars Palace from Howard
Hughes in 1971. Wynn then sold it back to Caesars at a handsome profit.
Thomas also maneuvered to set up Wynn with a wholesale liquor distribu-
torship, which forged invaluable connections to the city's hotel owners.[74]

Wynn steadily accumulated stock in the publicly traded company that
owned downtown's Golden Nugget, becoming president and chairman in
1973. Wynn cast out the cheats and thieves, fired 160 casino operators, and
hired employees he could trust.[75] He showed off his stylish sense of design in
renovating the aging casino and turning it into a surprising success in just
a few years. The casino's elegant Victorian theme stood out among its more
down-home Glitter Gulch competitors. In a 1978 interview for *The Merv
Griffin Show* at the Golden Nugget, Wynn discussed the effects of the shift
from gangsters to reputable businessmen like himself. "I think that anytime
the underworld leaves, that's good, because when it's all said and done, that
element of people in whatever business they're active, they don't contribute

a damn thing," he said. "But it was glamorous, and I think that Las Vegas in the era of the modern corporation—the post-Hughes—maybe lost a little bit of that."[76] Wynn knew he had to go big to get noticed.

Wynn made his first foray onto the Strip with the $630 million Mirage in 1989—the first large-scale casino to open in Las Vegas in many years. Rather than Teamsters pension funds or mob money, the Mirage was financed by the era's hottest financing tool: Wall Street junk bonds, which were rated below investment grade and thus carried a higher risk-reward potential for investors.

The Mirage was a master class in stagecraft. The frontage of the expansive Seven Seas–themed resort featured dramatic waterfalls and a fiery special-effects show culminating with an erupting "volcano" that attracted waves of tourists. The nightly display was the hook for pedestrians to venture inside the luxury hotel, where they found a steamy tropical botanical garden, a gigantic aquarium with sharks, and Siegfried & Roy's spectacular exotic animal act. Wynn's bold approach shook the Strip out of its decade in the doldrums. The Mirage needed to make $1 million a day just to break even. It exceeded expectations and earned $420 million in its first full year, easily outpacing the former leader and neighbor, Caesars Palace.[77]

Wynn tried to outdo himself with each project: Treasure Island (opened in 1993) boasted an elaborate gun battle between pirates and a British naval vessel in its man-made bay; the Bellagio (opened in 1998 on the former site of the Dunes) strove for a higher-end clientele with its dancing fountains, Dale Chihuly–created glass flowers blanketing the lobby ceiling, and art gallery showcasing Wynn's tasteful collection of masterpieces. Like his mentor, Jay Sarno, Wynn understood that he was in the entertainment business, not just the gambling business. "I'm not a gambler. I wouldn't go across the street to shoot dice except as a lark maybe twice a year. But I'd go regularly to see a wonderment or a new attraction. So would you," he said.[78]

In 2000 Wynn's Mirage Resorts agreed to a $6.4 billion buyout from Kerkorian's MGM Grand, creating the behemoth MGM Mirage with a portfolio of casinos stretching across the nation and overseas. The purchase heralded the era of corporate consolidation. MGM Mirage got even bigger in 2005 with its $7.9 billion acquisition of the Mandalay Resort Group, which included the Mandalay Bay, Luxor, Excalibur, and Circus Circus. Today it is a *Fortune* 500 company known as MGM Resorts International, with 58,000 employees and annual revenue of $9 billion.

In 2005 Harrah's Entertainment, which traces its roots to Bill Harrah's first bingo parlor in Reno in 1937, purchased Caesars Entertainment for about $9 billion and took the Caesars name, making it then the world's largest casino company. The Harrah's brand is still attached to dozens of casinos nationwide under the Caesars Entertainment Corporation. The company's Las Vegas holdings include Caesars Palace, Bally's, Paris, Flamingo, and Planet Hollywood.

As for Wynn, he stayed in the game by concentrating on the luxury market. He bought the decrepit Desert Inn as a birthday present for his wife in 2000. The old-school resort famous for hosting headlining acts, mobsters, and Howard Hughes was reduced to rubble to make way for the luxe Wynn Las Vegas, which opened in 2005. Wynn built a companion resort, Encore Las Vegas, three years later. The connected properties are known as much for their hot nightclubs and impressive restaurants as they are for their casinos.

These giant companies plus a fourth, Las Vegas Sands—owner of the Venetian and the Palazzo—not only dominate the Strip but also have a significant overseas presence, especially in Macau, the only Chinese territory that allows casino gambling.[79] Their global ambition, sheer scale of their resorts, and cooperation with governors and lawmakers would have been unimaginable in the city's gangster-dominated days. Government helped engineer the fall of the mobsters in Las Vegas and the rise of the casino corporations, which brightened everyone's bottom lines. The triumphant corporations needed new lands to conquer. Nevada gambling titans like Wynn fixed their gaze on competing for a tantalizing piece of the casino business far away in another town with a history of organized crime activity: Atlantic City.

PART II

All In

THE NEW MASTERS OF GAMBLING

CHAPTER 7

Siren Song

THE SPECTACULAR RISE AND
FALL OF ATLANTIC CITY

Everything dies, baby, that's a fact.
But maybe everything that dies someday comes back.
—Bruce Springsteen, "Atlantic City"

FRIDAY, MAY 26, 1978

Despite an overcast morning and thinner-than-expected crowds on the Boardwalk, Atlantic City did its best to put on a show for the day-trippers and gawkers who turned out on the Friday of Memorial Day weekend in 1978. The Boardwalk's ticky-tack souvenir shops, saltwater-taffy stands, and greasy snack bars braced for the annual surge in foot traffic as welcome as a beach breeze on a warm summer day. Steel Pier's arcades and amusement rides beckoned to children and teenagers; for their parents and older folks, the pier's music hall booked faded singer Eddie Fisher and comedian London Lee for shows all weekend.

In a hokey beginning-of-summer ritual that evoked Atlantic City's historic role as the home of the Miss America Pageant, a lifeguard playing the role of King Neptune carried two "mermaids" through the surf and deposited them in a boat.[1] The bikini-clad women—Miss Atlantic City Nancy Small and *Penthouse* Pet of the Year Victoria Lynn Johnson—were rowed out beyond the breakers where they dipped large wooden keys into the ocean, symbolically unlocking the ocean for the summer. As the mayor looked on approvingly and banks of photographers snapped away,

145

an observer asked which of the models had been featured in *Penthouse*, prompting one wiseacre to comment, "I don't know. I can't tell with their clothes on."[2]

The city and state hoped that the day would be remembered as much more than a routine exercise of nostalgia. They worked for years and overcame a host of doubts and setbacks to launch the greatest experiment in Atlantic City's colorful history—legalized gambling. In 1976 the state's voters had approved a referendum to make the city the only place in the United States with legal casinos outside of Nevada. With 60 million people living within a one-tank car trip away, the rewards had the potential to be enormous.

The state's daring risk was an appeal to the city's illicit history. For generations, illegal casinos and numbers rackets had been as much of a fixture of Atlantic City as the wooden planks that formed the Boardwalk. But by the late 1960s every symptom of urban decline afflicted Atlantic City: population loss, unemployment, poverty, and crime. New Jersey politicians believed that casinos could rejuvenate tourism and reverse the fortunes of the sagging city.

At ten o'clock in the morning on May 26, 1978, New Jersey governor Brendan Byrne joined other dignitaries at Resorts International Hotel for the opening of Atlantic City's first legal casino. Resorts hired husband-and-wife singers Steve Lawrence and Eydie Gormé to entertain patrons at the casino's 1,750-seat Superstar Theater. Lawrence had the honor of being the first to roll the dice, losing a ten-dollar bet at a craps table.

After the ribbon was snipped and handshakes were exchanged, the casino quickly filled to its 5,500-person capacity. As the day wore on the line to enter Resorts was shorter than projected, with many deterred by the threatening skies and authorities' warnings of nightmarish traffic jams on the three main causeways connecting the New Jersey mainland to Atlantic City.

For most of the players who made the trip, it was the first time they had been inside a legal casino. Joseph Cristofaro, a repairman from Philadelphia, cheered his $300 win at the roulette table, then frittered away half of it in two spins of the wheel. "As soon as I get in rhythm, I'm going to break this place," he vowed.[3] New Jersey housewife Caren Reich brought ten dollars and squealed after winning twenty-five dollars after only sixteen pulls on a slot machine. She happily scooped the coins into a cup and declared that her next stop would be the blackjack table.[4]

While the slot machines whirred and the craps players roared, about thirty people, mostly black, demonstrated on the Boardwalk near Resorts to protest alleged discrimination in the hotel's hiring practices. In recent decades, the city's year-round population had become increasingly black and Hispanic, and they felt that their needs went unnoticed in the corridors of power. The protesters complained that Resorts hired minorities for housekeeping and kitchen jobs but rarely for secretarial or managerial positions.

There were other problems. The state's comprehensive examination of Resorts delayed its ability to conduct the required background checks of prospective employees, leaving Resorts with a shortage of card dealers that forced ten blackjack tables to close. The hotel had too few cashiers to make change for players and not enough mechanics to repair the casino's nine hundred slot machines when they broke down, an all-too-frequent occurrence.[5] A woman who won a jackpot asked her husband to guard the slot machine while she chased down an employee who could pay her the remainder of her winnings. The hotel's restaurant closed several times during the day because of management disarray.

The crowds didn't seem to mind the inconveniences because Resorts was filled at the casino's scheduled closing time of six o'clock Saturday morning.[6] While employees prepared to reopen it later that morning, about a thousand people eager for more action waited behind velvet ropes. On the third day, many thousands more lined up for hours to enter the casino. A sense of feral desperation was in the air. Sleepless players reportedly relieved themselves into plastic cups to avoid losing their spots at their slot machines or tables.[7] The president of the hotel noted that "a lot of people abandoned their kids at the door of the casino and went in to gamble" at the adults-only casino floor.[8] Resorts imposed a dress code to screen out beach riffraff in shorts and T-shirts or bare feet.

All weekend, the casino floor was at or near capacity. A Resorts vice president estimated that it was the largest slot drop of all time and said that one hundred thousand people were in the casino on each of the weekend days. It took longer than expected to weigh the mountains of coins and count the piles of paper bills. When the results from the first six days were finally tallied, Resorts took in an average of $438,504 daily for a total of about $2.6 million in gross revenue.[9] "It's obvious from the turnout this weekend that we could have filled six casinos," declared Marvin Ashner, president of the Atlantic City Hotel and Motel Association.[10]

After so many years of neglect and ridicule, Atlantic City was hot again. The appetite for gambling was strong, but could it last? Would casinos really pull Atlantic City out of hard times, or would powerful business interests and their allies in government benefit at the expense of the people? Could New Jersey defend its vulnerable gambling industry from the mob and also carefully manage its growth?

There was a lot riding on the answers to those questions, not only for Atlantic City and New Jersey but also for governments across the nation. If Atlantic City's grand experiment succeeded, it would no doubt inspire other states to authorize casinos to revive depressed areas and bring in a fresh source of revenue to their treasuries. After all, most states in the Northeast had experience running lotteries, so the taboo against government-sanctioned gambling had long been broken.

And yet the potential of casino gambling's expansion to neighboring states loomed as an existential threat to Atlantic City. Yes, Resorts International was raking in big bucks as the only legal casino on the East Coast, but what would happen if casinos opened in nearby Philadelphia or Delaware or even in Connecticut? Would people still come out to the shore to gamble? Or would Atlantic City be stuck with a row of half-empty casinos along the Boardwalk? New Jersey would find that it could manage many things about Atlantic City's casino industry, but it couldn't control what other states would do.

Out-of-town entrepreneurs have always seen great resort potential in a narrow ten-mile-long barrier island in New Jersey along the Atlantic Ocean. In the early 1850s industrialists and land speculators—many from Philadelphia—backed a railroad company that would lay down sixty miles of track in a straight line from Camden, New Jersey, to Absecon Island. The men bought up the sandy land, developed the beach, and christened the town "Atlantic City." Train service began in 1854, the same year of Atlantic City's incorporation, and pleasure-seeking Philadelphians filled rail cars in search of good health and a respite from the stresses of urban life. In 1870 Atlantic City's first boardwalk was constructed as a beachfront boulevard elevated from the tides and sand.

The city billed itself as the nation's playground, a wide-open "Queen of the Resorts" where it seemed like anything could happen. The intoxicating whirl of sun and hedonism attracted day-trippers and year-long residents alike. The population more than tripled between 1890 and 1910, when Atlantic City entered its prime.[11] The Boardwalk evolved into a stage for the upwardly mobile to proudly display their status and a proving ground for the working class to test their social aspirations. Dignified hotels such as the Moorish-themed Marlborough-Blenheim, with its prominent dome and chimneys, catered to the upper classes and visiting dignitaries such as Winston Churchill.

Atlantic City also perfected its trademark blend of middle-brow and low culture, resembling a mix of a circus and a county fair. Steel Pier featured vaudeville shows and theaters but also a rogue's gallery of palm readers, pitchmen, and freak shows. The pier's lurid displays included a "diving" horse that fell off of a high platform into a deep pool while throngs watched. (Periodic attempts to revive the act have been squelched by the fierce opposition of animal-rights activists.)

Inspired by the siren song of the beach, the city organized a beauty contest in 1921, holding it in September to extend the tourist season. Tens of thousands of visitors flocked to the resort to admire the contestants. The winner was high school student Margaret Gorman from Washington, DC, who claimed the dual honor of "Inter-City Beauty, Amateur" and "The Most Beautiful Bathing Girl in America." Her titles were ultimately simplified to "Miss America," and the pageant became Atlantic City's signature event. The cavernous Atlantic City Convention Hall opened on the Boardwalk in 1929 to accommodate the pageant and other spectacles.

Engineers organized the city along a grid pattern: Avenues running parallel to the ocean took the names of bodies of water (Mediterranean Avenue, Baltic Avenue, Pacific Avenue), and they were intersected by streets with state names (Virginia Avenue, New York Avenue, North Carolina Avenue). Generations later the Depression-era game Monopoly named the properties on its famous board after Atlantic City's streets. The object of the game is to strategically buy property, accumulate enough money to build houses and hotels, and drive up rents to bankrupt other players. It's an all-too-fitting reflection of the city's history.

Power and wealth accumulated in the hands of a few, and no one wielded greater influence in Atlantic City than political boss Enoch "Nucky" Johnson, the inspiration for the heavily fictionalized central figure in the HBO series *Boardwalk Empire*. Johnson sat atop the Republican Party's machine in the city and county for thirty years and controlled the rackets. His dominance of the seaside resort began about a decade after the Victorian era, thrived during Prohibition and its repeal, and ended just before the attack on Pearl Harbor. Little of significance happened in the city or county without his approval. His influence over politicians and police was complete, and his right to take kickbacks from Prohibition-era bootleggers and speakeasies was unquestioned.

In 1929 Johnson hosted an important meeting of crime kingpins known as the Atlantic City Conference. It marked one of the earliest gatherings of bosses from cities across the nation, bringing together an astonishing constellation of underworld personalities—Al Capone, Charles "Lucky" Luciano, Meyer Lansky, Dutch Schultz, and Frank Costello. They came from Chicago, Cleveland, Detroit, Boston, Philadelphia, New York, and New Jersey with the aim of avoiding unnecessary competition (and violence) by forming alliances. Atlantic City's wide-open spirit made it the ideal place for such a convention and Johnson was a perfect host, arranging their hotel accommodations and ensuring protection from law enforcement.[12]

Atlantic City's illicit atmosphere attracted workaday visitors in the same way Las Vegas has long been a magnet for those seeking an escape. Illegal gambling dens, numbers running, and prostitution were as plentiful as the sand on the beach. "We have whisky, wine, women, song and slot machines. I won't deny it and I won't apologize for it," Johnson declared. "If the majority of the people didn't want them they wouldn't be profitable and they wouldn't exist. The fact that they do exist proves to me that the people want them."[13]

After repeal of Prohibition, Johnson focused on illegal gambling to keep his political patronage machine humming. An FBI investigation in the late 1930s uncovered twenty-five horse-betting parlors and casinos, nine numbers banks, and eight hundred retailers that handled numbers bets.[14] "Not a horse-race betting room, brothel, gambling casino, numbers banker, or petty racketeer could operate without cutting in the boss," a journalist wrote in 1942, a year after a tax-evasion conviction sent Johnson to prison and effectively ended his reign.[15]

The next in line to be the region's strongman, Frank "Hap" Farley, took Johnson's city and county party posts and maneuvered a seat for himself in the New Jersey Senate. Although he was a staunch Republican, Farley lobbied hard to secure Atlantic City as the host for the 1964 Democratic National Convention. When thousands of television and print reporters descended on the city that summer, they found the grand old resort to be in a shocking state of decline, especially in comparison to the glitter of San Francisco, where the Republicans had met about a month earlier. Presidential campaign chronicler Theodore White judged Atlantic City to be "run down and glamourless" and noted the tawdriness of the once-fashionable Boardwalk.[16] In the aging hotels, visiting journalists complained of cramped rooms, hapless room service, broken TV sets and air conditioning units, and plumbing problems.

By the late 1960s Atlantic City had fallen into a deep spiral of urban decay. Population dropped from 59,544 in 1960 to 47,859 in 1970, and about 80 percent of those who had moved out were whites, leaving behind an impoverished black population. Companies also headed for the exits, boosting unemployment. A 1965 report on poverty called it the poorest city in the state, with a third of its year-round residents on welfare.[17] Among small US cities, Atlantic City had the highest number of crimes in seven categories, according to the FBI.[18]

The grand Boardwalk hotels from the resort town's heyday had become poignant reminders of how far it had fallen. The Ambassador Hotel, which had counted President Warren Harding and author Arthur Conan Doyle among its guests in the Roaring Twenties, closed in 1966 and was auctioned off in bankruptcy court. The majestic Traymore Hotel, once described as the "Taj Mahal of Atlantic City," was demolished in 1972. (Years later New York developer Donald Trump swiped the palatial name for his opulent casino on the Boardwalk.)

In a nod to Atlantic City's gambling heritage, New Jersey politicians and business interests began to consider legalizing casinos as a way to revive the sinking resort. Farley, damaged by an array of investigations and nearing the end of his powers as political boss, failed to persuade the New Jersey Senate in 1970 to approve a referendum to legalize gambling in Atlantic City.[19] (Farley lost his reelection bid to a Democrat in the following year.)

The idea stewed in the legislature for a few years as lawmakers studied the issue and sought out the public's opinion on gambling. Voters had overwhelmingly approved setting up a state lottery in 1969, which had matured into the most lucrative in the nation. With the state essentially running a legal numbers racket as well as sanctioning wagering at racetracks, it was hard for some to see the moral case for restricting other forms of gambling. A state commission heard testimony from both sides—opponents worried about an increase in problems such as crime and compulsive gambling while supporters pointed at the potential of a new source of revenue without raising taxes—and concluded that the casino question should go before voters. A March 1973 poll showed that 57 percent of state residents backed casinos with only 29 percent in opposition.[20]

The push for casinos gained an important advocate when Democrat Brendan Byrne took office as governor in 1974. The Harvard-trained lawyer adopted a pragmatic attitude toward gambling during his stints as a prosecutor in an urban county and later as a superior court judge. After much negotiation, Byrne and lawmakers agreed to put a referendum on the November 1974 ballot that would allow state-operated casinos but prohibit private investment in them to guard against mob influence. Although the intent was to limit casinos to Atlantic City, the language in the constitutional amendment opened the door to casinos elsewhere in the state, subject to local approval. Political opponents worried about the specter of organized crime, and church groups mobilized their congregations. Voters soundly rejected the measure.

Pro-gambling forces assessed where they went wrong and drafted a proposal allowing private corporations to own and operate casinos, a response to public doubts that government alone would be equipped to perform those roles. Importantly, the new measure explicitly stated that casinos would be located only in Atlantic City. After it won approval from lawmakers, Byrne and other politicians campaigned for the measure as a redevelopment tool that would create tens of thousands of jobs. They argued that gambling would be a social good because state taxes on casino revenue would defray the costs of utility bills and property taxes for the elderly and the disabled. (The committee advanced its cause with the slogan, "Help Yourself. Help Atlantic City. Help New Jersey.") The pro-casino campaign courted big donors, collecting more than $1.3 million in contributions from business interests compared to a paltry $21,250 scrounged up by the opposing side.[21] The state's voters solidly approved the referendum in November 1976, setting off celebrations across the city. The next morning a banner headline in the *Atlantic City Press* blared: "CITY REBORN."[22]

One of the difference-makers in the 1976 campaign was a $200,000 pro-gambling campaign contribution from a shady company named Resorts International, which operated Paradise Island Casino in the Bahamas.[23]

In 1958 a group of investors purchased the Tampa, Florida–based Mary Carter Paint Company, a manufacturer of house paints. The chairman, James M. Crosby, showed more interest in real estate than home décor and bought up a swath of property in the Bahamas. The company opened the successful casino-resort in 1967 and changed its name to Resorts International a year later, leaving behind the paint business for good. (Crosby, the principal owner of Resorts, himself refrained from gambling: "I find it boring. And the edge favors the house.")[24]

After mostly staying on the sidelines during the 1974 effort, Resorts emerged as the biggest single contributor in the renewed campaign two years later. In the interim, the company's owners played a real-life version of Monopoly, which also designated Boardwalk as the most valuable space. Resorts purchased the aging Chalfonte-Haddon Hall Hotel on the Boardwalk near Steel Pier even before the state's voters weighed in, pledging to turn it into a world-class casino if the gambling referendum passed. Resorts applied for a gambling license, and its aggressive lobbyists shaped the enabling legislation that gave the company a monopoly on Atlantic City's casino business for the first year.

A December 15, 1976, public hearing before a New Jersey Assembly committee revealed the depth of desperation felt in Atlantic City. Speaker after speaker begged politicians to enact the casino bill as soon as possible to rescue the ailing city. "I am 100 percent in favor of destroying the quality of life in Atlantic City. Anyone who wants to maintain it couldn't have been in Atlantic City for at least the last 15 years," said Edmund Colanzi, the city's parks commissioner.[25] Richard Lavin, spokesman for the 42,000-member Atlantic City–Cape May Central Labor Council, told the panel that he was a bartender by trade but had no bar to tend. "There is a feeling all around us that this is our last Christmas of hunger and our first Christmas of hope," he said, calling the city a "slum-infested ghost town." "The purpose in having casinos in Atlantic City is to end hunger in Atlantic City and the surrounding area. The purpose in giving Atlantic City the right to have casinos is to provide jobs for the jobless."[26]

Despite the pleas, legislators were determined to take it slow and avoid the mistakes Nevada made decades earlier when weak oversight allowed crime syndicates to dominate the casino industry. They were mindful that mob interests in New York and New Jersey had every intention of infiltrating the new casinos in their backyard. New Jersey's Casino Control Act outlined a thorough licensing procedure to check the backgrounds of casino investors. At a crowded bill-signing ceremony on June 2, 1977, Byrne sent a clear message that New Jersey would not tolerate the mob. "Organized crime is not welcome in Atlantic City! And we warn them again: Keep your filthy hands out of Atlantic City and keep the hell out of our state!" Byrne declared in front of historic Boardwalk Hall overlooking the beach.[27]

To follow through on that ringing declaration, the state met with Nevada officials and set up two agencies: the Casino Control Commission to supervise the industry and the Division of Gaming Enforcement to patrol it. Resorts' application for a gambling license bogged down as the state struggled to trace the company's byzantine financing schemes and verify rumors of its ties to nefarious characters like Lansky, who had transferred his Caribbean casino interests to the Bahamas after the communist revolution in Cuba. In early 1978 Byrne pressed lawmakers to grant a temporary six-month license to Resorts that would allow it to open the casino in time for the summer season while the investigation continued.

Meanwhile, Resorts was busily keeping its promise to refurbish the Chalfonte-Haddon Hall Hotel. Resorts spent an estimated $50 million to demolish the Chalfonte part of the complex and convert the fifteen-floor, 1920s-era Haddon Hall into a lively hotel-casino—a striking pivot from its previous incarnation when Quakers ran it as a boarding house and forbade alcohol. Resorts officials and state regulators haggled over the size of minimum and maximum bets and the casino's operating hours. They compromised on five-dollar minimums for the vast majority of tables and allowed the casino's doors to be open eighteen hours a day on weekdays and twenty hours on weekends.[28]

The casino enjoyed a sensational first seven months, piling up $134 million in revenue, nearly triple the company's original investment.[29] In 1979 Resorts grossed $232 million.[30] However, the casino was still operating under a temporary gaming license because of lingering questions about Resorts International's dicey background. In December 1978 the Division of Gaming Enforcement reported that the company had associated with organized crime figures, maintained a fund to pay off public officials, and kept shoddy accounting records of its Bahamas casino.[31] Since Resorts was the first and only legal casino in New Jersey's history, no precedent existed for judging a company's fitness to own a gambling resort. The Casino Control Commission chose the path of flexibility and granted Resorts a license in February 1979 after failing to find a direct connection between Resorts International and organized crime.[32]

Despite its difficulties with Resorts, the state's Division of Gaming Enforcement did a credible job overall at repelling organized crime interests from holding ownership stakes in casino. New Jersey's stiff regulatory structure ensured that there would be no Bugsy Siegels in command of casinos on the Boardwalk. Atlantic City's original nine casinos all received temporary permits, a strategy that kept the companies on a short leash while the state weeded out sketchy executives and closed off sketchy funding sources.[33] "I do not think there was even a real effort to bring organized crime into any casinos, because we were so scrupulous in the licensing procedures," Byrne said years after he had left the governor's office. "I mean we have turned down somebody because they had once hired a lawyer who had once represented some mobsters. And we made it so tough, and I do not think they wanted to tackle us."[34]

Resorts International's smashing success in Atlantic City had entrepreneurs lusting for their place at the gold rush. The owners of the Howard Johnson and Regency hotel planned to lease their space to Caesars World, the operator of Caesars Palace in Las Vegas. Bob Guccione, the publisher of *Penthouse* magazine, bought two motels near the Howard Johnson's and bragged that his would be the next casino to open in Atlantic City.[35] Playboy Enterprises purchased land on the Boardwalk near Convention

Hall with an eye to building a casino-hotel. Bally Manufacturing Corporation acquired three Boardwalk hotels and planned to raze them for a new casino-hotel complex. However, many potential casino operators ran up against heavy-handed regulators who imposed stringent design rules and limited the types of allowable games.[36] People like *Playboy* magazine founder Hugh Hefner invested millions of dollars in projects only to be denied a permanent gambling license. Guccione was also among the spurned.

Resorts lost its monopoly in 1979 with the opening of Caesars Boardwalk Regency and then Bally's Park Place, built on the site of the demolished Marlborough-Blenheim hotel, a turn-of-the-century architectural gem. Concerns of preservationists were brushed aside as historic site after historic site fell to make way for casino magnates chasing fast money with their modern pleasure domes. Vacant lots and condemned housing projects were swallowed up with little regard for how such rabid land speculation would affect the surrounding neighborhoods. A study found that two thousand people had been pushed out of the city in a "systematic effort by landlords to evict Hispanic, poor and elderly residents from Atlantic City" to make way for the casino developers.[37]

The charismatic Steve Wynn, in the early stages of building his gambling empire in Las Vegas, visited Resorts soon after it opened and was struck by the teeming crowds who seemed almost desperate to gamble away their money. "I had never seen anything like it. It made Caesars Palace on New Year's Eve look like it was closed for lunch," he said.[38] The project was largely financed by a Drexel Burnham Lambert bond trader named Michael Milken, Wall Street's "junk-bond king" who later served a prison sentence for violating securities laws.

Wynn opened the Golden Nugget in Atlantic City in 1980 and flamboyantly signed Frank Sinatra to be the headliner at his hotels in Nevada and New Jersey. The Golden Nugget was Atlantic City's top-earning casino in the early 1980s, helped along by jokey TV commercials featuring Sinatra and Wynn. (Wynn sold the Golden Nugget to Bally in 1987, accurately foreseeing that the good times wouldn't last long in Atlantic City. The casino passed through several ownership groups and name changes before closing in 2014 as the dingy Atlantic Club.)

Another famed developer swooped in from his perch high above Manhattan to enter the real estate scrum in Atlantic City. Unlike Wynn, Donald Trump had never run a casino, but he couldn't resist entering such a red-hot market in a neighboring state. The brash dealmaker partnered with Harrah's to open Harrah's at Trump Plaza in 1984, but Trump soon fell out with Holiday Inn—then the owner of Harrah's—and seized a controlling interest in the thirty-nine-story Boardwalk property. He then purchased Hilton's nearly complete casino in the Marina District the following year, naming it Trump's Castle. Trump fell deeper into debt to pull off the $320 million deal that staved off a hostile takeover bid by Wynn.[39]

After the death of Crosby, the Resorts chairman, in 1986, Trump pledged to fulfill Crosby's dream of building an opulent "Taj Mahal" in Atlantic City. After a complicated boardroom minuet that involved Trump taking over and then unloading Resorts, he restarted construction on the hotel-casino next door to Resorts. Trump bragged that it would be "an incredible place—the eighth-wonder of the world" and pushed his contractors and stretched his financing to have it completed by 1990.[40] The $1 billion Trump Taj Mahal, a gaudy mishmash of architectural styles, stood as a five-hundred-foot-tall monument to excess: $15 million was spent on the Austrian-made chandeliers that illuminated the world's largest gambling floor featuring more than three thousand slot machines.[41] Trump ensured extensive media coverage when he persuaded Michael Jackson to attend the casino's grand opening. Trump's highly leveraged acquisitions propped up with high-interest junk bonds left him with three casinos—the maximum allowed under the state's Casino Control Act.

Big shots like Wynn and Trump had good reason to grab a piece of Atlantic City at any cost: in the 1980s, the small oceanfront city was the most popular tourist destination in the United States, outdrawing Las Vegas and Disneyland. Fleets of buses from the New York City area, the Philadelphia region, and other parts of New Jersey carried millions of gamblers into Atlantic City each year. The buses fed into underground bus depots that were as busy as any big-city transit station. As passengers stepped off the buses, they were handed rolls of quarters and buffet tickets and took escalators to the casino floor. Many didn't bother to venture out onto the Boardwalk or see other parts of the city since they were only there for the day.

If they had, they would have seen the persistence of urban squalor in the neighborhoods just a few blocks from the glitz of the Boardwalk casinos. The promise that casinos would pull Atlantic City out of decades of blight remained unfulfilled. New Jersey had already broken its pledge that casino taxes would aid the state's elderly; the money was channeled to the general fund instead. In addition, 2 percent of gross casino revenue was earmarked for redevelopment in Atlantic City, but it was triggered only when the companies had recouped their investments.[42] Confusion over who would control the funds and how they would be spent delayed the much-needed urban-renewal projects for years.

Violent and nonviolent crime surged with the influx of new visitors. The city's poverty rate actually worsened after the first legal casino opened in 1978: in the 1970 US Census, 22.5 percent reported living in poverty, a figure that jumped to 25 percent in 1980 and stayed at that level in 1990 despite the decade's casino building boom.[43] The city's demographics also shifted: in 1970 Atlantic City was 55 percent white and 44 percent black; by 1990 it was 35 percent white and 51 percent black.[44]

Employment did spike in the early years of gambling legalization: the service sector boasted a net gain of nearly fifteen thousand jobs from 1975 to 1980, and construction jobs were plentiful as long as high-rise casinos kept popping up along the Boardwalk.[45] The city's eleven casinos had more than forty thousand full-time workers (about three-quarters of the city's private-sector employment) and generated about $300 million a year in taxes to the state.[46] However, workers in the surrounding suburbs benefited the most from the job surge; unemployment remained stubbornly high in Atlantic City.

The rosy numbers masked the unsettling realities that the new resorts managed by giant companies were driving up real estate prices and property taxes and pushing small retailers out of business. Atlantic City had become too reliant on a single industry with the power concentrated in the hands of a few moneyed developers. What would happen once the casino market hit its peak in Atlantic City and restless speculators and gamblers looked elsewhere for their riches?

THURSDAY, MAY 23, 2013

Nearly thirty-five years to the day since Governor Byrne presided over the opening of Resorts International—then the only legal casino east of the Mississippi—a different governor held a pair of scissors at another ribbon-cutting ceremony at the same hotel. This time it was New Jersey governor Chris Christie inaugurating a $35 million Margaritaville project just before Memorial Day weekend in 2013. Like Byrne, Christie was a strongly pro-gambling governor and passionate about boosting Atlantic City as a tourist destination.

After Christie delivered a short speech to hundreds of guests and members of the media at Resorts, eager customers lined up to soak in the tropical vibe inspired by musician Jimmy Buffett. Though 1977's "Margaritaville" is his only Top 10 hit on the pop charts, Buffett's relentless touring schedule and laid-back charm has built one of the most rabid fan bases in pop music history. Legions of margarita-swilling, floral-shirt-wearing "Parrot Heads" fill arenas and summer sheds year after year to soak in Buffett's feel-good concerts with the Coral Reefer Band.

These days Buffett may be as famous for his business savvy as for his music. His upbeat "island lifestyle" brand is at the center of a global empire consisting of hotels, casinos, restaurants, and alcohol. His chain of Margaritaville eateries serves fish tacos, Key lime pie, and fruity boat drinks in outposts from Cincinnati to the Caribbean. While customers wait for a table, they are encouraged to browse in the adjoining store, carrying a full line of easy-living apparel, housewares, and collectibles.

Buffett's "it's five o'clock somewhere" attitude meshes perfectly with the escapist mentality of casino visitors and tourists. He owns Margaritaville-branded casino/restaurants in Las Vegas, Mississippi, and Louisiana, and his restaurants and bars are showpieces in several other casinos. Parrot Heads who still have money to spend after hitting the bar flock to Margaritaville-themed slot machines and gaming tables conveniently located near the restaurant. At Resorts, a Buffett-themed LandShark Bar & Grill sprawls out onto the beach.

Resorts had hit hard times, and Christie saw the addition of Margaritaville as a chance to "hit the reset button on things that we that we wish we would have done differently before." "What I feel in Atlantic City now is a renewed enthusiasm. And I do think that to some extent we've been presented with an opportunity," he said.[47] Christie praised the new investment as a signal to tourists that the Jersey Shore was back after the previous October's devastation wrought by Superstorm Sandy. For Atlantic City, its once-unassailable advantage in the gambling trade had in many ways become an albatross. Superstorm Sandy didn't hit Atlantic City as severely as other parts of the state, but the city was facing a slower-moving threat poised to spin the resort into a death spiral.

———

During the last thirty-five years, Resorts' fortunes swung between the high of being among the richest casinos in the world and the low of coming within days of closing its doors for good. In between such extremes were ownership changes that unfolded amid a dramatically altered gambling landscape in Atlantic City.

Legal casino gambling was no longer a novelty on the East Coast as it had been in the 1970s and 1980s: today betting chips tower on tables in riverboats and docks on America's rivers and shores, slot machines whir in big-city casinos and on remote reservations and old mining towns. There is no longer any reason for gamblers in Philadelphia or New York to board a bus to Atlantic City when they have a variety of gaming options in their own backyards. Competition has drained away Atlantic City's customer base, leaving the gambling-dependent town exceptionally vulnerable to economic downturns. The rocky road traveled by Resorts is a case study of how drastically the climate had changed.

In the late 1980s the company was at the center of a bitter public struggle between developer Donald Trump—owner of multiple Atlantic City casinos, including Resorts—and entertainer Merv Griffin, who wanted in on the gambling business. After fraught negotiations that noisily played out in the media, Trump took control of Steel Pier and got to keep the unfinished Taj Mahal project, and Griffin acquired the rest of the Resorts company, including its casinos in Atlantic City and the Bahamas. In his memoir, Griffin described Trump as "a person of extremes. There's no in-between with Donald. He's either your best friend or your worst enemy."[48]

Saddled with unpayable debts and mounting losses, Trump and Griffin became regular denizens of bankruptcy courts. About a year after it opened to great fanfare in 1990, the junk-bond financed Trump Taj Mahal entered bankruptcy when Trump, who personally guaranteed the mountain of debt, couldn't keep up with the high-interest-rate loan payments amid the recession. Trump endured additional Chapter 11 bankruptcies—in 1992, 2004, and 2009—that eroded his ownership share and day-to-day control of his Atlantic City casinos. He resigned from the board of directors of Trump Entertainment Resorts in 2009. Trump's Castle, which had been renamed Trump Marina, was sold off at a fire-sale price in 2011 and now operates as the Golden Nugget Atlantic City. Trump Plaza and Trump Taj Mahal fell into such an embarrassing state of disrepair that in 2014 the self-aggrandizing billionaire unsuccessfully sued to take his name *off* of the buildings. Trump Plaza closed in late 2014. Trump Entertainment Resorts went through bankruptcy for a fifth time and ended up as a subsidiary of Icahn Enterprises, which shuttered Trump Taj Mahal in October 2016, the last of the Atlantic City casinos once owned by Trump.

Trump's business record in Atlantic City emerged as an issue during his run for the presidency. He consistently brushed off the corporate bankruptcies as necessary business maneuvers even though they left stock investors and bondholders exposed while risking little of his own money.

"I left Atlantic City before it totally cratered, and I made a lot of money in Atlantic City, and I'm very proud of it," he said during a Republican primary debate on August 6, 2015. After his campaign steamrolled through the primaries, investigative journalists probed Trump's business failings and examined his financial dealings. Trump's Democratic opponent, Hillary Clinton, used the abandoned Trump Plaza as a backdrop for a campaign stop in July 2016, charging that his poor casino management led to thousands of job losses in Atlantic City. Trump weathered the scrutiny, effectively counterpunched his critics, and was elected the forty-fifth president of the United States on November 8, 2016.

Trump's rival in the battle for Resorts, the TV talk-show host Griffin, took the debt-laden company through two rounds of Chapter 11 bankruptcy. As a casino owner, Griffin tapped into his connections from a life in showbiz to entice celebrities to stay and improve the showroom's offerings. Stars like Burt Lancaster and Dinah Shore appeared at casino-related events. Griffin held contestant searches for his shows *Wheel of Fortune* and *Jeopardy!* at Resorts and hosted his New Year's Eve TV programs there.[49] Griffin's knack for marketing and promotion lifted the casino's cash flow and boosted the stock price of the company, renamed Merv Griffin's Resorts.

In the mid-1990s Griffin sold out to South African business magnate Sol Kerzner, creator of the Sun International hotel and casino chain. (His Sun City resort near Johannesburg was the target of antiapartheid protests in the 1980s.) Kerzner seemed more interested in developing the Caribbean part of the portfolio—he built the ambitious Atlantis casino-resort complex in the Bahamas in 1998—and sold the Atlantic City casino in 2001.

By then Foxwoods Resort Casino and its giant neighbor Mohegan Sun (which Kerzner helped bankroll) in rural Connecticut had grown into the largest casinos in the world. The Indian casinos siphoned off much of the business that had been flowing to Atlantic City, which heavily relied on day-trippers busing down from North Jersey, New York and Long Island, and Pennsylvania. Atlantic City casinos like Resorts designed their buildings to accommodate bus depots that process senior-citizen groups or social clubs on day trips to sample the buffet, play the slots or tables for a few hours, and then return to the bus with a few more stories and probably a little less money.

Additionally, Resorts and its Boardwalk neighbors seemed out of step with Atlantic City's trend of steering visitors to the Marina District a few miles away. The Borgata Hotel Casino and Spa, which opened in 2003, created a self-contained resort with décor and amenities similar to the finest casinos in Las Vegas. Like the Bellagio, the Borgata showcases artist Dale Chihuly's fanciful glass sculptures and boasts celebrity-chef restaurants, luxurious spas and pools, and high-end entertainment that set it apart from the third-tier comedians and cheap magic shows at Boardwalk showrooms.

Unlike the Boardwalk, the Marina District is unburdened by the weight of history and geographical limits. Highways and bluffs wall off the Marina District from Atlantic City's urban blight—no shiftless pedestrian traffic or spillover rowdiness from poor neighborhoods will disturb visitors. The Borgata and two other casinos in the district exist in an oasis without pawn shops, grind joints, and the other detritus of city life. In 2000 nearly a quarter of residents lived in poverty and 13 percent were unemployed—both figures were double the national rates.[50]

Atlantic City's decline accelerated as new casinos popped up in the Philadelphia metro area and Delaware in the 2000s, giving people in those neighboring states little reason to make the trek into Atlantic City, especially the Boardwalk. Resorts' dismal financial situation—its revenue was in free fall and among the worst of Atlantic City's eleven casinos—led its hedge-fund owners to stop paying the mortgage and hand over the keys to their lender in 2009.[51] New owners picked up Resorts at a bargain price and kept the doors open by slashing payroll expenses and promoting discount room rates and restaurant deals.

When Christie took office as governor in 2010, he made reviving Atlantic City a priority of his new administration. He seized control of Atlantic City's tourism district, launched a major marketing campaign called "Do A.C.," and pushed for new private investment on the Boardwalk. His big bet has clearly failed. Atlantic City's gross casino revenue fell each year during his governorship, from $3.6 billion in 2010 to $2.7 billion in 2014, the year when four out of Atlantic City's twelve casinos closed.[52] The losses left the city gasping for its very survival. In 2016 Christie and city leaders agreed on a five-year state takeover of Atlantic City's finances to avert municipal bankruptcy.

Meanwhile, the money-losing Resorts ironically found a savior in a competitor that presaged its downturn in the 1990s: Mohegan Sun, one of the nation's leading casino operators. With casinos in Pennsylvania and Connecticut, the 2012 deal tied in with Mohegan Sun's ambition to become a regional power. Among Mohegan Sun's business partners is Jimmy Buffett, who installed one of his Margaritaville restaurants in Mohegan Sun's resort in Uncasville, Connecticut. Buffett and Mohegan Sun agreed to undertake the project for Resorts.

The Margaritaville expansion is the latest in a long string of fresh starts for Resorts and Atlantic City as a whole. New Jersey was far ahead of its time in adopting a pragmatic view of gambling—that it was better to control it than to ban it—but other states gradually caught on and surpassed the Garden State. Still standing through it all is Resorts. As the first legal casino outside Nevada, Resorts is an important part of gambling history. How many more chances will it get to make more?

CHAPTER 8

Betting on a Boom

STATES PROMOTE CASINOS AS ENGINES OF REVIVAL

We're losing revenue every day because people are going to those casinos to play. . . . They now go to New Jersey, they go to Connecticut. Why don't we bring them to upstate New York?

—New York governor Andrew Cuomo,
arguing for more full-scale casinos in his state in 2013

Gambling's deep roots in American culture evoke a strong nostalgic pull in regions of the country outside urban areas such as Atlantic City. The colorful exploits of steamboat gamblers who plied their trade along the nation's great rivers and the optimism of gold and silver prospectors who journeyed west in the hope of pulling riches from the earth are the stuff of legend. Lionized in the nation's literature for their cunning and boldness, they are enshrined as American archetypes.

The steamboats themselves are seen as reminders of simpler times. In *Life on the Mississippi*, former steamboat pilot Mark Twain wrote that the prospect of a race between two big paddle-wheelers brought "a state of consuming excitement" to the Mississippi Valley that would dominate conversation for weeks: "Politics and the weather were dropped, and people talked only of the coming race."[1] Throngs gathered along the riverbanks to watch the departure of the grand steamers followed by their twin trails of charcoal-black smoke, and bets were staked in cities along the route. An estimated $1 million was wagered on the famous 1870 contest between the *Natchez* and the *Robert E. Lee* from New Orleans to St. Louis.[2]

With little to do and many hours and sometimes days to pass between ports, steamboat passengers socialized by playing cards in saloons and social halls. Professional gamblers—many would call them outright swindlers—clambered aboard the paddle-wheelers at will and operated with impunity throughout the lower Mississippi Valley. By their very nature, steamboats were beyond the reach of any local or state codes against gambling. Their lavish accommodations and high fares attracted a class of well-to-do travelers who were irresistible targets for the clever gamblers. "Most of the travellers had broad belts around their waists, filled with good honest twenty-dollar gold pieces. It was these belts which the professional gamblers sought to lighten," wrote one author from the period.[3]

The cardsharps performed as if they were actors using the "floating palaces" as their stages. They draped themselves in elaborate costumes to give the appearance of wealth: black high-heeled boots (some arranged to have them shipped from Paris), black coat, black tie, frilled shirt with a vest, diamond rings, and a heavy gold pocket watch. A well-known gambler named Col. Charles Starr went a step further: he hired blacks to come on board the steamers and treat him like a wealthy plantation owner.[4]

They traveled in teams—never alone—but made sure not to board a vessel together. At the card table, they pretended not to know each other and silently communicated by using prearranged signals such as a twirl of a cane or a puff of cigar smoke.[5] They were merciless at devising ways to cheat. One method was to use a razor to trim the edges of the high cards so carefully that the differences would go unnoticed by other players. Some gamblers wore a ring with a needle-like point to make tiny indentations or scratches on cards that would be cues to their confederates.[6] Inevitably, some blacklegs lacked the sleight of hand or the nerve necessary to avoid detection. Reporting disputes to police ashore was at the discretion of captains, the undisputed masters of their vessels. Most often, the gambler was able to keep his money and sidestep any legal trouble. Disagreements were usually settled with fists, not in courts.

Even professional gamblers and "sure-thing" players saw their fortunes come and go like the tides. The gambling life left them with little more than vivid stories. A story attributed to the flamboyant steamboat gambler and three-card monte operator William Jones, popularly known as Canada Bill, deftly explains a gambler's mentality. One night Canada Bill and a partner were stuck in a Louisiana river town, and Canada Bill set out on a desperate search for a game. He finally found one and began to play, but his suspicious partner sized up the action and exclaimed, "The game's crooked!" Canada Bill replied, "I know it, but it's the only one in town!"[7]

For states along the Mississippi, rekindling the glory days of the riverboat gamblers—without the fisticuffs and rampant cheating, of course—seemed like an ideal way to revive flagging river towns. The recession in the early 1980s hammered Iowa's farms and its manufacturing base: 8 million square feet of industrial space was abandoned, farming income plummeted, and unemployment jumped into the double digits.[8] Especially hard hit were the factory-dependent Quad Cities: Davenport and Bettendorf in Iowa and Rock Island and Moline in Illinois. Legislators in the eastern part of the state proposed riverboat gambling as a tourist attraction to stimulate the economy, arguing that it also honored the state's heritage. "We're selling the lore of Mark Twain," said Iowa House Speaker Bob Arnould, who represented the Davenport area. "We want to give Tom Sawyer and Huck Finn a home in Iowa."[9] A strong lobbying effort by developer Bernard Goldstein who promised to build a $57 million riverfront entertainment complex to serve his floating casinos led to the bill's passage in 1989.

Iowa governor Terry Branstad was reluctant to push the state deeper into gambling. Soon after taking office in 1983, the Republican signed a bill allowing wagering at horse- and dog-racing tracks to benefit farms and horse owners. But he subsequently vetoed two lottery bills because he felt uneasy with the idea of the state running its own gambling operation. When neighboring Illinois saw its lottery prize swell as high as $50 million, Iowans swarmed across the border to buy tickets. They defiantly mailed him their losing tickets. "Basically the message was, 'Governor, we're going to buy lottery tickets and we'll spend our money out of state if we can't do it in your state,'" Branstad said in a 2016 interview with the author during his second stint as governor.[10] Branstad finally agreed to sign off on the lottery, and the first tickets were sold in 1985.

With riverboat casinos, Branstad insisted on a battery of protections to avoid scandals and corruption. Counties needed voters to approve a referendum to proceed, casinos were barred from hiring anyone with a criminal background, and licensees were required to make substantial charitable contributions to local communities. "I learned from my experience with the lottery that when you're governor, you've got to listen to your constituents and respect the fact that a majority of people want to have legal gambling opportunities in the state," Branstad said.[11]

On April 1, 1991, the first legal riverboat casinos in modern American history launched in Iowa to great fanfare and national media coverage. In Bettendorf, actor Howard Keel, who portrayed a gambler in the 1951 film *Show Boat*, rolled a ceremonial pair of dice across a craps table aboard the *Diamond Lady* as *Wheel of Fortune*'s Vanna White and the press watched. On the same day in Davenport and Dubuque, two other refitted casino riverboats powered by diesel engines carried gamblers onto the water. "This may be as important to Davenport as the Bill of Rights and the Magna Carta," boasted L. C. Pike, chairman of Iowa's racing commission, about the *President*.[12] In their first year of operation, the state's five riverboat casinos paid $13 million in state taxes on $65 million in revenue—hardly earth-shaking but not insignificant either.[13]

Lost amid all of the hype, Mark Twain impersonators, and faux-Victorian décor on the ships was the hard truth that neighboring states were ready to barge in on Iowa's gambling business. Other states looked at Iowa's tight controls on the riverboat casinos—maximum bets of $5 per hand and maximum losses of $200 per passenger on a single excursion, a requirement that the vessels schedule cruises lasting at least three hours from April to October, and the restriction of gambling activities to no more than 30 percent of a ship's floor space—and drafted less cumbersome rules. For instance, Illinois imposed no betting or loss limits when it legalized riverboat casinos in 1990. The looser regulations enticed Iowans to travel across the Mississippi to gamble on Illinois's riverboats when they launched in the fall of 1991. In 1994 Iowa responded to its loss of business by lifting its betting and loss limits, waving restrictions on the amount of gaming space on the boats, and allowing them to operate twenty-four hours a day. But by then the state faced a crop of new competitors, with Indiana, Louisiana, Mississippi, and Missouri authorizing gambling on navigable rivers and designated waterways.

Surprisingly, politically conservative and deeply religious Mississippi set the region's pace for liberal attitudes toward gambling. In the 1980s parts of the Deep South state were mired in an extreme level of poverty shocking to see in modern America. *60 Minutes* correspondent Morley Safer took viewers to Tunica County, the poorest county in the poorest state in the United States.[14] Jesse Jackson called it "America's Ethiopia," and Safer likened the region's persistence of segregation to apartheid South Africa. The 1985 CBS report focused on Sugar Ditch Alley, a Tunica neighborhood with an open sewer running through it and residents living in crumbling shacks infested with insects and vermin. Soybean and cotton fields blanketed the town just downriver from Memphis, and, although a whiff of the plantation-era sensibility remained, mechanized harvesting eliminated many of the only jobs available to poor blacks in the region.

In 1990 legislators from the Delta counties and the Gulf Coast city of Biloxi—a place with a background of illicit gambling and corruption—took note of Iowa's legalization of riverboat casinos and advanced their own plan to enter the gambling marketplace. They argued that Mississippi, not Iowa, had a richer history of steamboat gamblers and worried about the effects of losing revenue to other states. Their bill not only waved limits on bets and losses, it also put no restrictions on the number of licenses that could be granted. One of the bill's sponsors quietly deleted the word "underway" in describing the operation of the casino "boats" on state waterways, ensuring that they would not be required to leave the shore.[15] Casinos would be permitted to operate in structures built on floating barges or in renovated riverboats permanently attached to a dock. The legalistic nicety allowed supporters to claim that the casinos would be set apart from communities because they would not be land-based. The bill became law with the condition that each county had the right to accept or reject the dockside casinos.

Some politicians said later that they felt blindsided by the seemingly innocuous law in which lay the blueprint for a large-scale casino industry in Mississippi. Gov. Ray Mabus, who had unsuccessfully pushed for a state lottery earlier in the legislative session, felt chagrined when he realized what the state had unleashed. "I frankly didn't think I was signing that important a piece of legislation when I signed that bill," he later said. "Neither I nor any of my staff had any idea of what doors we were opening."[16]

The state's pliant rules on gambling and low tax rate on casino profits attracted development and lured competitors from other states. The owners of two Iowa casino vessels—including the *Diamond Lady*, which had opened to such excitement just the year before—announced plans to move them to Biloxi. The decision outraged Iowans, comparing it to the actions of the con man in *The Music Man* who duped the trusting people of River City.[17] In 1992 the first three casinos opened in Biloxi and the riverboat *Splash* docked in Tunica, where county supervisors approved gambling without putting it on the ballot. Gamblers filled the dumpy *Splash* from the start, awakening national casino operators to the potential of the Mississippi market. By 1996 twenty-nine casinos in the state employed about twenty-eight thousand people and generated nearly $2 billion, putting it third behind Nevada and New Jersey in commercial casino revenue.[18]

Impoverished Tunica was instantly converted into a casino hub: Harrah's, Bally's, and Circus Circus opened outposts; Boyd Gaming Corporation's ambitious Sam's Town Hotel and Gambling Hall mimicked its Las Vegas counterpart except that it was constructed on barges; the Grand Casino's 340,000 square feet rivaled the biggest resorts in Las Vegas and Atlantic City. Casino companies had no trouble getting their way. A mile-long ditch extending inland from the river was dug out to allow casinos closer access to the Memphis market, which had no legal casinos.[19]

The ten or so casinos—several came and went within a few years—clustered in the county of about ten thousand people created jobs and generated tax money of a scale unimaginable just a few years before. By most measures, the superheated casino industry was a godsend to Tunica County. The child poverty rate, which stood at an alarming 66.4 percent in 1990, fell to 31.4 percent by 2000. Unemployment dropped from 13.6 percent in 1990 to 5.2 percent a decade later. More residents stayed in school, and literacy rates improved. ABC's *Good Morning America* featured the changing face of Tunica ten years after *60 Minutes* compared parts of it to a shantytown. "Before the casinos came, this was almost like a ghost town. People just didn't have hope," Mack Williams, a custodian at Sam's Town, told a *Fortune* magazine reporter in 2007, which turned out to be Mississippi gaming's high-water mark. "Everybody's got more hope now."[20]

Despite the perceptible gains in Tunica's quality of life, the casino boon was unevenly shared. A lion's share of the tax windfall went to interests serving the local business establishment, not the majority black population. The county returned a budget surplus to taxpayers in the form of a 25 percent cut in property taxes in 1997, a costly giveaway that benefited the area's mostly white landowners and businesses. Expensive museums and a $40 million airport expansion served the tourist market. Only 2.5 percent of the hundreds of millions the county took in from casino taxes from 1993 to 2015 went to social programs geared for the poor, who were predominately black.[21] When the initial rush of investment tapered off, economic indicators took a turn for the worse: the child poverty rate jumped above 40 percent and unemployment returned to pre-casino era levels in 2009 as a recession took hold. Life expectancy is among the lowest in America—sixty-seven for men and seventy-three for women—and one in four people don't maintain bank accounts.[22]

Like Atlantic City, Tunica became overly reliant on casinos for its well-being and was vulnerable when competition ramped up in the region, especially in Louisiana with its armada of riverboat casinos. At its height, gambling taxes made up more than four-fifths of the county's annual budget. In fiscal 2014 Mississippi River counties—which includes Tunica—generated just under $1 billion in gross gaming revenues, a 27 percent decline in just five years, according to the Mississippi Gaming Commission. That in turn has sliced the amount of tax money transferred to local governments: $103.7 million in fiscal 2009 dropped to $84 million five years later. The drying up of dockside casino tourism hit hard in 2014 with the closure of Tunica's largest casino, Harrah's, and the loss of 1,300 jobs.

States, too, fall into peril when gambling revenues are built-in parts of their budgets. Missouri launched its first riverboats in 1994 with the notion that they would be quaint references to its Mark Twain heritage. Just as in Iowa, the quest to keep up with other states resulted in rule changes that made it easier to gamble more money, more frequently. Two decades later, the thirteen casinos grossed about $1.7 billion each year.[23] Missouri's education budget has become increasingly dependent on taxes from casinos and the lottery, rising from 2 percent in 1995, to 6 percent in 2000, to as much as 11 percent in the early 2010s.[24] Critics argue that total education spending isn't going up that fast, meaning that the state is using casino money to pull back on the amount it contributes. With casino revenues falling every year since 2011 even without adjusting for inflation, will Missouri dig deeper into its general fund to maintain education spending or find new ways to encourage people to gamble more? Given the track records of other states when gambling money plateaus or declines, Missourians can expect to hear renewed pitches of how they can strike it rich.

———

A distinctly different region experimented with gambling for many of the same reasons but in a more limited way than states along the Mississippi River and in the South. Colorado and South Dakota decided to cash in on nostalgia for the Old West to revive tourism in former mining towns and ghost towns. Their appeal to history was fitting. The opening of the American West attracted waves of fortune seekers who were gamblers in every sense of the word. They left behind their families, their livelihoods, and their communities to follow the evanescent dream of finding a latter-day El Dorado. Their long, difficult journeys delivered them into lawless towns and crowded encampments. The riverbeds and streams did not yield riches to all who sought them, but all miners did encounter a culture unburdened with the strictures of polite society. The freewheeling way of life gave them license to engage in behaviors that would be unthinkable back home—namely, wide-open gambling and carousing.

Just like on the era's steamboats, professional gamblers stalked the camps and lured the impulsive miners into high-stakes games of faro and monte. They were easy marks. A prospector in California, William Swain, described the scene along the Yuba River in an 1850 letter to his mother and wife: "Here in the mountains it is no unusual sight to see hundreds of dollars staked on the upturning of a certain card. I have known a gambler on this bar in one evening to rob the miners of $500 by their own wills. They are fools and need no pity."[25]

Gamblers gravitated toward boom towns that popped up wherever miners were able to pull silver and gold from the ground. In an echo of the California gold rush nearly a decade earlier, the discovery of gold deposits near the confluence of the South Platte River and Cherry Creek transformed a desolate town of huts into a bustling city that soon became known as Denver. Prospectors streamed in from all directions to seek their fortune in the Rocky Mountains. The diggings yielded fewer riches than the streams of California, but gamblers made their presence felt from the start. Leadville, Creede, and Cripple Creek were among the dens of gambling and lawlessness. A pioneer wrote in March 1859, "The gamblers are very numerous, and [have] got most of the gold in their possession."[26]

In the Dakota Territory, a gold strike in 1874 drew thousands of fortune seekers to the Black Hills that gave rise to the wild town of Deadwood. Saloons popped up to relieve miners of their treasure. Gamblers cut an impressive figure in Deadwood, where they "strolled up and down Main street with a magnificent leisure," dressed in fine linen and freshly ironed broadcloth.[27] They could easily afford such finery. Author Estelline Bennett recalled riding in a carriage to run an errand in town when a passenger jumped out at a stop and announced he was going into a saloon to win his 50¢ fare. Time passed and the other passengers grew agitated at having to wait for him. Finally, a passenger went in to retrieve the stricken gambler, who had lost $1,700 in about thirty minutes.[28]

Sometimes, gamblers in Deadwood lost more than their money. Gun-fighter Wild Bill Hickok made his way to the town in June 1876 and sought out high-stakes poker games. On August 2 Hickok played with three friends in a saloon with his back to the door. A man named "Crooked Nose" Jack McCall entered the saloon, pulled out a revolver, and fatally shot Hickok. Witnesses reported that the cards that slipped from Hickok's dead fingers included two pair, aces and eights, which entered into poker lore as the "dead man's hand." McCall was convicted and hanged the following year.

More than a century later, the romantic appeal of the Wild West days of gold and gunfights motivated town leaders to propose limited-stakes gambling in the fading town in 1988, an idea supported by South Dakota's voters. The first gambling halls opened a year later, making South Dakota the third state to legalize commercial casinos. Deadwood's roughly two thousand residents hoped that gambling would revive the town, help preserve its stature as a National Historic Landmark, and still maintain its rural character. The "gaming parlors"—a term of art used by South Dakota to soften public perceptions—were modest by Nevada or New Jersey standards. No more than thirty gaming devices (slot machines, poker, and blackjack were the only permissible games) were allowed per building, betting limits were capped at five dollars per play, and no licensee could own more than three establishments.[29] In a nod to the town's history, a $2,000 annual licensing fee on each gaming device went to the Deadwood Historic Preservation fund in addition to unspent money allocated to the state's gaming commission.[30]

Deadwood's parlors welcomed their first gamblers on November 1, 1989, and business was brisk: more than $1 million in revenue in the first month and an average of $3.5 million during the summer months in 1990.[31] The parlors did boost local employment with mostly low-wage jobs, and a majority of gambling tax revenue stayed in town for preservation purposes. Investment poured into the Black Hills. Actor-director Kevin Costner, who used South Dakota as the setting for his Oscar-winning film *Dances with Wolves*, opened a casino and restaurant. The gleefully foul-mouthed HBO series *Deadwood* kindled interest in the town's roughneck past. Once the market matured, about three-dozen gambling halls lined Main Street. However, Deadwood's remote location, thin population, and seasonal climate put curbs on how much it could gain from gambling. Also, another Western state threatened Deadwood's gambling revenue.

Colorado lawmakers watched South Dakota's experiment in Deadwood and reasoned that they could apply the same strategy to bring back their declining mining towns. The state already ran a lottery and allowed pari-mutuel gambling, so it wasn't a great stretch to also sanction small-scale casinos. The old mining towns borrowed Deadwood's historic preservation argument to advance their cause. Proponents claimed that casinos would "revive the flavor of the true frontier gold mining life" and restore old Victorian buildings and dilapidated mining structures.[32]

Just as in Deadwood, an intensive petition drive placed a constitutional amendment on the ballot. In 1990 the state's voters strongly backed a referendum permitting limited-stakes gambling in the dying mountain towns of Central City, Black Hawk, and Cripple Creek. (Central City and Black Hawk are neighboring communities about fifty miles west of Denver; Cripple Creek is outside Colorado Springs.) The rules were tight when the first casinos opened in October 1991: five-dollar betting limits, restrictions on the amount of square footage devoted to gambling, and caps on the hours of play. Gambling activities were intended only for buildings with "architectural styles and designs that were common to the areas prior to World War I."[33] Initial revenues far outpaced Deadwood: $8.4 million in the first month and $8.1 million in December 1991, typically a slow time for tourism in the region.[34] Within a year, each of the three gambling towns in Colorado surpassed Deadwood in adjusted gross profits.

Colorado was much more aggressive than South Dakota in expanding gambling. By the end of October 1991 there were twenty-one casinos and 1,920 gambling devices (slot machines, table games, video poker terminals); just a year later, the three towns had seventy-five casinos and 11,578 devices.[35] The first chunk of casino tax money—$9.1 million—was disbursed in September 1992 with $4.1 million channeled to the state's general fund, $2.5 million to state historical preservation purposes, and the rest to county and local governments.[36] In 1996 casino tax revenue jumped to $52 million, further swelling municipal coffers.

However, many casinos came and went within a few years, creating instability amid increasing competition. In Central City only seven of the thirty-nine casinos remained a decade after legalization, leaving some newly refurbished buildings empty again.[37] When tax revenue stalled, Colorado followed the example of riverboat gambling states that liberalized the rules to bring in more money. Voters backed a ballot measure in 2009 that raised the maximum bet from $5 to $100 and allowed casinos to stay open twenty-four hours a day. (The following year, South Dakota raised its bet limit in exactly the same way.)

The introduction of gambling in Colorado and South Dakota paid for noticeable improvements of downtown facades, but there were some negative effects. In Deadwood, spikes in property values resulted in the conversion of seventy-eight businesses into casino operations in just the first year of gambling.[38] The influx of tourists brought a predictable surge in crime and traffic to the rural communities, supporting the perception that the new development was geared to visitors, not residents. Mindful of such consequences, voters were unwilling to extend gambling into urban areas. An effort to expand gambling to Denver's lower downtown area was voted down in November 1992, along with other amendments to bring casinos to other parts of the state. Struggling cities in other states would not be so reluctant to turn their downtowns into gambling-friendly zones.

Given its lively history, it was no surprise that New Orleans was among the first cities in modern America to approve land-based casinos. Its rich tradition of gambling stretched well before American rule. The expansion of river traffic in the early 1800s created a mélange of cultures and characters who mingled and gambled in the city's many taverns and grog-shops.[39] Legal high-end gambling clubs were open day and night to accommodate the city's ever-flowing stream of visitors, who found great appeal in the city's unofficial motto, "*Laissez les bons temps rouler*," or, "Let the good times roll."

A visitor to New Orleans in 1820 wrote a letter to the *Baltimore Chronicle* reporting that "gambling and sensual pleasures were practiced to such a degree to destroy domestic happiness and tranquility."[40] Flatboat men congregated in a notorious area of the city called the Swamp, which was "crowded with saloons, dance-halls, gambling-dens, bordellos, and so-called hotels, all housed in shacks."[41] Robberies, beatings, and murders were so common and the level of danger was so high that even the police dared not venture into the district.

The city was the headquarters of the sensationally corrupt Louisiana State Lottery Company, which for decades controlled a stupendously lucrative nationwide lottery monopoly. Later, bookies and illegal gambling houses thrived under the sway of organized crime: Meyer Lansky and Frank Costello were among the national mob figures who had interests in the city. Protection money paid to law enforcement ensured that gambling could carry on without interference, a revelation that embarrassed the city during the Kefauver Committee's visit to New Orleans.

Against that historical backdrop, Louisiana lawmakers and voters adopted a flurry of gambling measures: a state-run lottery in 1990; riverboat casinos in 1991; and video poker, also in 1991. Louisiana then proposed to go a step further than other Mississippi River states. Edwin Edwards, a political animal straight out of *All the King's Men*, was entering his third stint as governor in 1992 when he signed a bill to put the world's largest land-based casino in the heart of New Orleans at the site of a former convention center.[42] Edwards, a high-stakes craps gambler perennially dogged by scandal, argued that it would touch off redevelopment and create twenty-five thousand jobs.[43] "With the stroke of a pen, we've taken the largest step toward economic development and the creation of jobs undertaken in Louisiana in the last twenty-five years," Edwards remarked at the bill-signing ceremony.[44]

After a bidding process tangled up in a web of politics and special interests—many directly tied to Edwards—Harrah's won the license to operate the casino and entered into an Edwards-arranged partnership with local businessmen called the Jazzville group. The plan was for

Harrah's to open a temporary casino in the aging Municipal Auditorium while building a permanent casino closer to the river with 200,000 square feet of gambling space. When the converted casino opened in May 1995, dignitaries celebrated amid a swirl of Mardi Gras colors, fireworks, and confetti cannons. "Some will look at it as an abomination," Edwards said at the ceremony. "I view it as economic development. I supported it because of the jobs it will create and the tourists it will bring."[45]

But the tourists didn't come. The casino was in the city's Tremé neighborhood, a part of town that French Quarter–based visitors were reluctant to explore. In its first six months, the casino brought in only a third of Harrah's projected business, forcing Harrah's to shutter it, file for bankruptcy, and halt construction of the main casino in November 1995.[46] Thousands of construction workers and casino employees were laid off. Edwards was furious, telling a Harrah's official that "it's going to be a big, big black eye for the city and your organization, and for me and for the state."[47] Edwards was weeks away from leaving the governor's office anyway. His freewheeling ways finally had caught up to him. In 2000 a jury convicted Edwards on racketeering charges related to the awarding of riverboat casino licenses. He served eight years in federal prison. Meanwhile, a less-ambitious version of the main casino opened as Harrah's New Orleans in 1999, falling into bankruptcy again in 2001 before finding its footing.

The episode in New Orleans set a precedent for urban gaming that was followed by a bigger city: Detroit. The state and city grew weary of watching gamblers cross the Detroit River to spend their money at a land-based casino and a riverboat casino in Canada. Casino Windsor opened in 1994 and piled up $500 million in annual gambling revenues, with Michigan residents accounting for about 80 percent of it.[48] The state's voters approved a proposition in 1996 allowing the decaying city of Detroit to host three urban casinos, making it the largest city in the Western Hemisphere with legalized casino gambling.

MGM Grand and a group affiliated with Circus Circus received two of the licenses, and a local group was awarded the other one. The projects clustered in downtown Detroit with the opening of temporary casinos in 1999–2000 and permanent ones years later. The MGM Grand Detroit, MotorCity Casino Hotel, and Greektown Casino-Hotel performed well at the outset, netting a combined $1 billion in total adjusted gross revenues in 2001, the first full calendar year when all three were fully operational. Growth was steady until later in the decade when a recession, increased regional competition, and Greektown's Chapter 11 bankruptcy filing hampered the marketplace. Revenues have plateaued ever since and so have the state's returns. At its height in 2006, the state wagering tax on the casinos yielded nearly $158 million; only $108 million was sent back to the state in 2014 even though the same three casinos remain open.[49] Large-scale casino gambling could not stop the city's slide and eventual declaration of bankruptcy in 2013.

In the Mid-Atlantic, Pennsylvania's move to legalize slots at racetracks and stand-alone casinos in 2004 touched off a gambling arms race in the region. The intention was that proceeds would support property tax relief, reduce taxes on wages, and boost economic growth. About a dozen racinos—racetracks with adjoining slot parlors—and full-scale casinos sprouted in Philadelphia and Pittsburgh as well as in less populated parts of the state. Ed Rendell, the plain-spoken governor of Pennsylvania at the time, reasoned that it was a waste for the state's residents to go elsewhere and lose money gambling. "These people were losing their paychecks in Atlantic City, in Delaware, at the racetracks in West Virginia," he told Lesley Stahl of CBS's *60 Minutes* in a report broadcast January 9, 2011. "If they're going to lose it anyway, let's get the upside. We were getting all the downside and none of the upside." When Stahl pressed Rendell on the propriety of state-sponsored gambling, he turned combative. "These people would lose that money anyway. Don't you understand? . . . You're idiots if you don't get that!"

Rendell's gambit elevated Pennsylvania to the nation's No. 2 casino market by pinching revenues from neighboring states like Delaware, Maryland, West Virginia, and New Jersey, compelling them to upgrade their gambling portfolios just to maintain their returns from gambling.

Of those states, Maryland has been the most daring in expanding casinos. The state's first casino opened in 2010, and the industry ramped up quickly with four more in the next three years along with voter approval of table games. Among those new casinos was Maryland Live! Casino in Hanover, which adjoins the Arundel Mills Mall in suburban Baltimore. Maryland Live! itself is practically a megamall for gambling: 4,200 slot machines, 189 live-action table games, 52 poker tables, and a 5,000-vehicle parking garage. In 2014 the behemoth casino took in $1 billion a month in bets, capitalizing on its high-traffic location and proximity to the Baltimore and Washington markets.

But as in Missouri with its riverboat casinos, Maryland fell short of its promised results. Analysts projected that the state's Education Trust Fund would receive $660 million in the fiscal year that ended June 30, 2013, but only $284 million went into the fund because the number of slots were far below expectations.[50] Casino money was not the windfall for schools as was advertised; instead, critics argue that the new funds have simply allowed the state to earmark less money from its general fund to education. Meanwhile, the state is doubling down on its burgeoning gambling industry: Caesars Entertainment opened Horseshoe Casino Baltimore in the heart of the city in 2014 and MGM Resorts International launched the state's sixth casino in late 2016. The $1.4 billion resort, MGM National Harbor, sits on the edge of the Capital Beltway across the Potomac River from Alexandria, Virginia, and about eleven miles south of the White House.

Even if casino revenue figures are underwhelming, they become budgetary fixtures that states fight to protect at all costs. Delaware in particular has become reliant on gambling revenues—6 percent of the state's annual budget in 2014 was derived from gaming sources, including the lottery.[51] It may not seem like a big percentage, but the total revenue of casinos exceeds the amount of state income tax paid by all Delaware-based corporations.[52] The state's politicians have a direct interest in fostering the health of their casinos if they want to maintain services without raising income taxes.

Dover Downs, one of the state's three racinos, has keenly felt the impact of out-of-state rivals. When they were legalized in the 1990s, their only nearby rivals were in Atlantic City and Charles Town, West Virginia. Since then more than a dozen casinos have opened within a short drive of Delaware's borders, driving down slot machine revenue. In the meantime, the state has raised casino taxes seven times and now takes a hefty 43.5 percent for every dollar gambled in a slot machine. Those dollars are dwindling, and Dover Downs has struggled to stay afloat, cutting jobs and watching its stock price crash. In 2014 state lawmakers approved $9.9 million to assist the casinos in paying their slot machine vendors, an unusual government expense. More bailouts are undoubtedly on the horizon to prop up the state's faltering casinos and salvage their diminishing returns.

Politicians in bigger states turned to casinos as a quick fix, often overpromising what casinos could deliver. In 2009 Ohioans approved a plan for four casinos that advocates promoted as economic engines. They opened in the state's largest cities: Columbus, Cleveland, Cincinnati, and Toledo. However, projections were far too rosy, according to a *Columbus Dispatch* analysis published in 2014.[53] Casino supporters said there would be 34,000 new construction and permanent jobs, but only 15,640 materialized. Revenue figures were way off: $651 million was expected for governments in the first year, but only $519 million in tax revenue was paid in the first two years. Part of the problem was that many of the state's struggling racetracks combined to add thousands of slot machines to become racinos, undercutting the new urban casinos. The racinos were the product of an executive order signed by the governor, not a public vote.

Two latter-day entrants into the casino craze are Massachusetts and New York, and both have encountered delays in deciding where they will be located. In 2011 Massachusetts governor Deval Patrick signed the Expanded Gaming Act into law, which authorized up to three resort casinos and a slots parlor. The legislation mandated that each of three regions would get a resort, and the slots parlor would be allowed to be anywhere in the state. The directive touched off a torturous process in which East Boston voters rejected a $1 billion resort in 2013 and residents in smaller towns like Milford blocked casino developers' plans. Then, in 2014, a statewide referendum to repeal the casino law failed. The haggling over sites and the push and pull of the electoral process slowed the task: As of 2017 only the slots parlor at the Plainridge Park harness racing track had opened. MGM Resorts International won the bid for the western Massachusetts license and plans to build a resort in Springfield by 2018, Wynn Resorts has broken ground on a $2.1 billion casino-resort on a brownfield site in Everett near Boston for a 2019 opening, and the third license is still in limbo. At this pace, a decade will pass before the state makes good on what it promised.

Another high-stakes siting process is unfolding in neighboring New York. Gov. Andrew Cuomo has been a forceful advocate of gambling expansion, championing a plan by Malaysia-based gambling juggernaut Genting Group to bring a multibillion-dollar project to Aqueduct Racetrack in Queens, one of the state's nine racinos offering limited electronic gambling. In 2011 Genting welcomed visitors to its new gambling emporium with thousands of video lottery terminals (similar to traditional slot machines) and electronic table games. As the only casino in the five boroughs, Genting and the state had a big hit on its hands. In its full fiscal year, Resorts World Casino New York City took in $696 million in total revenue, of which $306 million was sent to the state to fund education programs.[54] An expanded casino is in the works, along with the nation's largest convention center, three major hotels, and an entertainment complex.

Emboldened by the flush partnership with Genting, Cuomo persuaded the legislature to place a referendum on the November 2013 ballot to authorize up to seven full-blown, commercial casinos across the state, joining the five tribal-run casinos scattered on upstate reservations. Casino interests spent heavily on the campaign despite the lack of organized opposition, and voters approved the amendment to the New York Constitution. On Election Day, Cuomo, himself a beneficiary of the industry's largesse via campaign contributions, advanced the well-worn argument that it would keep money in the state. "We literally hemorrhage people from the borders who go to casinos," he said. "I think it will keep money in this state, I think it's a major economic development vehicle for the Hudson Valley especially and for upstate New York."[55]

It was the last portion of his remarks that disquieted gambling operators like MGM, Caesars, and Wynn Resorts, who are far more interested in exploiting the New York City area than rural communities already served by Indian casinos. With more than five hundred commercial casinos and nearly five hundred tribal casinos in all but a handful of states, few markets remain untapped. Cuomo and lawmakers are calling for four new casinos exclusively in upstate regions such as in the Catskills and Albany that, in Cuomo's words, "will bring a new economic future to parts of this state that have been suffering too long."[56] But with the misbegotten record of promises and the fact that nearly everyone in New York state is within easy driving distance from a gambling hall, it's hard to see how four more in remote parts of the state will truly bring economic salvation.

CHAPTER 9

Rise of the Tribes

TRIBES AND STATES FORGE
UNEASY GAMBLING PARTNERSHIPS

Indians can't win too big without some attempt at retribution.
—Suzan Shown Harjo, Native American activist

The death of Elizabeth "Eliza" George on June 7, 1973, appeared to mark the end of the line for the Pequot people. The seventy-eight-year-old known as the "Iron Lady" was the only full-time resident on the tribe's wooded reservation in rural Connecticut. Although the 214-acre homestead in Ledyard offered few niceties of modern living such as indoor plumbing, Eliza tenaciously stayed on the property when the population dwindled down to just her. With unchained dogs and a shotgun, if necessary, she shooed away curious state health inspectors and other unwanted intruders.[1] As the sole representative of the Pequot people, Eliza stood defiant, proud to be the keeper of the tribe's dying flame.

The tribe's sorrows are remarkable even among the centuries of miseries suffered by the native population of North America. The arrival of English settlers threatened the tribe's hold on a swath of modern-day Connecticut. The colonists declared war on the tribe in 1637 and convinced the Narragansett and Mohegan tribes to fight against the Pequots. One day before dawn the English and their new allies encircled a Pequot village along the Mystic River and set it on fire while many were still asleep.[2] English swordsmen stabbed terrified residents who tried to escape, killing hundreds of villagers. Such a style of total warfare was an affront to their

Indian allies, who complained that it was "too furious and slays too many people."³ The Puritans simply viewed it as God's will. The colonists hunted down and dissolved the Pequots in the following years—some were sold into slavery and shipped elsewhere, most were bartered to other tribes in exchange for wampum.⁴ The English solidified their dominance of the area, going so far as to rename the Pequot River the Thames River.

Thirty years after the defeat of the Pequots, Connecticut's colonial government granted two thousand acres for the tribe's few survivors who were under the control of the Mohegan Indians. Over the years the government sliced away at the Western Pequot Indian Reservation, cutting it in half. In 1790 Congress passed the Indian Nonintercourse Act, which required the federal government to approve any transaction of Indian lands. However, Connecticut did not request federal permission in 1856 when it auctioned off eight hundred acres of the reservation to white settlers, leaving only about two hundred acres for the Pequots—the chunk of land that Eliza George knew during her life.

After Eliza George's death, one of her daughters, Theresa Hayward, moved her family from Maryland to the reservation in Ledyard. Theresa's son, Richard "Skip" Hayward, took a leading role in managing the family's affairs even though he had little connection to the tribe other than making summer visits to his grandmother. Hayward recalled Eliza's flashes of anger when she retold the story of the Pequot War, but it did not stir within him a sense of Indian identity. Hayward's mother was not a full-blooded Indian—her father was a French-Canadian woodsman—and Hayward's father was a Navy man who traced his ancestry to the Mayflower.⁵

Hayward had little preparation to wrestle with the complexities of the laws governing Indian lands—he ran a clam shack near Mystic Seaport and also worked as a pipe fitter at a shipyard defense contractor in Groton—but he was a quick study and possessed an innate talent for political gamesmanship. He learned that the land was held in trust for the Pequots, but what would the government do now that the tribe seemed to be extinguished? How could it be considered a reservation if no one lived on it?

Tom Tureen, a lawyer who represented the claims of tribes in Maine, believed that Hayward and his extended family had the right not only to the 214 acres that had been occupied by Eliza but also to the 800 acres of Pequot land sold without federal government approval in 1856. Hayward realized that he needed to organize to more effectively press his land claim. Hayward rounded up other family members—aunts, uncles, distant cousins, in-laws—to meet at his grandmother's weathered house on the reservation, and they formally incorporated as the Western Pequot Indians of Connecticut, Inc.

Although there was no tribal council or chief, Hayward asserted control by tapping into his skills of persuasion honed during his brief time as a preacher. With Tureen's help, a tribal government was set up, a constitution was adopted, and Hayward was named tribal chairman. The next step was to figure out who could join. Hayward and his family possessed precious little Indian blood. In fact, they had always identified themselves as "white" on official forms. But now they would need to profess their "American Indian" heritage no matter how tenuous it might be. They decided that anyone who could trace his or her ancestry to a Pequot Indian listed on the 1910 census could be a member.[6] Since Elizabeth George was on the census rolls as an Indian living on the reservation in that year, Hayward and his extended family would be eligible. (Genealogical studies published in author Jeff Benedict's book *Without Reservation* yielded no evidence that George had blood ties to the tribe. Benedict reported that her only documented tribal connection was to the Narragansett tribe in Rhode Island, not the Pequot tribe of Connecticut.[7])

The reconstituted Pequot tribe moved quickly to stake its claim on multiple fronts. Hayward secured a $1 million US Department of Housing and Urban Development loan that allowed the tribe to build fifteen houses on the reservation. Money came in from the state for historic preservation purposes and a Catholic group gave $45,000 to help Hayward with tribal expenses.[8] The tribe also sued to recover the eight hundred acres that it claimed was illegally sold by the state so many years ago. The case languished and the prospect of mounting expenses led the tribe, the people who had purchased the land, and the state to seek an out-of-court settlement. In 1982 Connecticut agreed to Tureen's proposal to transfer the disputed reservation land to the federal government and in exchange the tribe would drop its legal claims against the landowners.[9] It would then be up to the federal government to approve the deal.

Next the tribe had to think of an industry that could sustain the fledgling reservation. Tureen and Hayward knew that bingo halls were bringing in revenue to tribes on reservations from Maine to California, so they quietly made sure the bill kept that possibility open for the Pequots. The settlement legislation included the eight hundred acres formerly part of the reservation, a $900,000 payment from the federal government to the tribe to buy out the landowners, plus a crucial provision granting the tribe the ability to purchase additional land in Ledyard.[10] The tribe coveted a thousand acres of undeveloped land between the reservation and State Route 2, a busy highway that fed into Rhode Island.

Sen. Lowell Weicker, a Connecticut Republican, introduced the legislation. A staffer on the Senate's Indian Affairs Committee noticed that the bill failed to stipulate exactly where the tribe would be permitted to purchase land, so Hayward, Tureen, and a lawyer from the other side used a red felt marker to draw a boundary on a map that consisted of the tribe's desired two thousand acres. Anything within those boundaries stood to become federal Indian land that would be exempt from taxation and regulations because the tribe would be considered a sovereign entity. No questions were raised about the reservation's expanded borders.

Hayward, by now a persuasive public speaker well practiced in the airing of tribal grievances, appeared before the committee. He recounted the sorrows of the Pequot people dating to the massacre in 1637 and appealed to Congress to support their resurgence after suffering generations of injustice and neglect. The tribe had grown to 42 people living on the reservation and another 153 off the reservation, he said. "It was the desire of our predecessors that we hold and maintain the land," he said, adding that the tribe wanted to become "self-determining and self-sufficient through its economic development projects."[11] He decided not to outline his vision of a high-stakes bingo hall.

With the bipartisan support of the Connecticut delegation in Congress, the legislation easily won approval. The bill was sent to President Ronald Reagan for his signature, but he vetoed it on April 5, 1983. It shouldn't have come as a great surprise because the Reagan administration had publicly signaled its skepticism about the tribe's credibility. In his veto message Reagan seemed most concerned that the bill would grant the Pequots federal recognition as a tribe, a profound step that he felt "is not warranted at this time."[12] He also insisted that the state of Connecticut pay at least half of any settlement costs to lessen the financial burden on the federal government.

The veto infuriated Weicker, who pressed for another vote to override it. To avoid such an embarrassing spectacle for the White House, a compromise was hatched in which Connecticut would spend $200,000 on the settlement and the tribe would not need to supply documentation of its genealogy. Reagan signed it into law in October 1983. The outcome pleased the politicians, who emphasized that it respected the rights of Indians and would not force landowners to sell their property. The settlement seemed equitable at the time, but tribal members emerged as the biggest winners by far. They claimed the all-important prize of sovereign-nation status on what was formally called the Mashantucket Pequot Indian Reservation. That gave them governmental rights that a savvy tribe could use to their advantage.

Armed with that designation, Hayward lobbied reluctant tribal members to go along with his plan of building a bingo hall on the reservation's newly acquired land in Ledyard. Many Indian reservations are located in remote, thinly populated states, but Hayward's adjoined State Route 2, which offered easy access to Interstate 95. Ledyard, though a city of only about fifteen thousand people, is ideally positioned between Boston and New York City, with Hartford and Providence each only an hour's drive away. If done right, the rewards of big-time gambling in untapped New England promised to be immense.

Hayward lined up the Penobscot Indians as a partner to manage his bingo operation because they had run a profitable parlor in Maine before the state closed it down. Tureen had represented the Penobscots in their land-claim efforts, so he knew well the state/tribal conflicts that could ignite over gambling. Maine had asserted regulatory authority over the reservation, which meant the state's ban on high-stakes gambling also applied to the Penobscots. He didn't want the Pequots to go to the trouble of building a bingo hall only to have it deemed illegal and slammed shut by state regulators or local law enforcement.

The tribe's legal team went to work in court and inside the halls of state government to ensure there would be no resistance to gaming. Connecticut had a general statewide ban on gambling, but it did allow licensed bingo games at places such as churches and charities. The tribe argued in federal court that it had a right to run a bingo hall because it was not subject to state regulation. The state disagreed, threatening to shut down the bingo hall if it opened as planned. A federal judge sided with the tribe, ruling in January 1986 that the state's bingo laws were not part of its criminal code and thus not enforceable on the reservation. The victory opened a path for the Pequots to proceed without fear of prosecution. What they had in mind was a long way from church-basement bingo.

Tureen set out to find financing for the 34,000-square-foot bingo hall, steering clear of funding sources that had even the faintest of ties to organized crime. However, he had difficulty persuading bankers that the untested tribe had the know-how to launch such an enterprise. Finally, he convinced United Arab Bank to sign on when it grasped the size of the tribe's market. The risk-taking bank agreed to issue a $5 million loan, which was backed by a guarantee from the federal Bureau of Indian Affairs.

On July 5, 1986, Hayward and the tribe welcomed customers to the opening of the bingo hall in Ledyard. They came from all across New England and New York, clogging State Route 2 and filling the eight-hundred-space parking lot within hours. Some parked their cars along the highway and took long hikes to the hall; hundreds more were turned away because the crowds exceeded the building's occupancy limit of about 1,200 people. Nightly prizes started at $10,000, far above the $500 cap the state imposed on off-reservation bingo games. Three weeks after opening, the tribe announced a Super Bingo night offering $100,000 in cash and a new Cadillac as a door prize.[13] The increased $125 entrance fee didn't dampen demand; customers bought up the tickets and showed up several hours early to ensure good seats at the tables.

The bonanza from bingo surpassed everyone's expectations. Tribal profits averaged about $300,000 a month for the first year, and hundreds of thousands of customers visited the reservation.[14] A majority of the players were women and retirees lured by the promise of major money. "It's just your average next-door kind of people," said Howard Wilson, manager of the hall. "For twenty-five dollars, they get three-and-a-half hours of entertainment, and a chance to win some really big bucks. But even if they lose, they're happy."[15] The Pequots' high-stakes bingo hall spelled trouble for smaller bingo operators like charities and churches. Groton's Sacred Heart Catholic Church, which had raised nearly $500,000 during its forty-one years of bingo nights, closed down its game due to lack of player interest.[16]

Things were going so well for the Pequots that tribal leaders were flush enough to buy out the Penobscots after two years and fully take over management of the bingo hall. As successful as the bingo parlor had become, Hayward wanted something faster-paced and more profitable—a full-fledged, Nevada-style casino that he imagined would be the biggest in the world. His daring vision would pit his tribe directly against the wishes of the state of Connecticut. Meanwhile, a landmark Supreme Court ruling and a subsequent act of Congress reordered the nature of state-tribal relationships and forever changed the landscape of Indian gaming in America.

———

The status of American Indian tribal nations as distinct political entities with sovereign rights under federal government oversight has always been a source of tension. Tribes—at least the ones that survived the onslaught of colonists—were organized nations long before the existence of the

United States. Early laws recognized this and granted them sovereign status unique among America's racial and ethnic groups, but the Constitution also explicitly gave Congress the singular right to regulate commerce
with Indian tribes. The federal government and tribes negotiated hundreds of treaties with each one the equivalent of an agreement between
two sovereign nations.

In an important Supreme Court ruling, Chief Justice John Marshall
wrote in 1831 that tribes were "domestic dependent nations" whose relationship to the United States "resembles that of a ward to his guardian."[17]
The Bureau of Indian Affairs was organized to carry out policy, settle
claims, and reinforce the principle that only the federal government had
authority over tribes. Meanwhile, the government's Indian removal and
land allotment policies uprooted many tribes from fertile land desired by
white settlers, disbursing them across a vast archipelago of reservations
where the chances of prosperity would be bleak.

In the 1960s and 1970s, Indian activists tapped into the wider civil rights
movement and protested their mistreatment at the hands of government.
In response Congress approved the Indian Civil Rights Act of 1968. Two
years later President Richard Nixon advanced the cause of greater self-
determination in a special message to Congress. "The time has come to
break decisively with the past and to create the conditions for a new era
in which the Indian future is determined by Indian acts and Indian decisions," Nixon wrote.[18] In 1975 Congress gave tribes control over federally
funded programs for social services and health care.[19]

Starting in the 1970s some tribes decided to use their unique legal status to their advantage and set up reservation-based "smoke shops" selling cigarettes and other tobacco products at deeply discounted prices.
Since federally recognized tribes are sovereign governments, they imposed
their own taxes and did not collect state or local taxes. The trailers lured
bargain-hunting non-Indians to reservations and generated hundreds of
thousands of dollars in new revenue for tribes.[20] States resented the challenge to their cigarette tax money and sued, opening up a standoff over tax
enforcement and the nature of tribal sovereignty.

Cigarette sales were a welcome financial boost to tribes, but this alone wouldn't pull the tribes out of impoverishment. In 1980 eighteen of the thirty-six reservations with populations greater than two thousand people had poverty rates of at least 40 percent.[21] Unemployment reached as high as 50 percent in some tribal communities. Tribes took note that casinos in Atlantic City brought instant prosperity to that battered city in the late 1970s, so they hoped gambling would also be their salvation. Bingo seemed like a natural fit for tribes. Since the 1930s, states allowed designated charities and religious groups to operate bingo nights as fundraisers. In some places it was the first form of gambling to be decriminalized. The wide acceptance of bingo softened resistance to gambling—after all, if the local parish priest encouraged it, how much of a sin could it be?[22]

Among the first and most prominent tribes that entered the big-time bingo business was the Seminole tribe of Florida. In 1979 James Billie, a colorful alligator wrestler and newly elected chief of the tribal council, was convinced that high-stakes bingo could be the tribe's ticket out of squalor. When he took office, the tribe eked out $400 of revenue per Seminole each year by selling cigarettes and sponsoring the occasional rodeo.[23] Billie closely tracked Indian-related court rulings and believed that the tribe had the authority to operate a bingo hall without regard to the state's rules. Florida law permitted a single one-hundred-dollar jackpot per night for sanctioned charities, so the tribe's more lucrative prizes promised to poach gamblers in the same way its cheap cigarettes attracted smokers.[24]

The tribe's high-stakes hall opened in December 1979 and offered jackpots as high as $10,000—Billie sweetened the pot by giving away a Cadillac—and players flocked to the Hollywood reservation between Fort Lauderdale and Miami. The aggressively promoted bingo parlor angered the state's attorney general and the Broward County sheriff's office. They claimed the Seminoles were in violation of state gambling regulations and ordered the tribe to shut it down, prompting a lawsuit. A federal court of appeals ruled that Florida could enforce criminal prohibitions on reservation land but not civil regulatory statutes, which applied to gambling.[25] Since bingo was permitted in the state of Florida, the federal court concluded that the Seminoles could also operate bingo on its reservation. As a federally recognized tribe, the tribe had the right to run its bingo enterprise free of state or local regulation.

Encouraged by the favorable ruling and the Reagan-era policy of Indian economic self-sufficiency, bingo halls popped up on dozens of Indian reservations across the country in the 1980s. The Seminoles and the Mashantucket Pequots were not the only tribes that went far beyond the modest bingo games found in church basements and fraternal organization social halls: in Oklahoma, the Otoe-Missouria tribe built a 6,000-seat gambling hall and offered prizes of up to $400,000 in a weekend; in Arizona the Yaqui ran a 1,300-seat parlor that undercut bingo games in nearby Tucson; in North Carolina the Cherokee tribe hosted more than two thousand players paying $500 each for a shot at a $200,000 jackpot.[26]

In Southern California the Cabazon Band of Mission Indians phased out its smoke shop operation and tried its luck with gambling. In October 1980 the twenty-five-member tribe opened a small poker room on its reservation in the desert outside Palm Springs. Days later dozens of officers from the local Indio Police Department raided the facility, seized tables and chips, and made numerous arrests. The tribe's lawyers pointed out that California law permitted "card rooms" that included table games such as poker, so the Cabazons should be allowed to run a similar enterprise. The state claimed that a card room was legal only when local voters approved an ordinance, which was not the case in Indio. A judge let the tribe's poker room reopen while the arguments were hashed out in court. In 1982 the Ninth US Circuit Court of Appeals held that the city's gambling laws did not apply to the reservation.

The tribe doubled down by adding a bingo hall in 1983, which local authorities promptly shut down. Riverside County sheriff's officials confiscated cash and poker chips from the tribe's card room. In an echo of the earlier controversy, the tribe sued and a judge issued a preliminary injunction against Riverside County, which wanted to enforce its ordinances prohibiting card clubs and regulating bingo. The neighboring Morongo Band of Mission Indians also ran afoul of county authorities because its bingo operation featured prizes exceeding California's $250 limit. Like the Seminoles in Florida, the two California tribes said the state had no legal grounds to impose its gambling statutes on tribes running the same games on their reservations.

In a decision that shook the foundations of gambling in America, the US Supreme Court in 1987 sided with the tribes in *California v. Cabazon Band of Mission Indians*. In a 6–3 decision, the justices rejected local, county, and state efforts to enforce their gambling restrictions on tribal lands, finding that such laws were civil and regulatory in nature and thus not enforceable within Indian reservations. Justice Byron White, author of the court's majority opinion, noted that since California "permits a substantial amount of gambling activity, including bingo, and actually promotes gambling through its state lottery, we must conclude that California regulates rather than prohibits gambling in general and bingo in particular."[27]

White emphasized that tribal gaming was an acceptable means of achieving the federal government's stated goal of promoting economic self-sufficiency among Indians. "The Cabazon and Morongo Reservations contain no natural resources which can be exploited. The tribal games at present provide the sole source of revenues for the operation of the tribal governments and the provision of tribal services. They are also the major sources of employment on the reservations. Self-determination and economic development are not within reach if the Tribes cannot raise revenues and provide employment for their members. The Tribes' interests obviously parallel the federal interests," he wrote.[28]

Indeed, federal departments had had a hand in encouraging tribal gaming. The departments of Housing and Urban Development and Health and Human Services, and the Bureau of Indian Affairs issued grants and guaranteed loans to help tribes build bingo halls such as the Pequots' high-stakes bingo hall in Connecticut.[29] Federal agencies also assisted tribes by clearing bureaucratic barriers and defending their gambling rights. An Interior Department policy directive said it would "strongly oppose" any legislation to subject tribes to state gambling regulations. The director of

Indian services in the Bureau of Indian Affairs went so far as to file an affidavit to the Supreme Court declaring that "the development of tribal bingo enterprises is consistent with" Reagan's official policy of increasing tribal self-government.[30]

States worried about the ruling's practical effects—would the hundreds of federally recognized tribes build ever-bigger bingo palaces and poker rooms while states helplessly stood by? What would happen if the tribes decided to add slot machines in states where they were prohibited? Tribal gaming was poised to erode revenue from government-sanctioned casinos, lotteries, and pari-mutuel operations. The eighty or so tribes involved in gambling grossed $110 million in 1988, a figure that poised to soar after the resounding legal victory for tribes.[31] To governors, the worst part of expanded tribal gambling was that none of that revenue would be subject to state taxation.

The rattled governors turned to Congress for help. On Capitol Hill, Nevada and New Jersey representatives who were well-financed by the casino industry warned that something must be done on the federal level to avoid organized crime activity in tribal gaming. Lawmakers from states with large tribal populations saw such concerns as overblown and self-serving. "Let us be candid. . . . The gambling lords of Nevada and the race-track owners of this country perceive an economic threat to their profits" from reservation-based gambling, said Rep. Morris Udall, an Arizona Democrat.[32]

Members of Congress cobbled together legislation that sought to balance tribal sovereignty with state and commercial casino interests. Sen. Daniel Inouye, a Hawaii Democrat and chairman of the Senate Indian Affairs Committee, was a driving force in creating the Indian Gaming Regulatory Act, or IGRA. Inouye, a staunch defender of Native American interests, declared: "We must not impose greater moral restraints on Indians than we do on the rest of our citizenry."[33] He, too, believed that the self-interested states opposed to Indian gaming were concerned only about losing their economic advantage to tribes.

The bill divided Indian gaming into three categories. Class I—traditional games associated with Native American ceremonies—would be regulated exclusively by tribes; Class II—bingo, lotteries, and nonbanked card games—would be subject to tribal and National Indian Gaming Commission oversight. Class III covered the main ingredients of a typical Nevada-style casino: slot machines, dice games, and banked card games such as blackjack in which players bet against the house instead of each other. For this most lucrative class of gambling, Inouye and other bill drafters developed the concept of "compacts," or agreements between states and tribes. Both sides would negotiate as equals and agree on regulatory issues such as what games and how many would be allowed in a tribal casino and whether the state would receive a portion of the revenue. Class III forms of gaming would be permitted on tribal lands only in states that allow such games.

A few senators worried that the bill compromised tribal sovereignty by enshrining a special role for states. Sen. Tom Daschle, a South Dakota Democrat, said the tribes in his state opposed the bill and "strongly object to any form of direct or indirect state jurisdiction over tribal matters."[34] Others pointed out that if a governor opposed gambling, he or she could theoretically stonewall tribal efforts to open a casino. Inouye outlined a path that a tribe could follow if a state refused to engage in good-faith negotiations. If a state did not respond to a tribe's request for a compact within 180 days, the tribe could sue in federal court. If the tribe won in court, both sides would have 60 days to complete a compact. If the impasse continued, the state and tribe would submit their drafts to a mediator. If the state still refused to accept the mediator-approved compact, then it would go to the secretary of the Interior Department for a final decision. The remedy was good enough to satisfy most lawmakers, but its weaknesses would soon be evident. Congress easily approved the bill and Reagan signed it into law on October 17, 1988.

The Indian Gaming Regulatory Act had something for everyone to hate. Tribes viewed it as a betrayal of the *Cabazon* decision, states were unhappy that they had no say in regulating bingo on Indian lands, and the casino industry fretted about the specter of new competition. Some governors used their substantial authority over Indian gaming as a wedge to extract more money or other concessions from tribes that wanted casinos. Wisconsin governor Tommy Thompson tried without success to expand the state's taxing authority on cigarettes and motor fuel on Indian lands in exchange for supporting gambling compacts.[35]

Still, the uneasy compromise did create a legal framework for tribes to pursue high-stakes bingo and full-blown casinos. To some tribes, gambling was "the new buffalo" that transformed Indian country.[36] Between when the IGRA was approved in 1988 and 1996, about 110 federally recognized tribes opened 230 gambling operations, with about half of them casinos. Polls showed strong public approval of reservation-based gambling. A Harris Poll in 1992 showed that 68 percent of adults in states other than Nevada and New Jersey believed tribes should be allowed to have casino gambling on their land.[37] (When pollsters asked if respondents favored casinos in their local communities, support slipped to 42 percent.) Once governors and tribes were able to rise above the bitterness from their duels in court, they came to realize that there would be plenty of money to be made on both sides.

————

The Seminole tribe of Florida, which kicked off tribal resistance to state and local control over reservation-based gambling in 1979, earned $100 million per year from its bingo operations by the late 1980s.[38] Under the Indian Gaming Regulatory Act of 1988, the tribe's gambling revenues from its patchwork of bingo halls and video gaming parlors rose to $500 million a year by 1998, allowing the tribe to send a monthly dividend check of $1,500 a month to each of its roughly 2,500 members.[39]

However, the tribe's attempt to make the jump to full-blown casino gambling put it at odds with the state throughout the 1990s and into the 2000s. Florida's consistent refusal to agree on a compact culminated in a US Supreme Court decision in 1996 that voided the IGRA requirement that states must negotiate in good faith.[40] That meant the tribe had to appeal to the Interior Department to bring the parties together, which slowed down the process for years. The state and tribe continued their dispute in state court over Class III gaming.

Meanwhile, the Seminoles stunned the business world by winning a nearly $1 billion bid in 2006 to acquire Hard Rock International and its global network of music-themed cafes, casinos, and hotels. "Our ancestors sold Manhattan for trinkets. We're going to buy Manhattan back, one burger at a time," boasted Seminole council representative Max B. Osceola Jr. at an event hosted at the chain's Times Square restaurant.[41]

Finally, in 2007, Florida governor Charlie Crist agreed to a twenty-five-year compact allowing the tribe to install Nevada-style slot machines and banked card games such as baccarat and blackjack.[42] In exchange, the tribe would pay the state at least $100 million each year. The Florida House sued, and the state Supreme Court ruled that the governor lacked the authority to adopt the compact because it permitted types of gaming illegal in the state. The Seminoles argued that Florida operated a state lottery and allowed slot machines in selected counties, so it had no grounds to block the tribe. In January 2009 the Interior Department secretary approved the compact despite the court ruling. It was a big loss for the state. Regulators could not stop the tribe from adopting the Class III games, and Florida received none of the revenue because lawmakers opposed the compact.

Bowing to reality, Crist and the Florida legislature reached a deal with the tribe for a new compact in 2010. It gave the Seminoles the exclusive right to operate three banked card games—blackjack, chemin de fer, and baccarat—at five of its seven casinos as well as Nevada-style slot machines at four of its casinos outside Miami-Dade and Broward Counties. In return, the tribe agreed to pay the state $1 billion spread out over five years. The tribe's casinos, which include the high-traffic Hard Rock Hollywood and Hard Rock Tampa, flourished under the agreement. The tribe takes in more than $2 billion in annual revenue, far outpacing Florida's disadvantaged pari-mutuel casinos.

The benefits of the revenue-sharing agreement softened opposition to tribal gambling. With the compact set to expire, Gov. Rick Scott authorized a new deal in 2015 that he said would create twenty thousand jobs by expanding the tribe's casinos and guarantee $3 billion in tribal payments to the state over seven years. In exchange for the nation's most lucrative tribal revenue-sharing compact, the Seminoles would win the exclusive right to offer craps and roulette. Florida lawmakers, swayed by the state's other gambling interests, rejected the compact in 2016, putting the state's share of the revenue into doubt.

———

California's similar history of antagonism toward tribal gaming placed it on a twisted path to its current status as the highest-revenue Indian gaming state. In the 1990s Republican governor Pete Wilson argued that the California Constitution barred tribes from operating Nevada-style slot machines and instead favored less lucrative lottery-style machines. He grudgingly completed a compact with a small tribe in San Diego County that capped the number of video gambling machines at 975 and prohibited popular games like video poker.[43] Wilson then tried to apply those limited terms to all other gaming tribes, which responded by promoting Proposition 5 in 1998. The measure guaranteed that any eligible tribe could operate certain types of Class III games, including traditional slots and banked card games. It shaped up to be the most expensive initiative in American history to date. The tribes spent $63 million on the successful campaign, overwhelming the anti-Proposition 5 interests that spent $29 million.[44] The California Supreme Court later invalidated the measure because it violated the state constitution's ban on full-blown casinos.

Despite the setback, the tribes made clear that they were a formidable political force. Wilson's successor, Democrat Gray Davis, received hefty campaign contributions from tribes and was much more open to casino gambling than Wilson. He negotiated a model compact with tribal-friendly language similar to Proposition 5 and successfully pushed for

Proposition 1A in 2000 to amend the state constitution to exempt tribes from the prohibition of "casinos of the type currently operating in Nevada and New Jersey." Sixty-one of the state's 108 federally recognized tribes signed the compact with the state, officially bringing Nevada-style gambling to California.[45] The agreement limited each tribe to two thousand slot machines and set up a revenue-sharing trust fund to benefit small or nongaming tribes and another fund to ease tribal gaming's impacts on nearby communities by paying for roads and fire protection. The model compact also covered matters such as casino building codes, labor rules, and environmental standards, showing the depth of the state's involvement in the details of tribal operations.

Only a few years after the ballot measure's approval and tribal expansion of their casino offerings, Davis wanted to renegotiate the compacts to rescue the state from its chronic budget shortfalls. The governor proposed to boost the number of allowable slot machines if the tribes made $1.5 billion in annual revenue payments to the state.[46] The tribes were furious at Davis's attempt to squeeze more revenue from them. Davis's plan fell victim to his collapsing political support and he was removed from office in an historic recall in 2003.

The sober, technocratic Davis was replaced by his opposite in every possible way, the action-film superstar Arnold Schwarzenegger. The flamboyant Republican loudly campaigned that he would make gaming tribes pay their "fair share" to the state, implying that they had been getting a free ride. In 2004 he amended compacts with five big gaming tribes that permitted them to add more slot machines. But for the first time the compacts required that a cut of the net revenues go to the state's general fund, amounting to millions in new revenue. The Rincon Band of Luiseno Indians in San Diego County sued, and a federal court ruled against Schwarzenegger's gambit, saying that it amounted to an illegal tax. "Today, many tribes have struck figurative gold with casino gaming and, again, some state governments, just like their predecessors, are maneuvering to take, or at least share in, some of that figurative gold," wrote Ninth US Circuit

Court judge Milan Smith Jr. in his 2010 opinion, drawing a parallel to the federal government's assault on tribes when gold was discovered in the Black Hills of South Dakota a century earlier.[47]

That ruling has had a chilling effect on the state's subsequent efforts to grab a bigger chunk of tribal casino money. In 2015 Gov. Jerry Brown and the United Auburn Indian Community, operators of the popular Thunder Valley Casino Resort in Northern California, agreed on a compact that slashed by two-thirds the amount paid into the general fund. Most of the revenue-sharing money will be directed to poor tribes and local infrastructure projects, and the tribe will be making smaller annual payments overall under the new compact.[48] California tribal casino money sent to the state's general fund shrank to $241 million in 2014.[49] That's partly because statewide Indian casino revenue peaked at $7.8 billion in 2007, dropped sharply during the Great Recession, and has since plateaued at about $7 billion a year even as the number of tribal casinos has held steady at sixty or so.[50]

In the latest bid to extract more gaming revenue, California is among the states warming to the idea of putting Indian casinos on off-reservation lands. In 2011 the Bureau of Indian Affairs lifted a requirement that an Indian casino had to be within easy driving distance of the reservation.[51] The rule change showcased the clout of tribes, which donate millions to federal campaigns and spend tens of millions of dollars on lobbying each year. The loosened restriction has encouraged dozens of tribes to apply for federal recognition and allowed a handful to put casinos near major highways and closer to population centers. It has also put them at odds with politicians and even some tribes who deride it as "reservation shopping" and a threat to existing casinos. California voters decisively rejected a 2014 referendum that would have ratified two tribal compacts to build casinos on land dozens of miles from their reservations.

The industry-leading glitzy resort-casinos like Thunder Valley near Sacramento and Pechanga in Riverside County create an impression that all Native Americans have hit the jackpot, but there is a wide split between the "haves" and the "have nots" in California and in the United States.

High-volume casinos have undoubtedly improved everyday life for the communities they serve and have enriched the tribes that run them. But they are the outliers. Only 5.7 percent of the nation's 459 Indian casinos earned revenue greater than $250 million in 2014, yet that small sliver took in 40.3 percent of the overall tribal gaming revenue of $28.5 billion.[52] On the lower end of the scale, 35.8 percent of casinos earned less than $10 million, making up only 2 percent of total revenue.[53]

As with the riverboat and dockside casinos that emerged at about the same time as Indian casinos, economic gains have been uneven at best. In 2010 about 18 percent of the nation's tribal population was available for work but not employed, mirroring tribal joblessness in California even with its strong casino industry.[54] An estimated 23 percent of all Native American families earned incomes below the poverty line in 2010, significantly higher than the national rate of 15 percent.[55] Overall, Indian gaming revenue leveled off from 2008 to 2010 after years of spectacular growth. "People thought casinos were recession proof," said Leo Chupaska, chief financial officer of the Mohegan Tribal Gaming Authority in Connecticut. "Starting in 2008, we learned it's not recession proof."[56] Indeed, Connecticut exemplifies the boom/bust cycles familiar to any gambler.

———

Like other big gaming tribes, the extraordinary rise of the Pequots from near extermination to national fame owed much to its doggedness in the legal and political realms. Regardless of its debatable authenticity as an Indian tribe, the Pequots leveraged every inch of its federally recognized status when pursuing a Nevada-style casino on its wooded reservation in rural Connecticut. If revenue from the tribe's high-stakes bingo hall that opened in 1986 was any guide, the returns from a casino with banks and banks of slot machines and a floor crammed with table games were poised to be tremendous. Tribal officials hoped for a repeat of what happened in New Jersey when Atlantic City legalized casinos in the 1970s—a virtual monopoly in a densely populated region. The main difference, of course, would be that the tribe could keep all of the money because it was a sovereign government. Connecticut had no right to impose taxes on the Pequots, as states could do for commercial casinos. On the other hand, Congress did give states an explicit command to forge casino compacts with tribes, which made for often tense partnerships.

At first Connecticut was hostile to the tribe's effort to build a full-blown casino. Connecticut did not permit traditional casino gambling, but it did allow state-approved charities and nonprofits to run occasional "Las Vegas nights" offering card games such as poker and blackjack. The events were fundraisers and winnings were restricted to prizes other than cash.[57] The Pequots reasoned that if the state permitted "Las Vegas nights," it should have no problem with the tribe featuring similar games on its reservation.

The Pequots sought Class III gambling as defined under the Indian Gaming Regulatory Act, which meant the tribe had to enter into a compact, or agreement, with the state. In 1989, the year after Congress passed the landmark law, the tribe's legal team approached the governor and requested a start to talks. The state attorney general dismissed the tribe's use of the "Las Vegas nights" statute as justification for a casino and concluded that the state was not compelled to negotiate a compact. The tribe pushed back, suing in federal court to order the state to negotiate in good faith as required under the law.

Despite the delay, the tribe proceeded with plans for its casino, which they hoped would someday be the biggest in the country. Skip Hayward, the former pipefitter who had miraculously resuscitated the Pequots, believed his clan's ancestors were the "fox people," and so "Foxwoods" was adopted as the casino's name. The tribe hired as an adviser G. Michael "Mickey" Brown, the former director of New Jersey's Division of Gaming Enforcement and a lawyer for gambling companies. As a veteran of Atlantic City's casino wars, the tribe calculated that he could insulate the tribe from organized crime interests. Brown connected the tribe to Malaysia's Genting Berhad, a global gambling giant willing to finance the casino when traditional banks passed on the opportunity. The company approved up to $60 million to build the first phase, a building housing a casino and restaurants with expanded parking to accommodate the

expected influx of gamblers.[58] The tribe had come a long way from securing the $5 million loan to build its bingo hall a few years earlier.

In 1990 the same federal judge who cleared the way for the tribe's bingo
hall handed it another legal victory, ordering the state to complete a compact within sixty days. The state appealed, but the ruling was upheld. The
tribe's draft compact included a blueprint for a state regulatory system
modeled on New Jersey's, and the negotiators agreed to put a moratorium on the explosive issue of slot machines. Since the state missed the
sixty-day deadline, the tribal and state draft compacts were sent to a court-
appointed mediator, subject to final approval by the Interior Department
secretary. There was little difference between the compacts, so the tribe
withdrew its version as a show of deference to the state. The move angered
Connecticut officials because it made it seem like they were the ones pushing for the casino. When the mediator endorsed Connecticut's draft version, the state refused to sign it. Furthermore, the state made a long-shot
appeal to the US Supreme Court.

While the federal government pondered the compact, a familiar face
was sworn in as governor of Connecticut: Lowell Weicker, who as a senator
was instrumental in securing tribal recognition for the Pequots. Weicker
had fallen out of step with the increasingly conservative Republican Party
in the 1980s and restyled himself an independent political maverick. He
ran as a member of "A Connecticut Party"—a name deliberately chosen
to ensure his name would be at the top of the ballot—and scored a rare
win for a third-party candidate. He rose to power amid a recession that hit
Connecticut hard, and he promised to take bold action.

It soon became clear that he was not going to be on the tribe's side
this time. The US Supreme Court declined to hear Connecticut's appeal
on April 22, 1991, clearing the last legal roadblock to Foxwoods becoming reality. Weicker appeared on a radio show less than a week later and
declared, "I do not want casino gambling as a fact of life in our state."[59] The
governor instructed his aides to search for a way—any way—to block
the tribe's casino from opening. They decided to push for a repeal of the "Las
Vegas nights" statute, which shocked tribal officials. If the repeal passed,

that would effectively end any rationale for Foxwoods to exist because the compact had not yet been approved by the Interior Department.

The political battle lines were sharply drawn: on one side, lawmakers sympathetic to the complaints of churches and charities worried about the potential loss of a lucrative fundraising tool and the tribe who charged the state was about to renege on a deal; on the other, a governor and his allies who argued that Las Vegas-style gambling would change the state's culture by inviting organized crime and prostitution. Weicker barely got his way in the Senate but lost decisively in the House. Many lawmakers were uneasy at being perceived as obstacles to a tribe's chance at economic uplift. Others recounted the many forms of gambling already legal in Connecticut—the state-run lottery, bingo, raffles, off-track betting, live greyhound racing, and jai alai—and were unmoved that adding another category would somehow bring ruin. Soon after, the Interior secretary signed off on the compact, at last allowing the tribe to break ground on its casino.

Foxwoods High Stakes Bingo and Casino opened in February 1992, a scene that resembled the opening of Resorts in Atlantic City more than a decade earlier. Like Resorts, Foxwoods benefited from holding a virtual casino monopoly in a big market. But unlike the New Jersey casino pioneer, Foxwoods was nestled in a nonthreatening, woodsy environment far from the grit of urban life. Waterfalls and skylights accented by American Indian designs created a feeling of surprising openness among casino patrons. Many New Yorkers found it more appealing to gamble in rural Connecticut than to head down the Garden State Parkway. The emergence of Indian gaming marked the beginning of Atlantic City's decline in casino revenue.

Unlike operators of traditional commercial casinos, the Mashantucket Pequot tribe had the advantage of owning plenty of land with no environmental or zoning restrictions on how it could be used to feed demand. Casino operating hours and other basic business decisions were up to the tribe's discretion, not the state's. (Foxwoods has always been open twenty-four hours a day, seven days a week.) No tax money was sent to the state of

Connecticut or the federal government, a huge competitive advantage over the glut of heavily taxed casinos fighting to make a buck in Atlantic City.

Thousands of people came every day to try their luck at poker, black-jack, or the roulette wheel in addition to high-stakes bingo. Foxwoods was an immediate hit, garnering $148 million in revenues and $51 million in profits in 1992.[60] The casino created thousands of jobs badly needed in a region reeling from the recession and a spate of defense industry layoffs. Still, tribal leaders keenly felt the absence of the top revenue-generators of any modern casino: slot machines. They were prohibited under the state's "Las Vegas nights" statute, which meant Foxwoods also couldn't have slots.

The tribe had big plans for its reservation—soaring hotels, a major Indian history museum, and a championship-caliber golf course—that would only be achieved through the level of revenue that slots could bring. The Pequots had come too far to roll over and accept running a casino without slot machines. Plus, they knew they wouldn't have the New England market to themselves forever. Las Vegas and Atlantic City casino magnate Steve Wynn, impressed by the early success of Foxwoods, scouted around the state and proposed building casinos in Hartford and Bridge-port. Lawmakers took up the idea of legalizing casinos as a balm for the state's budget crunch. Worried tribal leaders realized that they might be able to stave off competition from Wynn if the tribe allowed the state to financially benefit from Foxwoods.

Weicker opposed statewide legalization of casinos but knew that Wynn's clout could be enough to persuade the legislature. The governor also realized that if the tribe defeated the state in court over the right to have slot machines, Connecticut would receive zero revenue from them. The governor's aides and tribal leaders met secretly to broach a compromise that would allow slots exclusively at Foxwoods in exchange for sending the state 25 percent of slot revenue. The timing was ideal because Weicker was $100 million short of balancing the state budget.[61] If the tribe had cor-rectly calculated that three thousand slots at Foxwoods could potentially gross $400 million a year, such a compromise would solve the state's bud-get problem.[62] The state pushed for a guarantee, and the tribe responded by promising $100 million minimum a year to the state, provided that an agreement could be drawn up quickly. The tribe offered $100 million or 25 percent of the slot gross revenue each year, whichever was greater, but said the agreement would be void if the state approved slots on non-tribal land. It was a deal Wynn would never be able to match.

Weicker was thunderstruck by the Pequots' proposal. "You're gonna give the state of Connecticut $100 million a year and it's not going to cost us *anything*?" Weicker asked after hearing the tribe's presentation in January 1993.[63] Brown, the acting president and CEO of Foxwoods, assured the governor that the tribe would pick up the tab for casino regulation and policing. Weicker was sold. Even better for the parties involved, he had the power to add slots to the compact without legislative approval. Plus, the state had the freedom to spend the money in any way it pleased. The deal effectively boxed out Wynn from Connecticut and formed the backbone of a gambling titan in New England. Foxwoods immediately began installing the first of about 2,000 slots planned for the first year, ramping it up as high as 6,500.

A few months after the agreement was signed, state leaders placed an urgent call to Brown telling him that legislators remained $13 million shy of passing the budget. If that revenue could not be found, the state would need to cut deeply into social programs affecting the elderly and children. Without a deal, a government shutdown was possible. If the tribe agreed to a one-time $13 million boost to its payment to the state, those tough choices could be avoided. Hayward and the tribal council agreed, and the Pequots basked in the positive publicity. It represented a remarkable power shift for a tribe to rescue a state given the history of American Indian humiliations at the hands of government.

Buying the allegiance of the state of Connecticut for $13 million was a bargain considering the volume of cash gushing into Foxwoods thanks to the slot machine deal. Foxwoods had enough sway to impress Frank Sinatra, who agreed to appear at a series of concerts to open the casino's Fox Theater in 1993. Sinatra declared the joint to be "very classy," high praise from the seventy-seven-year-old crooner who had worked them all.[64] At 250,000 square feet, Foxwoods was the biggest casino in North America, surpassing anything Sinatra would have ever seen in Las Vegas.

In 1995 Foxwoods made more money than any casino in American history—an astounding $1 billion in gross earnings and more than $300 million in casino profits.[65] Millions went to local charities and arts groups in an attempt to build goodwill in the community. The tribe paid for road improvements to offset the surge in traffic and bankrolled its own fire and police stations. In 1998 Hayward presided at the opening of the $225 million Mashantucket Pequot Museum and Research Center just around the corner from Foxwoods. The 308,000-square-foot complex includes a 185-foot tower providing sweeping views of the thriving reservation. An archive and library foster scholarly research into indigenous cultures, and the museum's exhibits and films educate the public about the history of the "first nations." A gallery chronicles the history of the Pequot people and gamely tries to connect it to the modern-day tribe. A hefty slice of the annual proceeds was divided into six-figure stipends for the adult members of the tribe, which numbered nearly four hundred.[66] Council leaders received fat expense accounts, generous travel allowances, and other benefits.

For Hayward, the museum ended up being a capstone on his tenure as tribal chairman. He reveled perhaps too much in being a political player, making frequent trips to Washington and approving $1 million in campaign contributions, mostly to the Democratic Party. The money catapulted Hayward into the upper ranks of contributors, earning him the perk of staying in the Lincoln Bedroom during the Clinton White House of the 1990s.[67] Hayward's commitment to his vision since the 1970s had delivered incredible riches to the tribe, but his penchant for empire building and taste for expensive travel and entertainment paid for by the tribe disconnected him from everyday affairs. He no longer lived on the reservation, lost interest in tribal council meetings, and fell out of step with the tribe's changing demographics. Hayward was voted out as tribal chairman in late 1998.

Meanwhile, the slot deal worked out well for Connecticut. By 2000 the state had received a total of $1 billion of revenue from Foxwoods's humming slot machines.[68] The state also gained indirectly from the surge of tourism from the tens of thousands of people who visited Foxwoods every day and from the wages earned by the roughly eleven thousand workers at the resort. In 1996 the Mohegans—the tribe that fatefully allied with the English settlers against the Pequots centuries ago—opened the Mohegan Sun across the Thames River in Uncasville, about ten miles from Foxwoods. Like the Pequots, the Mohegans agreed to give a percentage of slot revenue to the state as long as the ban on non-Indian casinos stayed in place. Foxwoods and the Mohegan Sun grew to be the nation's two biggest casinos, each with annual revenues exceeding $1 billion in 2000.[69] Foxwoods alone boasted more than five thousand slot machines, three hundred gaming tables, dozens of restaurants, and four hotels for its tens of thousands of visitors each day.

The Pequot tribe's free-spending ways—the $700 million MGM Grand Tower at Foxwoods that opened in 2008 was a notable misfire—drove up its debt to levels that could only be sustained if the boom never ended. Debt payments were stretched out over longer and longer terms, but the tribe's accumulated shortfall reached $1.2 billion by 1999.[70] The tribal council slashed payments to families and government spending to balance the budget. Tribal members accustomed to a luxe lifestyle were furious at the austerity measures. "I am here because of the money. My family came here because of the money. That is what this tribe is about," said council protester and tribal member Theresa Casanova.[71] The tribe ended the annual revenue-sharing payments believed to average $100,000 per member.

Increased competition in neighboring states slowed the money spigot. What Foxwoods and Mohegan Sun had done to Atlantic City, new casinos in New York and New England were doing to them. Combined slot revenue for Foxwoods and Mohegan Sun crested in 2007 at $1.7 billion and skidded during the recession and its aftermath to $1.2 billion in 2012, less than what it was more than a decade earlier.[72] The declining casino revenue ballooned Foxwoods's debt to $2.3 billion. The tribe's status as a sovereign nation meant that creditors could not simply seize assets and sell them off to restructure the debt as they could under bankruptcy laws. Foxwoods CEO Scott Butera described it as being stuck in limbo. "We have six layers of creditors and, within each layer, twenty to forty institutions," he told the *New York Times* in 2012. "It's unbelievable."[73]

Foxwoods forged a deal with creditors to reorganize and cut its debt to $1.7 billion in 2013, ending years of uncertainty. A financial report completed later that year provided a fuller picture of its tailspin. Up to then, only slot revenue data were available—the financial performance of table games and other elements of the casino's business were not publicly revealed. The report, dated December 27, 2013, disclosed severe revenue declines in gambling, hotels, entertainment, and food and beverage sales. Foxwoods's net operating revenue sank from $1.2 billion in fiscal 2011 to $1.04 billion in fiscal 2013, and net income followed the same downward track.[74] The tribe slashed about one thousand employees from 2012 to 2013 and terminated its licensing agreement with MGM Mirage for the new hotel tower. The report cited Resorts World Casino in New York City, two casinos in Rhode Island, the growth of gaming in Pennsylvania, and the prospect of three large-scale casinos in Massachusetts as mortal threats to Foxwoods. "If we are not able to compete successfully with existing competitors, we may not be able to generate sufficient cash flows to satisfy our financial obligations, including our indebtedness," the report said.[75]

There was good reason for the gloomy outlook. During fiscal 2014 the Pequots defaulted under outstanding debt obligations, forcing the tribe and its lenders to enter into a forbearance agreement. "These matters raise substantial doubt about the Enterprise's ability to continue as a going concern," independent auditors Deloitte & Touche LLP wrote in reference to Foxwoods. Net operating revenue sank to $923 million for the fiscal year ending September 30, 2015, an 11 percent drop from just two years earlier.[76] Gaming revenue fell nearly 14 percent, more than offsetting the casino's efforts to bulk up its retail offerings with a new outlet shopping center.

Foxwoods's financial disclosure report recited the familiar threats of regional competition and outlined a new one: online gambling. The tribe warned that Congress and a handful of states have "renewed efforts to pass legislation to license and tax Internet poker and other online gaming." The fear is that many people will choose to stay home and gamble rather than head out to their local casino. Tribes in particular tend to be wary of such legalization efforts because they fear states will insist on taxing all online gambling revenue, even on reservations. "We are very adamant that people understand we are governments, and expect to be treated like governments," said Ernie Stevens Jr., the chairman of the National Indian Gaming Association.[77]

Foxwoods's rival, Mohegan Sun, has taken the opposite approach. It has also foundered under a mountain of debt—the tribe's gaming authority held $1.7 billion in long-term debt as of 2015 after refinancing to cut its interest expense—but the tribe has aggressively targeted opportunities beyond the stalled Connecticut casino market. It is among only a handful of tribes that have ventured into nonreservation gaming. The Mohegan Tribal Gaming Authority acquired the Pocono Downs Racetrack in Pennsylvania, slapped the "Mohegan Sun" brand on it, and remade it into the state's first casino with slots in 2006. Six years later the authority took over management of the historic Resorts Casino Hotel in Atlantic City.

When New Jersey legalized online gambling in 2013, the tribe's gaming authority embraced it. MoheganSunCasino.com allows people in New Jersey over the age of twenty-one to gamble in a real-money online casino. Players can earn VIP rewards as they do in a traditional casino, including free hotel rooms and chances to win cash and prizes. "Our goal is for MoheganSunCasino.com to become the premier online destination for both serious gamers and those who simply want to relax and have fun," said Bobby Soper, president of the Mohegan Tribal Gaming Authority. The website is intended to position the tribe as "a leading force within the online gaming space."[78]

Tribes in states where online gambling is illegal are at risk of being left behind. Although federally recognized tribes are sovereign entities, the last few decades of gambling policy show the considerable authority state and federal governments wield on their reservations. Tribes were dependent on governmental approval when they wanted slot machines, and the same is true of online gambling. Like struggling commercial casinos that push for looser betting limits and more table games to boost revenue, vulnerable tribes are desperate to stabilize their businesses and grow any way they can. While they wait, the biggest resorts are taking a cue from Las Vegas casinos and adding nongaming attractions such as golf courses, nightclubs, spas, and high-end restaurants to keep people coming. In a saturated market, the only way to do that is to expand into new frontiers. But that leads to the biggest question of all: Will the federal government allow that to happen?

CHAPTER 10

A Tangled Web

AMERICA'S DEEPLY CONFLICTED
APPROACH TO ONLINE GAMBLING

All I want is a safe place to play poker.
　　—Brian Boyko, a writer and online poker player who turned to a small
offshore site after the federal government's crackdown on poker sites in 2011

After a colorful history that stretched back to the steamboat era on the
Mississippi, the popularity of the great American pastime of poker seemed
to have leveled off by the 1990s. High-volume slot machines swallowed
up ever-more floor space in modern casinos, pushing traditional poker
rooms to the margins. Some casinos even closed them due to lack of revenue. The first-place prize at the game's signature event, the World Series
of Poker at Binion's Horseshoe in Las Vegas, remained flat at $1 million
throughout most of the decade. The tournament and the Horseshoe itself
felt like throwbacks out of step with the flashy megaresorts rising a few
miles away along the Strip.

But bubbling underneath was a new generation of young players mastering the game not in smoke-filled casinos or neighborhood cardrooms
but on their home computers. The dawn of the digital era meant that anyone with an Internet connection and a credit card could play high-stakes
poker whenever and wherever they wanted. They could compete with
players across the world and hone their skills by playing multiple games
simultaneously. Online players better versed in game theory than physical
tells began infiltrating poker's elite level.

If online poker had a big bang, it was Chris Moneymaker's triumph at the World Series of Poker in 2003. Moneymaker, the providentially named Tennessee accountant who had never before sat in a live tournament, spent $40 to win a PokerStars-sponsored satellite competition and claim a $10,000 seat at the No-Limit Hold'em main event of the World Series of Poker.[1] The amateur outclassed the field of 839 players and ended up sitting across the table from professional player Sam Farha with the $2.5 million grand prize at stake. Moneymaker executed what an ESPN commentator called "the bluff of the century" and snatched the victory from the seasoned pro.[2]

The phenomenon known as the "Moneymaker effect" kindled a poker renaissance. Casinos reopened or expanded their poker rooms to accommodate the surge in interest. Online players flooded into tournaments, hoping to replicate Moneymaker's instant fortune. The year after his victory, the first-place prize at the World Series of Poker doubled to $5 million, and the number of entrants in the main event tripled to 2,576. Just two years later, in 2006, the winner received $12 million and the field swelled to 8,773. By then Harrah's Entertainment had purchased the tournament from Binion's, ending the family's involvement with the enterprise.

The World Series of Poker had been televised as far back as the 1970s, but an innovation in how the game was covered expanded its audience. The cameras traditionally showed players glowering over their cards and pondering their next move—not exactly compelling television for the nonexpert viewer. In 1998 a British program called *Late Night Poker* installed a table with glass panels that revealed "hole cards," which are dealt face-down and not revealed before the showdown.[3] Showing those cards to viewers at home gave them the irresistible chance to match wits with the players and learn the game from the inside. The Travel Channel adopted the under-the-table camera technique for its presentations of the World Poker Tour starting in 2003 and suddenly televised poker programs cropped up all over. The rigorously edited shows made it seem like poker games were nothing but suspenseful showdowns when in fact they are rare. Players in hoodies and hats emblazoned with PokerStars and Full Tilt Poker logos became fixtures on cable and network TV. Poker-playing celebrities such as actor-director Ben Affleck joined in, injecting a dose of star power to the game.

Some poker players were winning their fortunes away from the glare of TV. In 2011 the *New York Times Magazine* profiled Daniel Cates, a twenty-one-year-old Floridian who made millions in high-stakes online poker playing under the online handle jungleman12. He applied the skills he picked up from his childhood obsession with video games to the virtual world of online poker, playing constantly and with multiple hands at once. After accumulating a level of game experience in a year or two that took players from an earlier era a lifetime to acquire, Cates went head-to-head with the elite professionals and got the best of them in each match by hundreds of thousands of dollars. Cates, who was then too young to sit at a poker table in most casinos, believed that his fearlessness separated him from more risk-averse older players. "Most of us young kids who play at nosebleed stakes don't really have any clear idea about the actual value of the money we win or lose," Cates explained. "Most of us see the money more as a points system. And because we're all competitive, we want to have the highest score. But really, we don't know what making $400,000 or losing $800,000 means, because we don't have families or whatever."[4]

The connectivity of the web fostered an international community of online players, swelling the amounts of money at stake. Top players experienced swings of as much as a few million dollars in a single day. In 2009 Swedish poker professional Viktor Blom (Isildur1) won $500,000 from Cates, earned another $700,000 in a contest with another player, then lost $4.2 million to Brian Hastings (Stinger) in just a few hours.[5] Cates's roommate, Ashton Griffin (theAshman103), said he won $7 million in three months but gambled away the lion's share of it over five months.[6]

Although some acted as if the figures in their online accounts were merely credits in a video game, they represented real dollars (or British pounds, or euros) tied to offshore accounts because online poker, at least in America, existed in a legal gray zone. Both the George W. Bush and

Barack Obama administrations had targeted payment processors involved in Internet gambling in the United States.

On April 15, 2011, a day ruefully remembered in gambling circles as "Black Friday," the federal government unleashed a stunning crackdown on online poker. The FBI shut down the three dominant sites—PokerStars, Full Tilt, and Absolute Poker—and eleven executives and payment processors were charged with bank fraud, money laundering, and illegal operation of gambling sites. The warning signs from the government were there for years, but no one in the poker world expected such a swift blackout. Casual players suddenly frozen out of their favorite sites feared that they would have no recourse to recover the money sitting in their government-seized offshore accounts.

Black Friday dealt a devastating blow to online poker. The boom went bust practically overnight. The industry's top executives stood accused of criminal activity, TV networks canceled their shows and fled the tainted business, and professional players considered moving to countries where they could continue their vocation without harassment. The federal government's hard-line stance cast doubt that any form of online gambling would ever be legalized in America. But within a matter of months, a surprising opinion from the Justice Department encouraged states to enter the Internet arena and, of course, benefit financially from it.

―――――

The roots of the federal government's hostility to online gambling can be traced to the underworld-controlled race wire that carried horse racing information to illegal betting parlors in the first half of the twentieth century. Poolrooms and bookies across the nation subscribed to the race wire, creating such a lucrative business for crime syndicates that Sen. Estes Kefauver called it "America's Public Enemy Number One." Cutting off the race wire was considered a federal issue because it crossed state lines. Congress passed the Wire Act in 1961 banning the use of a "wire communication facility for the transmission in interstate or foreign commerce of bets or wagers or information assisting in the placing of bets or wagers on any sporting event or contest, or for the transmission of a wire communication which entitles the recipient to receive money or credit as a result of bets and wagers, or for information assisting in the placing of bets and wagers."[7]

The sweeping action resembled the federal government's decision at the turn of the century to cut off mail service to lotteries when they were deemed to be a public scourge. (The exiled Louisiana State Lottery Company shifted its headquarters to Honduras to keep ahead of the law in the same way online poker companies moved to offshore sites to sidestep US regulations.) The ban on the interstate transportation of lottery-related materials persisted until the 1970s when state-run lotteries picked up momentum.

Betting-oriented websites popped up in the mid-1990s, and American regulators reflexively banned them as they had done with any new form of gambling that they couldn't easily operate or understand. Sportsbooks found a foothold in places like Antigua and Costa Rica and catered to US bettors, but the federal government insisted that the Wire Act applied to Internet communications and prosecuted operators.

Although US land-based casinos were reluctant to enter the online arena and risk losing their gambling licenses, everyday Americans showed no such hesitation. The digital revolution seeped into every corner of daily life, keeping them constantly tethered to their desktop computers, laptops, smartphones, and tablets allowing them to do whatever they want, wherever they want, whenever they want. Only the truly naïve would believe that gambling would not be part of that.

The trick for players was to find gambling websites and payment processors they could trust. It was one thing to bet on a game or horserace in which everyone knew the odds and the outcome; it was quite another to spin a virtual roulette wheel or slot machine without assurances that the results were legitimate. If the sites didn't pay as promised or folded without warning, there was no regulator to complain to as there would be in a land-based casino. Americans who gambled online were engaging in an illegal activity, so their government wasn't going to be there to help them out of a fix.

As the Internet's global penetration deepened, so did the number of websites taking real-money bets. In 1996 only about fifteen sites accepted wagers; three years later, the number jumped to 650 and then tripled by 2002.[8] Computer users displayed increasing confidence in websites and their ability to simulate casino play. Advancements in interfaces, wireless connections, and payment processing made the games more enticing for online gamblers. The websites managed small "sit-and-go" tournaments in which a player could play at any time. Larger multitable tournaments charged a small entry fee to thousands of players vying for a huge prize. In 2006 an estimated $6 billion of the worldwide online gambling market stemmed from US players.[9] That made the United States the leader in the amount and percentage of money gambled online even though such wagering had long been legal in many countries in Europe and elsewhere.

Planet Poker in 1998 was the first online card room to award actual currency instead of virtual points. Poker websites got rich by collecting tournament fees and keeping a percentage of the total amount wagered, or the rake. Unlike physical card rooms where fire codes limited occupancy, websites could accommodate as many players as their servers could handle. The top sites routinely handled thousands of players at any given time, and leading poker operator Full Tilt hosted up to fifty-four thousand players in an online tournament.[10] Mainstream casino companies, fearing being left behind in the digital age, began looking into how they could benefit. Nevada approved a bill in 2001 that drew up a blueprint for licensing and regulating online gambling in the state if the federal government ever loosened its restrictions.[11]

If anything, the feds stiffened their resistance. The State Department in 2004 blasted gambling sites as "the functional equivalent of wholly unregulated offshore banks."[12] Congress drafted a get-tough measure in 2006 to block American banks and credit card companies from processing electronic payments for "bets and wagers" defined as "the staking or risking by any person of something of value upon the outcome of a contest of others, a sporting event, or a game predominantly subject to chance."[13] It failed to attract sufficient support on its own, so Republican leaders in the Senate attached it at the last minute to a must-pass piece of legislation to ramp up security at the nation's ports.

Senators reported later that the vote was so rushed that they didn't have time to read the entire bill, which became known as Unlawful Internet Gambling Enforcement Act. The hastily written legislation worried some in Congress who considered it as unenforceable as Prohibition was in the 1920s and early 1930s. Rep. John Conyers, a Democrat from Michigan, thought it better for the government to regulate and tax online gambling as it belatedly had done with alcohol. "State regulation will ensure that gaming companies play fair and drive out dishonest operators," he said.[14] Other allies of online poker pointed out that the government was losing out on a potentially rich source of revenue.

Such arguments failed to derail momentum for the measure, which Congress passed and President George W. Bush signed into law on October 13, 2006. Online poker players perceived the law as a direct shot at them. They also resented the backdoor shenanigans members of Congress employed to pass it. "The American people should be outraged that Congress has hijacked a vital security bill with a poker prohibition that nearly three-fourths of the country opposes," said Michael Bolcerek, president of the Poker Players Alliance.[15]

What really galled poker aficionados was the perception that their game was just another form of online gambling. To advocates, poker belonged in a different category than slot machines, roulette wheels, or even blackjack in which players bet against the house, not each other. A 2009 study by the software consultant Cigital analyzed 103 million hands of Texas Hold'em played at PokerStars and found that more than three-quarters were decided before a showdown, meaning that results depended more on player strategies than the randomness of the cards dealt.[16]

The Unlawful Internet Gambling Enforcement Act set off a chain of events that had severe, long-lasting effects on the burgeoning industry.

Some leading foreign sites stopped accepting bets from US-based players, slashing their revenues. The stock price of Britain's PartyGaming, owner of the popular online card room PartyPoker, tanked 60 percent the day after passage of the bill.[17] Other publicly traded poker companies watched their shares crater. PartyPoker decided to bow out of the American market to avoid the risk of prosecution. Federal authorities cracked down on payment processors by indicting their founders and freezing their bank accounts.

The shrinking pool of available online talent had a ripple effect on entries into the main event of the World Series of Poker, which plummeted from 8,773 in 2006 to 6,358 in 2007. Accordingly, the first-place prize dropped from $12 million to $8.25 million during those same years (and have yet to return to their 2006 peaks).

Poker websites that defiantly chose to continue serving American players had their headquarters in foreign locales: PokerStars in the Isle of Man, Full Tilt in the United Kingdom's Channel Islands, and Absolute Poker in Costa Rica. They reasoned that if they were based in countries where online gambling was legal, the American government couldn't stop them. The hard part, though, was figuring out how to process payments from American players that didn't rely on American financial institutions. That problem is precisely what led to the Black Friday shutdown of PokerStars, Full Tilt, and Absolute Poker on April 15, 2011.

That the most popular poker sites in the United States were based overseas had raised alarms in the Justice Department about the potential of money laundering. Federal prosecutors charged Allied Systems and Account Services in 2009 for processing poker money illegally and seized $34 million owed to about twenty-seven thousand players.[18] The poker companies agreed to reimburse the customers and knew that they had to get more creative if they couldn't use mainstream payment processors. It was hard to overlook the swelling pile of cash being spun off by the red-hot business. The global online poker market was believed to be about $5 billion with about 2 million players in America accounting for $1.4 billion of the total revenue.[19] PokerScout, an online tracking site, estimated that online poker sites received $16 billion in wagers from US players in 2010.[20] The true numbers were as unknowable as they were in the era of illegal numbers games and underground casinos.

On September 20, 2011, the Justice Department amended its scathing suit to accuse poker executives of defrauding players of hundreds of millions of dollars. According to the complaint, Full Tilt's owners paid themselves millions by fraudulently draining players' accounts when money from the United States dried up once the 2006 law began to take effect. "Full Tilt was not a legitimate poker company, but a global Ponzi scheme," wrote Preet Bharara, the US attorney for the Southern District of New York.[21] Bharara added that the twenty-three owners of the site had withdrawn $444 million in total distributions. Two Full Tilt founders, pro players Howard Lederer and Chris "Jesus" Ferguson, were accused of receiving $38 million and $24 million in distributions, respectively.[22] (They and others charged in civil cases reached separate settlements with the government in which they forfeited millions of dollars with no admission of wrongdoing.) The government also charged the sites with bank fraud for allegedly working with third-party processors to create false companies. Banks were supposedly unaware that illicit gambling money was being routed through the websites of those seemingly legitimate companies.

At the time of the shutdown, Full Tilt customers had $390 million in their accounts, but the company had only $60 million in the bank, the filing said. Players with money sitting in the suspended accounts were left to wonder when or if they would ever see it again. Brian Mogelefsky made about $5,000 a month when he made his online poker hobby into an occupation. After Black Friday, the North Carolina resident said that he had nearly $29,000 frozen in his Full Tilt account. "I was in complete shock," he said. "I felt completely blindsided."[23] Players didn't dare join other poker sites for fear the feds would also shut them down and seize their assets, too. Some set up temporary residences in places like Canada and Costa Rica to continue their avocation. Professional poker player Walter Wright moved to Costa Rica to live in a housing complex with other pros, leaving his wife and children behind in North Carolina.[24] He realized that he had no other way to quickly replace his poker income and pull the family out of its financial morass.

PokerStars and Full Tilt reached a settlement with the government on July 31, 2012, more than a year after the crackdown. PokerStars agreed to forfeit $547 million to the federal government and acquire Full Tilt under the court-approved deal. Full Tilt forfeited virtually all of its assets and reimbursed $184 million it owned to foreign players. Neither PokerStars nor Full Tilt admitted any wrongdoing, ending litigation between the government and the companies. Bharara, the US attorney in Manhattan, praised the agreement as a means of compensating the bettors whom he described as "victims." "Today's settlements demonstrate that if you engage in conduct that violates the laws of the United States, as we alleged in this case, then even if you are doing so from across the ocean, you will have to answer for that conduct and turn over your ill-gotten gains," he said.[25] Absolute Poker, which weathered a major cheating scandal in 2007 involving an employee hacking into its software and bilking players, later agreed to a similar settlement.

Of the eleven people charged in the Black Friday raid, eight were arrested and pleaded guilty and three remain at large, presumably out of the country. Among the eight defendants, payment processor Ira Rubin received the stiffest sentence, three years in prison for his role in helping the poker websites disguise their illegal transactions. Prosecutors claimed that he tricked US banks into processing the gambling payments by setting up phony front companies and pretending they were transactions of legitimate companies. Rubin, a con man with a long criminal history, pleaded guilty in 2012 to conspiracy charges involving bank fraud and money laundering. The sentencing included a $5 million forfeiture order that was going be hard to claim because Rubin transferred $2 million to accounts in Costa Rica and also slipped gold bars to an acquaintance for safekeeping there.[26]

It took years, but the bulk of poker players with money stuck in the suspended accounts received their balances. By July 2014 the Justice Department estimated that the poker companies had made more than $1 billion in settlement payments.[27] Among the recipients was Daniel Cates, the online poker whiz kid who reportedly had millions in his Full Tilt account when the feds swept in. Like many pros who felt burned by the government's action, Cates felt that Black Friday permanently ruptured players' trust in online poker. "Poker sites are much less professional than I once thought, and personally I think that the entire online poker industry is dying," he said in 2014 after receiving his Full Tilt money. "My win rate has gone down by about 25 to 30 percent since Black Friday happened and that's largely due to there being so much less action."[28]

The crackdown and the ensuing wave of bad publicity had a chilling effect on online poker. Roughly 2 million Americans had online poker accounts before Black Friday; a year later, only 350,000 people had them.[29] Revenue from US players dried up accordingly, from about $1.4 billion to $223 million, according to data tracker H2 Gambling Capital. Cates's grim outlook pointed to the problems that would ensue if legalization ever came to online poker.

———

While the Justice Department was prosecuting poker companies, it was quietly adopting a softer tone toward online gambling in general. On September 20, 2011—the same day prosecutors detailed their charges against online poker websites—the department issued a legal opinion that stunned the gambling community. The document, written by Assistant Attorney General Virginia A. Seitz of the Office of Legal Counsel, was not made public until December 23, 2011. It addressed the narrow question of whether Illinois and New York's proposals to use the Internet and out-of-state transaction processors to sell lottery tickets to in-state adults would be a violation of federal law. Seitz concluded the "interstate transmissions of wire communications that do not relate to a 'sporting event or contest' fall outside of the reach of the Wire Act," meaning that Illinois and New York were free to proceed.[30] The memo said the Unlawful Internet Gambling Enforcement Act of 2006 did not apply to the case because the transactions would take place within a single state.

Although not on the level of an act of Congress or a Supreme Court ruling, legal opinions from the office have a force of their own and are followed by other government agencies.[31] The department's surprisingly liberal interpretation of the Wire Act encouraged states to pursue nonsports online wagering within their boundaries. It also seemed to allow online wagering across state lines. The green light enticed states to benefit from online gambling as they had done decades earlier with lotteries.

Nevada, always a gambling trailblazer, was the first state to legalize real-money online poker in 2013. "This bill is critical to our state's economy, and ensures that we will continue to be the gold standard for gaming regulation," said Gov. Brian Sandoval upon signing the bill into law.[32] Nevada imposed a 6.75 percent tax on revenues. Sandoval, a former chairman of the Nevada Gaming Commission, still believed that there should be some kind of federal action as a check on money laundering and fraud. "The advent of Internet gaming has introduced a borderless element that state regulation alone cannot address," he wrote in support of legislation backed by Sen. Harry Reid of Nevada, also a former chairman of the gaming commission.[33]

In any case, the potential riches of being at the front of the line were too great for the state to wait for Congress to act. Online poker in the United States had a projected market value of up to $10 billion, but Nevada first had to figure out how to manage it within its own boundaries. On April 30, 2013, Ultimate Gaming's UltimatePoker.com was the first site to go live. Play was limited to people physically within the state, and users were required to submit detailed identification verifying that they were over twenty-one years old. "Players won't have to worry if their money is safe. They are going to be able to play with people they can trust and know the highest regulatory standards have been applied," said Ultimate Gaming CEO Tobin Prior.[34] He touted his company's marketing deal with the mixed martial arts powerhouse Ultimate Fighting Championship as a way to hook younger people on online poker. However, the momentum toward legalization didn't impress professional poker player Matt Stout, who moved to Costa Rica after the 2011 crackdown on online poker. "It's going to be a long time before it's lucrative enough to convince me to move back to the US full-time," he said.[35]

Four months later, Caesars Entertainment launched the World Series of Poker-linked WSOP.com and was later joined by the South Point Casino–backed Real Gaming. The three operators struggled to gain traction even with a big marketing push. Revenue peaked at $1.26 million in October 2013 and gradually declined to $641,000 in November 2014.[36] That was the month Station Casinos-owned Ultimate Gaming folded its Nevada online poker operation after only nineteen months. The company's chairman reported that profitability came in far below expectations, blaming the slow pace of legalization in the United States for creating "an extremely cost-prohibitive and challenging operating environment."[37] Near the end of its run, UltimatePoker.com averaged just sixty players participating in a typical sitting.[38] At least this time, players didn't have to wait years to retrieve money from their accounts. So far online poker's impact has barely caused a ripple in Nevada: Interactive poker revenue accounted for only 7 percent of total poker revenue since legalization. As of December 2014, the state no longer reports interactive poker revenue.

Online gambling has also failed to live up to expectations in New Jersey, which began offering a full suite of casino-style games along with online poker in November 2013. It restricted online licenses to brick-and-mortar casinos in Atlantic City that could run their own websites or team up with companies like bwin.party. Just as in Nevada, specialized geolocating software ensured that only people in the state can place bets linked to designated websites. "We can be the Silicon Valley of Internet gaming," said Raymond Lesniak, a New Jersey state senator and the primary sponsor of the bill. "It's the wave of the future."[39]

So far Gov. Chris Christie's latest attempt to prop up Atlantic City and shore up the state's shaky finances has not lived up to expectations. New Jersey collected $11 million in taxes on online gambling revenue in its first eight months—far short of the state's wildly optimistic $180 million initially forecast.[40] (Independent analysts were much more realistic; one of them, H2 Gambling Capital, had estimated $45 million in annual tax revenue.[41]) State officials blamed technical glitches for creating barriers for customers. Some banks were unwilling to allow customers to use their credit cards for online gambling purposes, and not all mobile devices were equipped for gaming. In the first full fiscal year of online gambling, the state took in about $20 million in online gambling taxes—an improvement to be sure, but not exactly on par with "Silicon Valley"-level projections. Since then poker has been stagnant and other online games have far outstripped its revenue.

Delaware, the only other state with regulated online gambling, has also had its struggles. It kicked off online poker and other games in November 2013 partly to stay ahead of neighbors like Pennsylvania that poach the state's gamblers. Delaware's small population generated skimpy returns, with total online gaming revenue in the first full calendar year amounting to barely $2 million. That was bad news for the state because officials budgeted $7.5 million in additional tax revenue in fiscal 2014.[42] Startup costs and operating expenses meant that online gambling made no net contributions to the budget, state officials reported.

In Delaware and New Jersey poker makes up only about a quarter of the total online gambling win. Professionals accustomed to playing multitable tournaments with tens of thousands of players around the globe aren't going to be impressed with the much lower stakes offered in individual states. "Poker doesn't work in a small state like ours," said Nevada attorney and online gambling expert Anthony Cabot. "Poker requires liquidity. . . . House-backed games are different. It doesn't make any difference if you have liquidity or not. It's a person against a slot machine or a blackjack game."[43]

States are beginning to realize that their best chance for success in the online world is to band together and drive up the pots. The governors of Delaware, Nevada, and New Jersey have discussed forging an interstate online poker network, as states have done with Powerball and Mega Millions lottery drawings. But as of early 2017 they remain the only three states (plus the District of Columbia) with legal online gaming, making any kind of critical mass difficult to achieve. The biggest state, California, has considered entering the fray, but the competing interests represented by the state's card rooms, powerful Indian casinos, and racetracks have complicated negotiations for years. Supporters of legalization say they are trying to protect consumers from unscrupulous websites and prevent the state's hundreds of millions of dollars in wagers from flowing overseas. Other states like Mississippi and Washington have taken note of the underwhelming results elsewhere and dropped their efforts to legalize online gambling. About a dozen states have imposed bans on online gambling altogether.

The old-reliable state-run lotteries have fared somewhat better with the shift to the Internet. The reinterpretation of the Wire Act at the request of the Illinois and New York lotteries cleared the way for states to accelerate online play. In 2012 Illinois became the first state to sell individual lottery tickets online. (Other states had sold lottery subscriptions online but not single tickets.) Business was slow as customers and regulators adjusted to the geolocation software to screen out out-of-state players. Ticket sales totaled about $3 million in the first six months, well below the $26 million the state expected for the first year.[44] The lottery's operator redesigned the website, dropped the requirement that players needed to register a special debit card to receive winnings, and added Powerball to its lineup. Sales picked up online and via a mobile app and generated $68 million for the state in its first four years.[45]

As of 2017 more than a dozen states allow lottery sales online, a small but growing channel of new revenue. However, one of the wealthiest men in the world is standing in the way of it expanding much further.

———

Sheldon Adelson, chairman of the Las Vegas Sands Corporation that owns the Venetian and Palazzo on the Strip, is leveraging his $25 billion fortune and considerable clout in the casino industry to fight the legalization of online gambling. Adelson, who ranked number 22 on *Forbes* magazine's list of the world's richest people in 2016, charted an unlikely path to his wealth. Born in 1933 to a Lithuanian-immigrant father who drove a cab and a mother who ran a knitting shop, Adelson was raised in a shabby one-room tenement in Dorchester in South Boston. He showed little aptitude for school but learned how to hustle early on by selling newspapers and starting a candy vending machine business as a teen. After serving a stint in the Army, Adelson experimented with an array of businesses—everything from packaging toiletry kits for hotels to developing a spray to clear frozen windshields—and saw his financial success rise and fall over the decades.

His breakthrough came in 1979 when he founded COMDEX, a computer trade show in Las Vegas, which had blossomed into an attractive city for conventioneers. The city's expanding airport, abundance of cheap hotel rooms, sprawling convention center and meeting space in new hotels like Kirk Kerkorian's International lured out-of-towners. The constant influx of professionals such as doctors for medical conferences and sales-people for trade shows went a long way toward improving the reputation of Las Vegas in America. In 1970 the region attracted 269 conventions that brought $63.6 million into the local economy. A decade later, 449 meetings had an economic impact of $227 million.[46] The man at the vanguard of that booming business was Sheldon Adelson.

In 1989 Adelson had built up enough capital through his blockbuster computer trade show to buy the Sands from Kerkorian, inspiring the name of his company. Adelson constructed the nation's largest convention center next to the hotel and capitalized on the 1990s tourism boom, selling COMDEX in 1995 to the Japanese telecommunications company SoftBank for $862 million of which Adelson's share was reportedly $510 million.[47] Adelson knocked down the Sands—long past its Rat Pack heyday—and erected the Venetian on the property. It opened in 1999 at a cost of $1.5 billion. Adelson personally saw to it that the all-suite resort boasted the biggest rooms in Las Vegas, which ran counter to the conventional wisdom that hotel guests didn't care about such amenities. He dictated vintage Vegas "can-you-top-this" touches, such as a simulacrum of Venice's Grand Canal complete with singing gondoliers gliding along on startlingly blue waters. Adelson followed up with the adjoining luxury resort Palazzo in 2009.

Adelson astutely turned his focus to China, specifically the former Portuguese colony of Macau, the only part of the communist country where authorities permit casino gambling. Adelson's political connections and record of success in Las Vegas allowed him in as the first non-Chinese casino operator when he opened the Sands Macau in 2004. He earned back his initial investment within a year and became a multibillionaire overnight when he took his company public later that year.[48] Adelson has since built a casino in Singapore and added three more gigantic resorts to his portfolio in Macau, which has surpassed Las Vegas as the world's gambling capital.

After cashing in his golden ticket in Macau, Adelson asserted his authority in the political realm. The billionaire is a hawkish backer of Israel and lavishly contributes to Republican and Israeli politicians who share his strident opposition to a two-state solution to the Israeli–Palestinian dispute. Adelson has also written sizable checks to Jewish causes such as Yad Vashem, Israel's Holocaust museum and memorial, and Taglit-Birthright Israel, which funds free trips to Israel for young American Jews. In the 2012 presidential race Adelson and his wife, Miriam, singlehandedly kept alive Newt Gingrich's faltering bid for the Republican nomination with $15 million in contributions to a pro-Gingrich super PAC during the primaries. In all, the Adelsons spent $93 million (and reportedly many millions more in unreported "dark money"), making them the election cycle's biggest donors. Adelson clearly revels in his self-styled role as kingmaker, hosting events where candidates fly in to dutifully pay homage in the hope of winning the mogul's financial backing. He secretly purchased the *Las Vegas Review-Journal* in 2015 and has shaped the newspaper into a megaphone for his views.

Adelson's vast wealth and willingness to influence the political process make him the most formidable opponent of online gambling, an attitude that puts him at odds with much of the casino industry. "In my fifteen years of working with him, I don't think I have ever seen him this passionate about any issue," said Adelson political adviser Andy Abboud.[49] In 2014 Adelson launched the Coalition to Stop Internet Gambling and hired lobbyists to put pressure on politicians on the state and federal levels. He signed up Democratic and Republican leaders to promote the advocacy group's mission via talk shows, speeches, and opinion pieces. Adelson's argument for a federal ban is twofold: to shield children and problem gamblers from predatory websites and to protect the business model of brick-and-mortar casinos. He worries about the potential of tech giants like Google and Facebook dominating online gambling if it was legalized. "They'll come in there, they'll squash the other guys like . . . you squash the little ant running across the table or the floor and that's going to be the end of all of it," Adelson said in 2014.[50]

Adelson has allies in Congress who are upset at the Justice Department's shifting attitude about online gambling. "We can't have an office in the bowels of the DOJ going against decades of legal precedent without Congress having any say," complained Rep. Jason Chaffetz, a Republican from Utah.[51] In 2015 Chaffetz cosponsored the Restoration of America's Wire Act to prohibit all forms of Internet gambling, but the bill and its companion in the Senate have languished in committees.

The chronic gridlock in Congress has also stymied groups opposed to Adelson's absolutist approach. Weeks after the Black Friday shutdown of online poker sites, gambling executives and lobbyists decamped to Capitol Hill to press for federal regulation of online gambling. The American Gaming Association, the casino industry's leading lobbying group, dangled the figure of $2 billion as the estimated revenue governments would enjoy each year if it legalized online poker. The lobbyists also appealed to Congress and its historic role as the protector of the people. "The millions of Americans who are playing poker online deserve to know they are playing safely with law-abiding operators," said Frank J. Fahrenkopf Jr., then the president and CEO of the American Gaming Association.[52] Despite Fahrenkopf's political clout as a former chairman of the Republican National Committee, the movement went nowhere.

Reid, the Nevadan who led Senate Democrats until his retirement in 2017, called Internet poker the most important issue in his state since the debate to store nuclear waste at Yucca Mountain, yet his halting attempts to do something about it ran aground. In 2012 he floated an idea to create a federal regulatory office for online poker but curb states from authorizing other forms of online gambling. Lottery directors lashed out at the legislation for fear it would trample on states' rights, and they succeeded in squelching it. Reid's efforts included designating the Nevada Gaming Control Board as the main issuer of online poker licenses, a proposal that was never going to fly with other states. The bill was never formally introduced.

So far Adelson's crusade against online gambling has achieved a stalemate on the federal level. The issue is complicated by a swirl of warring interests: conservatives in Congress who see online gambling as a states' rights matter, governors who want new revenue, casino companies that want a piece of the digital revolution, and practical lawmakers seeking to bring order to an unregulated black market. Government's push-and-pull of regulation and prohibition is still playing out for online gambling, but it remains decidedly hostile toward embracing gambling's final taboo: sports wagering.

CHAPTER 11

Games without Frontiers

SCANDALS, BOOKIES, FANTASY SPORTS, AND AN UNCERTAIN FUTURE

It may be a little immoral, because it really is a tax on the poor, the lotteries. But having said that, it's now a matter of national policy: Gambling is good.

—David Stern, NBA commissioner in 2009 interview

March Madness is to bookies what the holiday shopping season is to department stores: an annual extravaganza that pulls millions of casual customers into their orbit. Both events are crucial to their businesses and create an exciting, almost frenzied atmosphere. An estimated $250 million is wagered at Nevada sportsbooks each year on conference tournaments and the National Collegiate Athletic Association's men's basketball tournament, which consists of sixty-eight teams.[1] The bracket itself is an instantly recognizable piece of popular culture. As president, Barack Obama diligently filled one out every March on ESPN while offering detailed rationales for each pick.

In Las Vegas basketball fans buy up blocks of hotel rooms at premium prices and camp out in plush sportsbooks to place bets on the bonanza of games. Although most bettors are only dimly aware of the strengths and weaknesses of the more obscure teams, they get caught up in the tournament's frenzied opening days when thirty-two games are played in two days. Dozens of big-screen TVs in sportsbooks show the drama of every missed free throw, key turnover, botched call, and buzzer-beating finish. Upsets and teams that fail to cover the point spread elicit as much raw emotion inside the books as in the basketball arenas. The single-elimination tournament culminates with the Final Four and national championship game, typically played in early April.

As big of a draw as March Madness is for gamblers in Nevada, it is only a sliver of the total amount wagered nationally on the tournament—almost all of it done illegally. The tens of millions of people who participate in office pools, gamble in real-money online tournaments, and wager with bookies are technically violating the law. Sports gambling is prohibited outside of four "grandfathered" states: Delaware, Montana, Nevada, and Oregon—and of them, only Nevada has truly full-blown sports betting. The FBI estimates that about $2.5 billion is wagered illegally each year on March Madness, much of it involving untraceable cash.[2] The American Gaming Association's estimate for the 2016 tournament was much higher: $9.2 billion wagered with only $262 million bet legally in Nevada.[3] Roughly 70 million brackets were filled out, more than the number of votes Obama received when he won reelection in 2012. The casino advocacy group reported the total illegal sports betting market in the United States swelled to about $150 billion in 2015.

The vast amount of illegal money being wagered on sports has serious repercussions, as it did when other forms of gambling were prohibited. A recent international report estimated that 80 percent of sports betting worldwide is conducted illegally, and $140 billion is laundered every year via sports betting, a vital tool for global organized crime interests that makes them well-positioned to manipulate athletic contests. The volume of illegal bets "has developed a significant underground economy with links between organized crime and sports as well as the impossibility to detect suspicious odds movements," warned the 2014 study by the International Centre for Sport Security and the University of Paris I. Much of this illegal activity stems from the United States, where sports wagering is largely prohibited and all of the major leagues—the NCAA, Major League Baseball, the National Football League, the National Basketball Association, and the National Hockey League—have traditionally been opposed to sports gambling.

March Madness is a prime example of the mixed messages that leagues send to fans about gambling. Four conference tournaments are played each March in Las Vegas, but the NCAA bars the city from hosting any NCAA Tournament games. The ostensible reason is the NCAA's fear that gambling could somehow taint the tournament, even though point shaving and game fixing have been shown to have no relationship to the proximity of legalized gambling.

Professional and amateur leagues piously warn of gambling's threat to athletic "integrity" and "public confidence," but they are keenly aware of how illegal betting and fantasy leagues stimulate interest in games and drive television ratings. The higher the viewership numbers, the more money the leagues can charge broadcasters for the right to carry their games. Only self-interested gamblers and fantasy players are likely to stay tuned to a lopsided game featuring two dull teams. In 2016 the NCAA agreed to an eight-year, $8.8 billion extension of its multimedia rights deal with CBS and Turner to broadcast the NCAA Tournament. The agreement runs through 2032 and allows for every game to be shown on multiple platforms. "Everybody in this country bets on sports," said Billy Walters, the nation's best-known sports gambler. "If you were to take away the office pools, fantasy pools, people betting on sports, I guarantee the [TV] viewership would be cut in less than half."[4]

In an unusual alignment of the business and sports worlds, mortgage lender Quicken Loans sponsored a contest paying $1 billion to anyone who picked a perfect bracket in the 2014 tournament. Warren Buffett's Berkshire Hathaway stepped up to insure the biggest-known bet in the history of sports. "This will be the most fun," said Buffett, the legendary investor with more than a few billion dollars to his name. "Just imagine if there's one person left at the last game. I will go to that final game with him or her and I'll have a check in my pocket. . . . I think we'll be rooting for different teams."[5]

There was no entry fee—although Quicken Loans gleaned invaluable data from online forms filled out as part of the registration process—so the challenge didn't run afoul of antigambling laws. Millions participated even though the odds of winning the grand prize were much longer than Powerball—a staggering 1 in 9,223,372,036,854,775,808. Buffett didn't have to worry for long about making the billion-dollar payout because no contestant's bracket survived the opening round. (The top twenty finishers each received $100,000 from Quicken Loans.)

An intriguing subtext of the contest was the background of Quicken Loans founder and chairman Dan Gilbert. Few are as schooled in the intersection of gambling and sports as Gilbert. He is the majority owner of the NBA's Cleveland Cavaliers (along with a handful of minor-league franchises) and is the founder and chairman of Jack Entertainment, which opened a casino in downtown Cleveland in 2012. The casino in Tower City Center is just a few blocks from the home of the Cavs—Quicken Loans Arena. Gilbert's company also has partnerships in casinos and thoroughbred racetracks in Kentucky, Maryland, and Michigan.

Gambling today is so widely accepted and thoroughly homogenized that few question the propriety of Gilbert's holdings. Indeed, cracks are beginning to form in the leagues' historic wall separating sports and gambling. In January 2014 the New Jersey Devils and Philadelphia 76ers signed a deal with PartyPoker, which enables players in New Jersey to play real-money online poker games. The deal—the first of its kind for American sports teams—is integrated with the teams' websites, advertising, and promotions.[6] Yankee Stadium features the Mohegan Sun Sports Bar in center field above Monument Park, and the Padres dismantled their display of retired numbers on top of the batter's eye at Petco Park in 2016 in favor of a large sign advertising a local Indian casino.

Most notably, NBA commissioner Adam Silver said in late 2014 that the federal government should legalize sports betting. The shift in attitude is a sign that teams and leagues sense that they can profit from partnership deals with betting sites and daily sports fantasy companies like DraftKings and FanDuel. But the weight of history and the borderless world of the Internet have consistently thwarted attempts to broaden sports gambling's legality.

———

Just as with horse racing, wagering and organized athletic contests have always been intertwined. So too has the temptation to fix the outcome. Boxing has a troubled past, with organized crime interests dictating who would win and who would take a dive; basketball, both professional and collegiate, has suffered from a host of point-shaving episodes and refereeing scandals; and many of the NFL's founding fathers were involved in illegal bookmaking or worse. The oldest continuous professional sport in America—baseball—has endured the highest-profile scandals that have done the most to shape public opinion about sports gambling.

The sport's first recorded gambling impropriety occurred during its amateur club days in 1865 when a gambler paid the catcher of the Boss Tweed–owned Mutuals of New York to bribe two teammates to assist him in fixing a game.[7] (The catcher allowed six passed balls before he was moved to right field in the loss.) The glaringly poor play kindled an investigation, confessions, and expulsions. The formation of professional leagues boosted attendance and encouraged bookies to roam the grandstands looking for bets. John Morrissey, the proprietor of tony New York gambling clubs and founder of Saratoga Race Course, had an ownership interest in his hometown Haymakers of Troy, New York. He supposedly wagered $60,000 that his team would beat the Red Stockings of Cincinnati, an undefeated professional team in 1869.[8] With the game tied in the sixth inning, the president of the Troy club pulled his players off the field because of repeated bad calls by the umpire. Many historians believe the true motivation for the forfeit was to protect Morrissey from gambling losses.

Rampant bribery warped the quality of play on the field and gamblers got into the act by throwing stones at outfielders so they would drop easy fly balls or by running out on the field to tackle ballplayers.[9] "Baseball, as a professional pastime, has seen its best days in St. Louis," lamented the city weekly *Spirit of the Times* in 1878. "The amount of crooked work is indeed startling, and the game will undoubtedly meet the same fate elsewhere unless some extra strong means are taken to prevent it."[10]

The sport's signature event—the World Series, or the "World's Championship Games" in the parlance of the time—was dogged by gambling-related corruption from the beginning. Gamblers tried to fix the first series in 1903 (a player declined a $10,000 bribe), and rumors spread that the 1905, 1914, and 1917 contests were also fixed.[11] Modern scholarship has cast serious doubt on the integrity of the 1918 World Series won by the Boston Red Sox.[12] A close examination of the Chicago Cubs' curious play on the field and court testimony alleging that some Cubs players were on the take have heightened suspicions that Chicago let Boston win. The economic impact of World War I cut players' pay in half, and they faced the potential of being drafted after the season, creating an atmosphere ripe for them to jump at a last-chance pay day.

Low player salaries were a factor in the fixing of the following year's World Series, known as the Black Sox scandal. The series, in those days a best-of-nine arrangement, pitted the heavily favored Chicago White Sox against the Cincinnati Reds. White Sox players despised the tight-fisted ways of owner Charles Comiskey, who refused to discuss raising salaries even though the war had ended and fans flocked to Comiskey Park to cheer on their first-place team. Some players talked openly of going on strike, unheard of in an era when owners had near-absolute control over their players. They backed down, but the team's best pitcher, Eddie Cicotte, burned with fury at the mistreatment. The veteran racked up twenty-nine wins in the 1919 season on a $6,000 salary—a pittance compared to other players of his caliber.

Disgruntled first baseman Chick Gandil approached Cicotte about whether he'd be receptive to fixing the World Series. He demurred, but the difficulty of paying off his mortgage on his meager salary weighed on him. The aging pitcher buckled and said he would do it for $10,000. Gandil hurriedly collected other key players, including starting pitcher Claude "Lefty" Williams and outfielder Shoeless Joe Jackson, who ranked with Ty Cobb as the best hitter in baseball. They all made the same or less than Cicotte and leaped at the opportunity to instantly double or triple their annual pay. If the eight players followed through on the fix, gamblers in the know stood to make a killing. But first the players needed to be paid to ensure their compliance, and one man in the gambling world had the resources and boldness to pull it off: Arnold Rothstein.

Like his protégé Meyer Lansky, Rothstein had a mind for numbers at a young age and applied it to loansharking and gambling operations in New York's East Side. He built a bookmaking empire in New York and emerged as a leader in the city's Jewish mob. Despite his gangster ties, he styled himself as a refined gambler in the manner of Richard A. Canfield. Rothstein ran horses at Saratoga, opened a high-toned gambling club there in 1919, and cultivated relationships with politicians and police to protect his illegal enterprises.[13]

Rothstein, always a master at hedging his bets, perfected the "layoff" system of betting. Ideally, bookies want a balanced book—equal amounts of money bet on each side (or on each horse)—so that they won't be burned by any possible outcome. Bookies make money by charging a commission, called a vigorish or "vig." Achieving such a balance is difficult because of the inexact science of handicapping: weather conditions change, key players get hurt, upsets happen. Many bookies were just one damaging bet away from going broke. If too much money went to one side, bookies looked to other bookmakers to offset the bet to reduce risk. If they couldn't find the money to even out the scales, bookies would need to turn away customers.

Rothstein, nicknamed "The Brain" as well as "The Big Bankroll," agreed to take all layoff bets but at discounted odds, meaning that if a bookmaker had offered 3:1 odds, Rothstein would offer the bookie 5:2 odds.[14] Bookies were usually willing to accept his tough terms and layoff money rather than face possible ruin. Rothstein profited from the premiums he charged for layoff bets, and he coordinated a national bookmaking syndicate tied to his Manhattan headquarters.

Among those betting men was Joseph "Sport" Sullivan in Boston, who told Gandil that he would ask Rothstein to supply the bribe money to throw the 1919 World Series. Then began a series of double-crosses and clandestine money exchanges involving a network of gamblers and middlemen. At first Rothstein apparently turned down the scheme as unworkable but changed his mind and worked through intermediaries to finance the fix. Sullivan came through with a $10,000 down payment for the players, not the $80,000 in upfront cash they had demanded.[15] The $10,000 went to Cicotte, the opening-game starter who was adamant about receiving his whole share in advance. (He spent the night carefully sewing the bills into the lining of his coat.) Cicotte drilled a Reds batter square in the back with his second pitch of the game, a signal to gamblers that the fix was in. Cincinnati easily won the game thanks to Cicotte's poor effort.

Even though the players were angry about not being paid as promised, too much money had been wagered on the White Sox to lose for the eight players to back out. Before the eighth game of the World Series, Williams received an intimidating visit from a hitman supposedly hired at Rothstein's request. Williams was ordered to dump the next game to avoid a decisive ninth game or else "something is going to happen to you."[16] A rattled Williams surrendered four runs and retired only one batter in the first inning, picking up his third loss and allowing the Reds to clinch the World Series.

Doubts in the press about suspicious play on the field and persistent rumors of off-field chicanery persisted into the following season. An investigation by the American League concluded in September 1920 that the White Sox deliberately lost the World Series and that Rothstein was the man behind the fix. A grand jury in Chicago secured signed confessions from Cicotte and Jackson and heard testimony from Rothstein in which he pleaded his innocence and pinned the scheme on one of his go-betweens. The eight players and five gamblers—but not Rothstein—were indicted on conspiracy charges. Before the trial began the following year, the confessions and other grand jury evidence went missing. The players exercised their Fifth Amendment right to decline to answer questions about their earlier confessions. The thinness of the case led to acquittals all around. The courtroom erupted in cheers, and the players partied deep into the night.

They received a harsh reality check the next morning when newspapers carried a statement from Kenesaw Mountain Landis, the stern federal judge who owners had installed as baseball's first commissioner. Landis said: "Regardless of the verdict of juries, no player who throws a ball game, no player that undertakes or promises to throw a ball game, no player that sits in conference with a bunch of crooked players and gamblers where the ways and means of throwing a game are discussed and does not promptly tell his club about it, will ever play professional baseball."[17] He had the power to back up his declaration. Landis, a tightly wound man with the visage of an Old Testament prophet, possessed absolute authority to suspend or banish any players acting against what he believed to be the best interests of the game. Landis banned the eight players for life.

No one went to jail because of the Black Sox scandal, but its aftermath tainted all involved. Rothstein was never indicted, but his involvement was so obvious that he inspired the character Meyer Wolfshiem in F. Scott Fitzgerald's *The Great Gatsby*. In the 1925 novel, Jay Gatsby tells narrator Nick Carraway that Wolfshiem was the gambler who fixed the World Series in 1919. "It never occurred to me that one man could start to play with the faith of fifty million people—with the single-mindedness of a burglar blowing a safe," Carraway reflected to himself before asking Gatsby why Wolfshiem wasn't in jail. "They can't get him, old sport. He's a smart man," Gatsby replied.[18]

Rothstein was indeed smart enough to use interlocutors to contact the players, gather intelligence, place bets, and plausibly deny that he had any direct role in the scandal. The official record shows that Rothstein did not throw the 1919 World Series, but his crime-sullied reputation blocked him from his aspirations to join the upper echelons of society. Like many gangsters, Rothstein branched out into bootlegging during Prohibition in the 1920s. He was slain by an unknown gunman in 1928 not long after failing to pay $322,000 in losses in a marathon poker game.[19]

The "eight men out" saw their careers cut down in their prime. Jackson, an illiterate country boy, suffered perhaps the worst fate of them all, given his greatness on the field. Despite taking bribe money, he performed brilliantly in the World Series, hitting .375 with no errors in the field. Jackson had an outstanding 1920 season with the White Sox, but it would be his last in the major leagues. Jackson knocked around in semipro ball playing under assumed names and ran a liquor store in his native Greenville, South Carolina. Public appeals for his reinstatement went unheard. He died in 1951 as a baseball pariah. Jackson remains on baseball's permanently ineligible list and thus cannot be considered for induction into the Hall of Fame. Jackson's playing career was unquestionably Cooperstown-caliber: his .356 lifetime batting average trails only Cobb and Rogers Hornsby.

Baseball's vigorous response to the Black Sox scandal sent an unmistakable message to players that gambling on games was the sport's equivalent of a scarlet letter. Every team put up signs in their clubhouses admonishing players from betting and promising severe punishment for violators. The rule would be invoked seventy years later in a shattering scandal also involving a Hall of Fame–level talent.

———

The National Football League, which decades ago surpassed baseball as the true national pastime, has gambling encoded in its DNA. Many of the league's founding fathers were big-time bettors or connected to bookies and horse racing. Tim Mara, who worked as a runner for bookies as a youngster and later ran a successful bookmaking business at New York racetracks, paid a $500 franchise fee to found the New York Giants in 1925. (His descendants still retain ownership of the Giants, now valued at more than $2 billion.) Mara's close friend and fellow bookie Art Rooney bought the Pittsburgh Pirates in 1933 and changed the team's name to the Steelers in 1940. Rooney maintained his gambling habit as an NFL owner and reportedly won $256,000 in a two-day spree at racetracks that helped keep his team solvent.[20]

His friend Bert Bell also bought into the league in 1933, renaming his team the Philadelphia Eagles. Bell was born to great wealth but felt at ease in less refined settings. "He was just as comfortable with Alfred Vanderbilt as he was with Al Capone. Oh, sure, he knew Al Capone. He knew all the gamblers because he was a gambler himself at one time," said his son

Upton Bell.[21] Like Rooney, Bell had ties to Frank Erickson, head of the mob's gambling syndicate in the East Coast.[22]

Organized crime's tentacles reached so deep into bookmaking that practically any heavy bettor would at some point have a link to unsavory characters. Chicago businessman Charles Bidwell, a bookmaker connected to Capone associates, purchased the Chicago Cardinals in 1933. Bidwell owned Hawthorne Race Course near Chicago, dog racing tracks in Florida, and was president of a company that printed the programs and pari-mutuel tickets for racetracks. In Cleveland, Mickey McBride, a veteran of the bare-knuckled newspaper circulation wars and a major investor in the mob-controlled Continental Press Service race wire, founded the Browns in the newly formed All-America Football Conference in 1946. The Senate's Kefauver Committee questioned McBride and accused him of creating a national network that meant "the Capone affiliates and the Mafia are now in control of the distribution of racing wire news with a resultant source of enormous profits and power over bookmaking," according to the committee's final report.[23] McBride never faced formal criminal charges and maintained ownership of the Browns.

Bell ascended to the post of NFL commissioner in 1946 and immediately faced a serious gambling scandal tied to that season's championship game. The Giants and Bears were the top teams that year, and New York had defeated Chicago 14–0 during the season. But in the title game involving the same teams, the Bears were listed as ten-point favorites, raising suspicions of a fix.[24] Just before the game, New York mayor William O'Dwyer summoned Giants running back Merle Hapes and quarterback Frank Filchock for police interrogation. The mayor called Bell and informed him that Hapes admitted to consorting with a felon who attempted to bribe him. Hapes was suspended, but Filchock was allowed to play in the Giants' 24–14 loss. Filchock later confessed that gamblers approached him about throwing the game, and Bell suspended him as well even though neither player accepted bribe money.[25]

Just as baseball did in the wake of the Black Sox scandal, owners handed Bell strong powers to root out the threat that fixing posed to the sport. The

commissioner possessed the sole authority to suspend players or team officials for life if they were part of a fix or if they failed to pass along information about a conspiracy. After an internal investigation into the 1946 title
game, Hapes and Filchock were dealt indefinite suspensions, effectively
ending their NFL careers. "Professional football cannot continue to exist
unless it is based upon absolute honesty. The players must be not only
completely honest; they must be above suspicion," Bell said in 1947. "In
short, the game and its players must be kept free from corruption, from all
bribes and offers of bribes and from any possible 'fixing' of games."[26] The
admonition against gambling would be posted in every locker room in
the league. Bell also ordered teams to post a list of injured players well
before each game to avoid gamblers from profiting from inside information on last-minute roster changes.

The next prominent betting scandal to hit the NFL involved two Pro
Bowl–quality players and a young commissioner who used the case to
define his command of the league. In 1962 and 1963 the league hired a team
of former FBI agents to investigate rumors that some players were wagering on games and palling around with bookies. The inquiry focused on
Paul Hornung, the glamorous Green Bay Packers halfback, and Alex Karras, the hard-nosed Detroit Lions defensive tackle. Hornung befriended
Barney Shapiro, owner of a pinball and slot machine company and a former investor in a Las Vegas casino. Shapiro called Hornung every week
during the season to get the star's evaluation of the teams and recommen-
dations on how he should place his legal bets in Las Vegas. Then Hornung
asked Shapiro to bet for him on college and NFL games, often on the Packers but never against them.[27]

Hornung's actions put him squarely at odds against the antigambling
clause embedded in the NFL's standard player contract. Pete Rozelle, a
public relations specialist who was only thirty-three years old when owners selected him to succeed Bell as commissioner in 1960, accumulated
damning evidence that Hornung and Karras had broken the rules. Rozelle
secured a signed confession from Hornung that he had placed bets on NFL
games in the 1959, 1960, and 1961 regular seasons. In April 1963 Rozelle used

his powers as commissioner to place Hornung and Karras, who was also found to have gambled on NFL games, on indefinite suspension. Rozelle also fined several Lions players who had bet on the 1962 championship game. Hornung and Karras missed the entire 1963 season and were granted reinstatement the following year.

Rozelle picked up strong support from the press for taking decisive action against two of the league's most popular players. "Rozelle had to protect the game rather than the players," wrote *Los Angeles Times* columnist Jim Murray. "He had to show the owners, the players—and the public—that pro football was a big boy now, a public trust that the public could trust."[28]

Rozelle harnessed the boost in public confidence in the sport's integrity and the growing power of television to lead the NFL into an era of unprecedented prosperity. The rival American Football League agreed to have its champion meet the NFL's champion in the first AFL-NFL World Championship Game at the Los Angeles Memorial Coliseum on January 15, 1967. More than 50 million viewers watched the NFL's Packers rout the AFL's Kansas City Chiefs in what became known as the first Super Bowl. The leagues completed their merger by the start of the 1970 season, the same year ABC launched *Monday Night Football*, a ratings and cultural phenomenon.

The elevation of the NFL as America's preeminent sport owes much to gambling and the advent of the point spread, which was developed in the 1930s but didn't come into wide use until after World War II. The point spread has the same goal as the layoff betting system: to balance the books as evenly as possible to minimize risk for the bookie. Point spreads have proven to be more appealing to gamblers than the more rigid oddsmaking system in which a bettor wins only if his or her team wins. If a point-spread bettor wants to put money on a favored team, that team must win by a certain number of points for the bettor to win. That means a bettor on an underdog can win even if the team loses as long as the loss is narrow enough to be within the margin of the spread. If bargain-hunting bettors perceive the opening line of a game to be inaccurate, the point spread can shift according to the amount wagered on a particular team. For the business interests of the NFL and the networks, it has the important side effect of keeping fans interested in games long after the outcome is decided. They are watching the money as much as they are watching the play on the field.

Demetrios Georgios Synodinos, a celebrated handicapper and gambler better known as Jimmy "The Greek" Snyder, brought the tough-guy world of bookmaking into America's dens on NFL Sundays. Snyder made his mark as a bookie in Las Vegas in the 1950s. Snyder ran afoul of Attorney General Robert Kennedy's enforcement of the Wire Act when he was caught on a wiretap in Las Vegas discussing the odds on a college football game with an associate in Utah. Snyder was convicted of felony illegal interstate gambling charges, paid a $10,000 fine, served probation, and lost his "turf club" in Las Vegas. (He later received a presidential pardon from Gerald Ford.)

Snyder rehabilitated his image via a syndicated newspaper column on oddsmaking and positioned himself as a public relations expert, including a stint working for Howard Hughes. In 1976 Snyder landed a role as an analyst on CBS's *The NFL Today* preview show to offer his picks for the day's slate of games. Snyder looked the part of a neighborhood bookie, with his wavy gray hair, tinted glasses, gold chain dangling under his neck, and gruff manner. The NFL and the network's lawyers cautioned him against explicitly discussing point spreads or mentioning gambling, but his winking predictions of scores and inside dope on teams sent clear signals to gamblers in the know. By then point spreads were hardly a secret because betting lines were published every day in mainstream newspaper sports sections. Snyder's lucrative perch at CBS came to a sudden end in 1988 when he was fired after making racist statements about black athletes during an on-camera interview.

Snyder's prognostications on CBS came at a time when casino sportsbooks reemerged after decades in the shadows. One of the few legislative results of the Kefauver Committee's investigation into the mob and its control of gambling was the passage of a 10 percent federal excise tax

on sports wagers and a $50 annual "occupational stamp" for bookmak-
ers in 1951.[29] After a flurry of initial prosecutions against illegal bookies,
the underground industry continued on as it had before. In Nevada, the
only state where bookmaking was legal, the tax deterred casinos from running their own books because it exceeded their typical commission. Small,
unrefined "turf clubs" that did their best to sidestep the tax were the only
places to bet on sports in the state. It wasn't until 1974 when Sen. Howard
Cannon of Nevada successfully pushed to lower the tax to 2 percent that
legal bookmaking took off in Las Vegas. (The tax was cut even further to
0.25 percent for legal books in the early 1980s.)[30]

In 1975 the Union Plaza in downtown Las Vegas opened the city's first
casino sportsbook since the days of Bugsy Siegel and the Flamingo.[31]
Nationally respected oddsmaker Bob Martin was hired to manage the
book and set the Las Vegas betting line by blending tips from his network
of national contacts, voluminous consumption of sports pages, and intu-
ition. At the Stardust, Frank "Lefty" Rosenthal, a mob-connected convicted bookie, installed large-screen televisions and electronic odds boards
to appeal to hard-core bettors as well as casual sports fans.[32] The Las
Vegas Hilton spent $17 million to build its gigantic sportsbook, and rival
casinos like Caesars Palace and MGM tried to keep up by adding bigger
screens and comfortable seating to their books.[33]

On their own, sportsbooks aren't huge revenue-drivers for casinos. In
2015 about $4.2 billion was wagered on sports in Nevada, and the books
kept $232 million—a small figure compared to the win amounts counted
in the billions from slot machines and table games such as baccarat or
blackjack.[34] But a book on an exciting sports night will draw crowds that
might decide to stay for dinner and drinks, see a show, and gamble elsewhere in the casino. Hotels jack up room rates during major sports events
like NCAA's March Madness or a high-profile boxing match to accommodate fans and gamblers. In addition to the traditional point-spread wagers
on the game, casinos offer a dizzying buffet of proposition bets based on
individual performances and more esoteric matters such as whether a
football team will record a safety in the second quarter.

One of the most important days of the Las Vegas calendar is the Super Bowl. No single game each year is bet on more than the NFL title game, an unofficial American holiday complete with over-the-top house parties, halftime entertainment extravaganzas, and companies willing to pay $5 million to air thirty-second commercials. The top seven most-watched broadcasts in American television history are Super Bowls, according to Nielsen. The 2015 game between the Seattle Seahawks and the New England Patriots drew the biggest average audience: 114.4 million viewers. An impressive 71 percent of US homes with televisions in use were tuned into the game.

The Super Bowl is the ultimate example of the marriage of television and gambling that has fueled the NFL's popularity. It also exposes the great disconnect between what's legal and how people actually behave. In Nevada, gamblers bet $132.5 million at sportsbooks on Super Bowl 50 in 2016—a tiny fraction of the $4.1 billion wagered illegally across the nation, according to an estimate by the American Gaming Association.[35] There have been no reports of prosecutions of people who participate in office pools, make informal wagers with friends, or place bets with illegal bookies. If a technically illegal activity is so widely practiced with little threat of punishment, then why not sanction it and allow states to benefit from it as they have from other forms of gambling, advocates of legalization argue. However, making such a change will be far more difficult than legalizing lotteries or casinos.

———

Despite the best effort of commissioners to protect the integrity of their games, scandals have routinely popped up over the years: the suspension of Brooklyn Dodgers manager Leo Durocher for the 1947 season for associating with known gambling figures; the point-shaving scandals that rocked college basketball to its core in 1951; and quarterback Art Schlichter's suspension from the NFL for his compulsive gambling problems in the 1980s.

Sometimes skittish commissioners have been roused to action even when no betting or conspiracy to bet has taken place. When Willie Mays accepted a job as a "greeter" at Bally's casino in Atlantic City in 1979, MLB commissioner Bowie Kuhn declared that the retired Hall of Famer was barred from employment in baseball. "It has long been my view that such associations by people in our game are inconsistent with its best interests," Kuhn said.[36] Mays was deeply disappointed to see his coaching position with the New York Mets come to an end, but decided not to challenge Kuhn's authority.[37] Another legendary New York center fielder, Mickey Mantle, was exiled from the sport when he took on a similar glad-handing role at another Atlantic City casino. The ex-players were paid well for playing golf with big spenders, signing autographs for patrons, and entertaining casino clients at dinners. But neither was ever accused of illegal gambling or betting on baseball as a player or coach. Peter Ueberroth, Kuhn's successor, recognized the absurdity of the bans and swiftly reinstated Mantle and Mays in 1985.

That case was simple compared to what loomed at the end of the decade: the sport's worst gambling scandal since the 1919 World Series. Pete Rose, who picked up the nickname "Charlie Hustle" for his aggressive style of play, was winding down his illustrious career when the Reds reacquired the Cincinnati native in 1984 and named him player-manager. In 1985 Rose broke Ty Cobb's career record for base hits and retired after the following season, closing out a remarkable twenty-four-year playing career at age forty-five. Rose stayed on as manager and earned a thirty-day suspension and a fine for shoving an umpire while arguing a call during a game in 1988. National League president A. Bartlett Giamatti meted out the tough penalty, showing that he would not show leniency even to a popular figure like Rose.

Two people could hardly be more different than Rose, the rough-neck baseball lifer, and Giamatti, the worldly literature professor and former president of Yale University. For many years it was an open secret in baseball that Rose, like many athletes, loved to gamble. He indulged his thirst at racetracks and through bookies, leaving a trail of unpaid debts. Team executives were apparently aware of Rose's heavy betting habit as early as the 1970s but chose not to step in. Rose's gambling became so blatant that

Ueberroth ordered an investigation, hiring Washington attorney John Dowd to investigate whether Rose bet on baseball. In response to the Black Sox scandal, baseball had enacted a tough antigambling edict to its constitution. The portion of Major League Baseball Rule 21 relevant to Rose's case reads: "Any player, umpire, or club or league official or employee, who shall bet any sum whatsoever upon any baseball game in connection with which the bettor has a duty to perform shall be declared permanently ineligible."

On May 9, 1989, Dowd presented a report to Ueberroth's successor, Giamatti, strongly arguing that Rose had violated Rule 21 by betting on baseball in 1985, 1986, and 1987, including games involving his team. The report presented reams of testimony and evidence such as betting slips with Rose's handwriting and phone records gleaned from bookies, middlemen, drug dealers, and weight-lifting pals associated with Rose. One of Dowd's sources was Ron Peters, a bookmaker in Franklin, Ohio, who revealed that Rose placed bets directly with him. For its July 3, 1989, cover, *Sports Illustrated* overlaid a damning excerpt of Peters's testimony on a tight close-up photo of Rose:

Q: And when [Pete Rose] bet on baseball, did he bet on the Cincinnati Reds?

A: Yes, he did.

Q: And was this at a time that he was the manager of the Cincinnati Reds?

A: Yes, sir.

Q: Is there any doubt in your mind?

A: Absolutely not.[38]

The findings shocked Giamatti and stunned baseball fans who just four years earlier were applauding Rose for breaking Cobb's hallowed record. Rather than acting like Judge Landis and rendering an immediate punishment, Giamatti gave Rose a chance to answer the charges. Rose's lawyers proceeded to poke holes in the report, pointing out its reliance on circumstantial evidence and testimony from unreliable witnesses to support its claims that Rose bet on baseball.[39] They also argued that Giamatti

had shown his bias against Rose during the investigation, citing an unsolicited letter the commissioner wrote to the judge handling a drug case
involving Peters that praised the defendant for his helpfulness in the Rose
investigation.[40] Giamatti's letter angered the judge, who released it to
the public. Rose sued Giamatti over his conduct and asked for a delay in
his hearing. Rose continued to serve as Reds manager while the legal battle
dragged on through the summer.

With neither side wanting an open trial, the parties hashed out a settlement that satisfied no one. In a deal reached on August 23, 1989, Rose
agreed to be placed on baseball's permanently ineligible list in accordance
with Rule 21 but did not admit or deny that he bet on games. At a news
conference the following day, Giamatti went beyond the narrow scope of
the agreement and said he believed Rose did bet on games. Giamatti, a
chain smoker who showed signs of stress during his deposition, died of
a heart attack eight days later. Rose lost his job as manager and was invited
to apply for reinstatement in a year under the terms of the deal, but
by then he was serving a five-month prison sentence after pleading guilty
to two felony counts of income tax evasion.

After Rose's banishment, the National Baseball Hall of Fame board
of directors approved a rule in 1991 barring anyone on baseball's permanently ineligible list from consideration for the Hall of Fame. Rose's name
has never been listed on a Hall of Fame ballot despite his overwhelming
credentials. He is suspended in baseball purgatory along with Shoeless Joe
Jackson. Rose has since defiantly shown up during Hall of Fame induction
weekends in Cooperstown to sign autographs and pose for pictures with
fans at a memorabilia shop just down the street from baseball's shrine.

In many ways Rose has been his own worst enemy since his banishment.
An early, unqualified apology coupled with tangible proof of a reconfig-
ured life could have brought him back into baseball's good graces years
ago. Instead Rose has swung from issuing steadfast denials and claiming
unfair treatment to offering belated apologies for his conduct while main-
taining he never bet on the Reds to lose. Rose profits from his tragicomic
case by selling autographed baseballs with the inscription "I'm Sorry I Bet

on Baseball" for $299.99 each. (A version signed in gold pen on a black baseball goes for $399.99 on his retail website.)⁴¹ He signs autographs as often as six days a week at a high-end collectibles shop at Mandalay Place in Las Vegas, the city where he makes his home. Rose continues to play the ponies and bet on team sports, including baseball. Though such wagering is legal in Nevada, it creates a perception problem in the eyes of those deciding on his case. Rose's latest application for reinstatement, in 2015, was denied by new MLB commissioner Rob Manfred principally because Rose appears to lack "a mature understanding of his wrongful conduct, that he has accepted full responsibility for it, or that he understands the damage he has caused."⁴²

Over a quarter-century, Manfred and his predecessors have held firm on barring Rose from baseball despite his enduring popularity among fans. He remains the only living person on baseball's permanently ineligible list. "The Pete Rose case represents the larger issue of gambling's prevalence in America," said former MLB commissioner Fay Vincent, a close adviser to Giamatti during the Rose investigation and his immediate successor. "It is always out there and it is a real threat to professional sports, which tells you why a commissioner has to keep such a hard line against it."⁴³ The understandable concern that a player, coach, or referee can steer the course of a game to fit his or her betting interest has in turn influenced a federal law that severely restricts traditional sports gambling in the United States.

———

Protecting the integrity of athletic contests whether through drug testing or guarding against game fixing is of paramount concern to sports executives. Otherwise, the Super Bowl would be little different than WrestleMania—an entertaining but choreographed piece of theater. Congress has historically been reluctant to wade into gambling matters, though in 1964 lawmakers made it a federal crime to commit bribery in sports contests. After the searing experience of the Rose scandal, the climate was primed for Congress to further cement into law the leagues' opposition to gambling.

In 1991 Congress held hearings on a bill to prohibit states from legalizing sports gambling. League commissioners lined up behind the legislation. "Sports gambling threatens the character of team sports," said NFL commissioner Paul Tagliabue, according to the measure's legislative history. "With legalized sports gambling, our games instead will come to represent the fast buck, the quick fix, the desire to get something for nothing. The spread of legalized sports gambling would change forever—and for the worse—what our games stand for and the way they are perceived."[44] Vincent, then the baseball commissioner, argued that sanctioning sports gambling would create many new gamblers who will seek out "wagers with higher stakes and more serious consequences."[45]

The bill's final language included a "grandfather" clause for states that had some form of legal sports gambling between 1976 and 1990: Delaware, Montana, Nevada, and Oregon. Of the four, only Nevada boasted full-blown sportsbooks. Delaware launched a "football lottery" in the 1970s that was poorly received and abandoned; Montana permitted modest sports pools in bars with video gambling machines; and Oregon experimented with basketball and football lotteries.[46] None of the three states generated significant revenue from their limited forays into sports betting. The desultory track record of such state-sponsored schemes didn't stop legislators from acting as the guardians of the sanctity of athletic contests. Congress easily approved the Professional and Amateur Sports Protection Act, also known as PASPA or the "Bradley Act," and President George H. W. Bush signed it into law on October 28, 1992.[47]

The law slammed shut the possibility of legal sports gambling in forty-six states, but some restive governors chafed under what they perceived as federal overreach. Since 2009 New Jersey has waged a battle in the courts to overturn the ban. (The law had actually provided a timetable for New Jersey to authorize sports gambling because it already had legal casinos in Atlantic City, but state lawmakers failed to act before the window closed in the 1990s.) The state's voters approved a 2011 referendum permitting sports gambling at casinos and racetracks, and Gov. Chris Christie signed a bill allowing such betting by the fall of 2012.

The NCAA and the four major professional sports leagues—the NBA, NFL, MLB, and NHL—collectively sued New Jersey in federal court for trying to circumvent the 1992 law. Publicly, the leagues' commissioners presented a united front on the need to maintain integrity by keeping the gambling ban intact. But in depositions, the leaders sounded less convincing about the perils of sports gambling. The attorney representing New Jersey pressed NFL commissioner Roger Goodell about whether he was aware of any cases of gambling-related fixing during his thirty years with the league. "I can't think of a specific incident off the top of my head," he said in late 2012.[48] When NCAA president Mark Emmert was deposed, the opposing attorney asked him if he agreed with the logic that a potential fixer would prefer to work in an underground gambling environment than in a legal, regulated market. Emmert replied meekly, "I, I have no idea. I really don't."[49]

After losing in lower courts, New Jersey took its appeal to the US Supreme Court, which in June 2014 allowed the federal ban on sports gambling to remain. The state pressed ahead with a revised law and planned to open a sportsbook at Monmouth Park racetrack that fall, which was blocked by a federal judge. In August 2016 the Third US Circuit Court of Appeals ruled 10–2 in favor of the five sports organizations. New Jersey may well find support for its challenge during a gambling-friendly Donald Trump administration. New Jersey's messy legal fight could have national implications—or at minimum might inspire other states to mount similar challenges—but the controversy over the legality of fantasy sports has overtaken the debate over traditional sportsbooks.

———

The digital revolution that has upended so many industries has transformed sports gambling in unexpected ways. Online betting was considered to be illegal in the United States under the interpretation of the Wire Act, so bookmakers shifted their money to offshore websites. In the mid-1990s the twin-island nation of Antigua and Barbuda in the West Indies emerged as a leading clearinghouse for offshore sportsbooks.[50]

By 1998 more than two dozen online sportsbooks in Antigua accepted bets—some just for fun, some for real money—on all manner of contests. The websites pushed for American customers through aggressive advertising and promotions.

The websites claimed that they were legal businesses under Antiguan law, but in 1998 the US Department of Justice charged fourteen operators in the Caribbean with violating the Wire Act.[51] A few of the individuals were in the United States at the time and surrendered, but the rest were abroad and were safe from American prosecution as long as they stayed overseas. The federal government tried to choke off electronic bets by persuading banks and credit card companies not to accept such money transfers. Antigua went to the World Trade Organization to fight the incursion into its flourishing and legal sports betting business. Antigua won its case in 2004 and prevailed in subsequent appeals but has had difficulty collecting on its WTO-approved sanctions.

The federal government's disapproval of online gambling culminated with the 2006 Unlawful Internet Gambling Enforcement Act, which was primarily a response to the thriving online poker industry. The law prohibits the transfer of online payments relating to wagers on "a sporting event, or a game subject to chance." Importantly, it carved out an exemption for "any fantasy or simulation sports game or educational game or contest in which (if the game or contest involves a team or teams) no fantasy or simulation sports team is based on the current membership of an actual team that is a member of an amateur or professional sports organization."[52] The law requires that "all winning outcomes reflect the relative knowledge and skill of the participants" and are based on the accumulation of individual statistics in multiple games or events. A betting outcome cannot be based on the score or point spread or performance of a single real-world team.

That fateful exemption relied on a pre-Internet understanding of how fantasy sports operated. Traditionally, participants paid an entry fee to join a league and assembled teams by drafting players on current rosters. The league kept track of the teams' statistics as the season progressed, and team managers traded or released players if they got injured or performed poorly. At the end of the season, the manager of the top-scoring team received the bulk of the money in the pot plus bragging rights. Some leagues consisted of a handful of participants and modest winnings; others were larger with more at stake. All generally waited six months or whenever the season ended to pay out winnings.

Improvements in computer software eliminated the hassles of paper-and-pen statistical tabulations or setting up complicated spreadsheets. Fantasy league participants with home computers or smartphones suddenly had access to an avalanche of real-time news, video, and stats about players, giving them the knowledge to make well-informed decisions. The pace of fantasy leagues accelerated to weekly and even daily contests played for money, compressing a season into a single day. The fantasy sports industry caters to a young, male clientele who crave instant gratification and a daily adrenaline rush.

Here's how it works: Fantasy team managers assemble lineups composed of real-life players while staying under a salary cap. Each lineup accrues performance-based points, and the managers with the highest-scoring lineups receive immediate cash payouts. Fantasy participants can play head-to-head, in pools, or in tournaments. Professional football is by far the most popular fantasy sport, followed by professional basketball and baseball. Individual sports like NASCAR and golf are also part of a typical fantasy site's menu.

Proponents of fantasy sports insist that they are a game of skill, a crucial distinction because games of chance are generally considered to be gambling. Fantasy also manages to sidestep traditional sports gambling because the lineups consist of a blend of players from many real-life teams, not just a single team. Critics point out that traditional sports betting is also based on knowledge of the teams and of individual players and how their strengths and weaknesses stack up against a designated opponent. Sports contests are inherently unpredictable. A random piece of bad luck like having your team's quarterback knocked out of a game or a poor outing from a Cy Young Award–winning starting pitcher can afflict a fantasy lineup just as much as it can hurt a point-spread bettor.

Well-established companies like Yahoo that had hosted season-long fantasy sports for more than a decade have jumped into daily and weekly fantasy games played for money. Tens of millions of users play Yahoo Fantasy Sports for free, so the company is trying to entice them to pay entry fees for a chance to win large cash prize pools. In 2015 industry expert Eilers Research estimated that companies collected $2.6 billion in daily fantasy entry fees and expects that figure to soar to $14.4 billion in 2020, with mobile apps expected to power much of that growth.[53] More than 57 million people in the United States and Canada played fantasy sports in 2016, double the number who participated just seven years before, according to industry group Fantasy Sports Trade Association.

FanDuel and DraftKings emerged as the dominant players in the daily fantasy sports arena. The upstart companies control more than 90 percent of the market and assiduously court teams and leagues to prove their legitimacy. New York–based FanDuel, founded in 2009 and the market leader, counts the NBA as among its investors and signed advertising deals with dozens of NBA and NFL teams. DraftKings, a Boston-based company founded in 2012, has received investment money from MLB, the NHL, and Major League Soccer. Individual MLB teams have sponsorship deals with DraftKings, and the company's logo is plastered in ballparks across the league. New England Patriots owner Robert Kraft and Dallas Cowboys owner Jerry Jones have equity stakes in DraftKings.

The sites are always careful to say they are American-based companies and are not "gambling" enterprises and thus fully legal. (Real-money fantasy sports is illegal in only five states: Arizona, Iowa, Louisiana, Montana, and Washington.) However, DraftKings has blurred the line with its partnership with the World Series of Poker. Top fantasy sports players are given an opportunity to win a seat at the tournament's main event, an activity that is indisputably gambling under current law.

Fantasy sports companies are also cozy with broadcasting networks: DraftKings counts 21st Century Fox as among its investors and had an exclusive marketing agreement with ESPN that has since been severed, and NBC Sports and parent company Comcast own stakes in FanDuel.

Networks and leagues know participants in fantasy sports are among the most passionate viewers of live events, so they want to do all they can to encourage the connections. In the run-up to the 2015 NFL season, Draft-Kings and FanDuel unleashed an extraordinary advertising blitz. During a three-week stretch, their ads appeared every ninety seconds on national networks, outspending pizza chains and beer companies.[54]

The hundreds of millions of dollars the companies spent on TV ads had the desired effect of driving tens of thousands of new signups every day but they were also disturbing to those unaware that million-dollar prizes could be won by playing fantasy sports. Although the websites cling to the notion that their games are "for entertainment purposes only," their ads resemble a state lottery's classic "low risk, big reward" pitch. A 2015 FanDuel ad features player "Scott H." who claimed he "deposited a total of thirty-five dollars on FanDuel and won over $2 million." The clear message was that you too can be a winner, but only if you get in the game. The ads promote contests with entry fees of just a dollar or two and try to hook sports fans with promo codes and deals to match their initial deposits up to a certain amount. FanDuel's 2015 fantasy football championship offered a $12 million purse with the overall winner's share $3 million. For context, those amounts exceed the prizes offered at the US Open, golf's national championship.

Of course, for every million-dollar winner there are always many more losers. Success in high-volume daily fantasy relies entirely on analytics, not on gut instincts or sentimentalism for your hometown team or favorite player. The reputation of daily fantasy sports has been sullied by the reality that a tiny percentage of elite players win all the big prizes. Full-time fantasy participants enter hundreds of lineups each week of the NFL season, and the very top fantasy players do it as a full-time job. A *Wall Street Journal* article in 2014 explained how Notre Dame business graduate student Cory Albertson got rich playing fantasy sports.[55] The former professional poker player devised a complex algorithm that crunches players' statistical data and accounts for factors such as injury reports and weather patterns in each city and stadium to select the optimal lineup for a specific game.

On a single NFL weekend, he won $100,000. "It is like securities trading and athletes are the commodities," he said.[56]

Leveraging inside access to sports information in daily fantasy is akin to engaging in insider trading on Wall Street. In October 2015, the industry was rocked by allegations that a DraftKings employee mistakenly released crucial ownership data before the third week of the NFL season. The proprietary information revealed which players were the most heavily used in lineups for the upcoming slate of games. That same week he won $350,000 on FanDuel. Both companies issued statements to reassure the public about the integrity of their contests and banned employees from playing daily fantasy on any site. (Previously employees were prohibited from playing only on their own site.) The employee was cleared of any wrongdoing.

For some states, fantasy sports' lavish spending on TV commercials, gigantic jackpots, and the apparent lack of internal controls raised uncomfortable parallels to the online poker boom. Authorities worried that consumers lacked adequate protections in the fast-growing, unregulated market. The FBI, New York state, and a Florida grand jury launched inquiries into allegations of the unfair use of inside information at FanDuel and DraftKings, and other politicians wondered if the sites were pushing too far into the realm of illegal gambling. Rep. Frank Pallone Jr., a New Jersey Democrat, pressed for a hearing on the issue. "I really think if they had to justify themselves at a hearing, they wouldn't be able to," said Pallone, a backer of legalized sports betting in his home state.[57]

Soon after the DraftKings scandal broke, Nevada regulators ruled that fantasy sports should be treated as gambling and ordered fantasy sites to stop operating in the state unless they secured gaming licenses. Attorneys general in states like Illinois and Texas have issued opinions that daily fantasy sports are not games of skill and thus violate state gambling laws. In November 2015 New York state attorney general Eric Schneiderman ordered DraftKings and FanDuel to stop taking bets in the state, calling them the "leaders of a massive, multibillion-dollar scheme intended to evade the law and fleece sports fans across the country."[58] In his cease-and-desist letters, Schneiderman said the department's investigation found that the top 1 percent of the sites' winners receive the vast majority of the winnings. These high-volume gamblers feast on new entrants who face a huge competitive disadvantage, he said. In response, the companies sued Schneiderman.

The parties in the legal standoff in New York agreed to give lawmakers a chance to draft a daily fantasy legalization bill, which Gov. Andrew Cuomo signed in August 2016. Fantasy sports companies must register with the New York State Gaming Commission, operate under its rules, and pay an annual $50,000 fee and a 15 percent tax on revenue. "Daily fantasy sports have proven to be popular in New York, but until now have operated with no supervision and no protections for players," Cuomo said in a statement. "This legislation strikes the right balance that allows this activity to continue with oversight from state regulators, new customer protections, and more funding for education."[59]

New York was only the eighth state to legalize and regulate fantasy sports—a small number that the industry will need to boost if it is to survive. The valuations of DraftKings and FanDuel have been slashed and neither one is profitable. In late 2016 the companies announced plans to merge. A dozen or so other states are considering legislation to regulate fantasy sports by mandating stringent age-verification procedures, adding more beginners-only pools, and requiring disclosures in the companies' ads. Fantasy sports companies will be fighting an expensive, state-by-state war of attrition to save their business through a patchwork of regulations.

A series of investigative reports by the *New York Times* and PBS's *Frontline* in 2015 and 2016 focused on fantasy sports, arguing that they had evolved into an industry not envisioned in the 2006 Unlawful Internet Gambling Enforcement Act. Daily fantasy has clearly tilted closer to a game of chance than a game of skill. The reporting also exposed the law's utter ineffectiveness in its aim to stop online gambling. The stories concluded that "the industry thrives not on online payments but on an old-fashioned shadow banking system where billions of dollars pass through paper bags, car trunks, casino chips and various money-laundering schemes."[60]

Offshore sites were found to use servers in the United States and foreign networks that regulators were unable to trace.

As for sports leagues, the emergence of daily fantasy has complicated their traditional stance against gambling. For years the NFL has played regular-season games in London, in a country where legal sports betting is ingrained in the culture. The league signed a deal with DraftKings allowing the fantasy site to plaster its logo inside Wembley Stadium, where the games are played. (Tellingly, DraftKings needed a gambling license to operate in the United Kingdom.) Goodell doesn't view fantasy sports to be gambling, admitting on ESPN's *Mike and Mike* program in April 2016 that "all of us have evolved a little bit on gambling." Now nearly every NFL team has a sponsorship deal with a daily fantasy site. The NHL broke a longstanding taboo in June 2016 by approving an expansion franchise for Las Vegas, the largest US city without a team from one of the four major sports leagues. The Oakland Raiders, a perpetual relocation threat, received approval from NFL owners in 2017 to move to Las Vegas where the team will play in a domed stadium to be built near the Strip.

Data is king in the digital world, and leagues have formed alliances with gambling-related companies to stay at the leading edge of technology. The NFL has an ownership stake in Sportradar US, the subsidiary of a Swiss company that provides real-time statistics to offshore books that offer illegal gambling to the US audience. Three NBA owners, including Michael Jordan of the Charlotte Hornets, are investors in Sportradar US, which distributes NFL data to FanDuel. With an eye at detecting suspicious activity that could suggest a fixed game, the NBA and MLB have signed agreements with data tracking companies that analyze fantasy sports and betting lines.

Under the leadership of Commissioner Adam Silver, the NBA is now the league most receptive to daily fantasy and even legalized gambling. On November 12, 2014, the league announced a deal with FanDuel to make it the NBA's official fantasy partner. In addition, the league acquired a small financial stake in the company under Silver's theory that the NBA is "much better off being inside the tent than outside the tent" when it comes to daily fantasy sports.[61] The next day the *New York Times* published an op-ed piece by Silver in which he called on Congress to set up a "federal framework that allows states to authorize betting on professional sports, subject to strict regulatory requirements and technological safeguards." He concluded: "I believe that sports betting should be brought out of the underground and into the sunlight where it can be appropriately monitored and regulated."[62] The sentiment was strikingly pragmatic for a sports commissioner, especially from a league that weathered an embarrassing betting scandal involving referee Tim Donaghy in 2007.

Enforcing blanket bans on sports gambling has always been a difficult task, but now it's nearly impossible in our borderless online world. Silver's point is that federal and state governments are better off accepting the reality of gambling by regulating it and taxing it to choke off organized crime and uncover fixing schemes. Sports leagues are benefiting through sponsorship deals with fantasy companies and higher TV ratings fueled by fantasy players and traditional bettors. The iron triangle of sports leagues, TV networks, and gambling is likely to strengthen as governments figure out how to address daily fantasy and sports betting.

The history of gambling in America lays bare the pitfalls of unregulated markets: street gangs and the numbers rackets, organized crime and illegal casinos, offshore websites and online poker. Prohibiting gambling only drives it deeper underground and fosters official corruption and rank hypocrisy. Where states have gotten into trouble is in losing sight of their primary responsibilities of stamping out fraud and protecting consumers and instead looking at gambling primarily as a revenue source. Once they get used to the additional money and build it into their public education or general fund budgets, governors usually push for more. That leads to more casinos, more slot machines, higher betting limits, bigger lottery jackpots, and oversaturated markets. It also has the worrying side effect of putting gambling within easier reach of people vulnerable to addiction.

Double or Nothing

STATES NEGLECT THE HUMAN COST OF PROBLEM GAMBLING

Even on my way to the gambling hall, as soon as I hear, two rooms away, the clink of the scattered money I almost go into convulsions.
—Fyodor Dostoyevsky, *The Gambler*

Governors' vested interest in expanding gambling revenue means they need to encourage people to lose more money and tempt the vulnerable who shouldn't gamble at all. To boost gambling proceeds year after year, states mount flashy advertising campaigns to promote their lotteries, raise the price of scratch-off lottery tickets, relax casinos' betting and loss limits, approve more kinds of table games and more slot machines, and push novel forms of betting. Although legalized gambling is pervasive and widely accepted, it is clearly not just like any other business. The perception persists among many that gambling is a vice, and it is heavily regulated and taxed like other potentially harmful products. States impose "sin" taxes on such things as tobacco, alcohol, and even sugary drinks, but governments do not encourage people to smoke more or drink more as ways to drive up revenue. Quite the opposite: punitive excise taxes are intended to reduce the usage of those items in the interest of public health.

Modern-day casinos resemble malls with their shopping arcades and gourmet restaurants, with gambling portrayed as a similarly benign, easily consumed commodity. But casinos are engineered to be ruthlessly efficient at extracting money from customers. Slot machines' whimsical animation, flashing lights, and sounds are signals designed to keep players riveted. Slots are plastered with trusted brand names like *Wheel of Fortune* and *Monopoly* and use images of celebrities like Elvis Presley and Michael Jackson to create an environment of chummy familiarity.

Advancements in slot machine technology have made gambling as frictionless as possible. Players who once lugged around plastic cups filled with quarters now insert special "players reward" cards and bar-coded cashless voucher slips into terminals that operate with a push of a button instead of the pull of a handle. Change machines automatically break bills and cash out tickets, eliminating the need to wait in line for a cashier. High-fee ATMs inside casinos provide easy access to cash for those who want to keep up a fast pace of play. Video poker gamblers can play a hand every three to four seconds, or up to 1,200 hands an hour.[1] In 2013 former San Diego mayor Maureen O'Connor admitted to taking more than $2 million from her wealthy late husband's charity to feed her gambling addiction. O'Connor claimed her brain tumor partly influenced her to squander a fortune on video poker, which she called "electronic heroin."[2] O'Connor made more than $1 billion in bets at casinos over the course of a decade, with net losses totaling about $13 million.[3]

People with gambling problems find help in groups like Gamblers Anonymous, which was founded in Los Angeles in 1957 and follows a twelve-step program similar to Alcoholics Anonymous. At a Gamblers Anonymous meeting observed by the author in suburban San Diego, about two dozen recovering problem gamblers shared stories about how their addiction wrecked relationships and drained bank accounts. A few said they contemplated suicide when they bottomed out. They discussed how their lives revolved around gambling—the next hand of blackjack, the next horse race, the next pull of the slot machine—and how freely they lied to their spouses and coworkers to cover up their whereabouts and expenditures.

They also applauded attendees who reached milestones ranging from ninety days to more than ten years and celebrated with slices of sheet cake and words of encouragement. For them, recovering from problem gambling is a lifelong journey made easier in the fellowship of others who

understand their pain. The small yellow booklet read aloud at the beginning of the meeting contains these stark words: "The idea that somehow,
someday, we will control our gambling is the great obsession of every
compulsive gambler. The persistence of this illusion is astonishing. Many
pursue it into the gates of prison, insanity, or death."

Compulsive or pathological gambling is a relatively recently recognized psychiatric illness. Nearly a century ago, Sigmund Freud analyzed
Russian author Fyodor Dostoyevsky's writings on his gambling problem
and concluded it was a form of self-punishment rooted in an unresolved
Oedipal complex and masturbatory urges.[4] In the 1950s psychoanalyst
Edmund Bergler viewed excessive gambling as "a uniquely convenient way
of expressing childish megalomania" but urged addressing it with medical
therapy, not moral contempt.[5]

It wasn't until 1980 when "pathological gambling" was listed for the
first time in the American Psychiatric Association's *Diagnostic and Statistical Manual of Mental Disorders*. It is characterized by a patient's lack
of control over or a dependence on gambling and the harm that results
from it. A few years earlier a federal government panel reviewing gambling
policy estimated that there were 1.1 million compulsive gamblers in the
United States and another 3.3 million people with the potential to fall in
that category.[6]

Groups like Gamblers Anonymous pressed for inpatient treatment programs and educated the public about the poorly understood issue, lik-
ening it to an addiction to drugs or alcohol. States were slow to realize
that they were being confronted with a widening public health problem.
In 1978 Maryland approved a bill to fund a treatment program at Johns
Hopkins Hospital for pathological gamblers. Maryland, which then had
a state lottery and racetrack betting, "has an obligation to provide a program of treatment for those persons who become addicted to gambling to
the extent that it seriously disrupts lives and families."[7]

The most recent edition of the American Psychiatric Association's
manual, published in 2013, classified the illness as "gambling disorder"
and for the first time listed it under the banner of addictive disorders.

Advocates tend to use "problem gambling," a term covering a wider range of behaviors than "pathological gambling," which is reserved for more severe, debilitating cases.

Advocates today estimate that 2.2 percent of American adults, or more than 5 million people, are problem gamblers. Keith Whyte, executive director of the National Council on Problem Gambling, cautioned in a 2016 interview with the author that such estimates rely on state studies and don't measure the severity of cases or the rate of relapses. There are no national surveys conducted on the issue, for instance. "This is a disease with deep roots in our biology and psychology—it's very complex," he said. "If you expand gambling, you will increase gambling problems."[8]

The proximity of casinos appears to correlate with problem gambling rates. A survey for the National Gambling Impact Study Commission reported that people within a fifty-mile radius of a casino were more than twice as likely to be pathological gamblers than those outside that zone. "I stopped going to Las Vegas, but then Las Vegas came to Maryland," lamented a woman in the Baltimore area trying to kick her gambling addiction.[9]

Dr. Richard J. Rosenthal, clinical professor of psychiatry and codirector of the UCLA Gambling Studies Program, said in an interview that this greater accessibility is crucial given that problem gambling is an impulse disorder. Early on in his long career treating problem gamblers, Rosenthal said his patients were mostly middle-aged men involved in slower-burn forms of gambling like horse playing or sports wagering. With the expansion of slot machines, he is noticing women as well as men getting into trouble, and much more quickly. They are also less likely to stick with treatment programs. The digital revolution has further accelerated the progression of problem gambling in patients, he said. "Now you're walking around with a casino in your pocket," he said. "Our culture is so fixated on distraction."[10]

The convenience of online gambling presents a major challenge for groups trying to combat problem gambling. Youngsters who grew up on immersive video games and mobile apps like Candy Crush are susceptible to gaming sites that mimic the playful spirit of social media. Some sites let users play for free to get them accustomed to the rhythms of the game and then bait them into entering their credit card information. Like the old-time slot machines that skirted regulators by offering nonmonetary prizes, other sites convert real-money bets into virtual coins that can't be cashed out.

The rise of the high-speed daily fantasy sports industry that targets young, risk-taking men is also uncharted territory for advocates. The *New York Times* profiled Joshua Adams in 2015, a man in his thirties who lost $20,000 playing daily fantasy and contemplated suicide.[11] He went to rehab for nearly a month and attended Gamblers Anonymous meetings to break his addiction. "I wish I never would have gotten back into playing fantasy sports, because for me, and I think for compulsive gamblers, it leads us right back into a destructive state," he said.[12] Adams believes daily fantasy sites are dishonestly claiming that their games are not gambling.

States feel a vague sense of responsibility to address this negative effect of expanded gambling, but their muted response indicates that they see it as an acceptable social cost. Thirty-nine states provided a total of $60.6 million in public funding for problem gambling services in 2013.[13] But those programs are vulnerable to cuts in states like Florida, which slashed funding by 90 percent for a nonprofit group that coordinates treatment for pathological gamblers. In Pennsylvania, the state sent $17.5 million to its Problem Gambling Treatment Fund between 2007 and 2012, a pittance compared to the $2.3 billion in gambling revenue received in 2010 alone.[14]

Other states are even more stingy in funding problem gambling treatment programs. Arkansas, which has a lottery, casinos, and pari-mutuel wagering, gave only $200,000 to problem gambling services in 2013.[15] Georgia's lottery also allocates $200,000; in 2013 the whole sum was spent on a contract with the University of Georgia for developing an online certification course to train counselors.[16] There were no helplines or treatment programs to fund. Eleven states, including Kentucky and Texas, spent zero money on problem gambling services.

Advocates like Whyte strongly believe such states are shirking their duty to protect the public health of its residents. "If you legalize gambling, you have a higher responsibility to take some of the proceeds and fund treatment programs," said the official with the National Council on Problem Gambling. "If you are literally running your own gambling monopoly, you have an even greater obligation to address problem gambling," he said, referring to state-run lotteries.[17] Whyte says even states with little to no legalized gambling have a responsibility to fund programs for problem gambling as they do for other medical diseases. Too often, he said, lawmakers are indifferent to problem gambling and see it as a moral failing, not a matter of protecting public health. His group recommends that states with gambling should earmark 1 percent of that revenue to treatment and prevention programs.

Rosenthal, the psychiatrist who created California's first inpatient gambling treatment program in 1990, also believes that states are not doing enough. Government funding for gambling services is a tiny fraction of what's spent on drug and alcohol treatment programs, and no federal agency provides funding for gambling research. In fact, the only way to get such funding is to combine it with drug and alcohol research, he said. "I think that the fact that there's not a substance involved has made it more difficult" for problem gambling to secure an equivalent level of financial backing, he said.[18]

In many states, the tepid support for treatment and counseling programs is not keeping pace with demand for the services. When Ohio voters weighed in on a 2009 ballot proposal to legalize full-blown urban casinos, the state promoted the projected economic benefits but did not estimate the potential social cost of creating new gambling addicts.[19] Two percent of tax revenue from casinos goes to problem gambling programs, which experienced a surge in traffic once the casinos started opening. In 2013 the first year all four casinos were in operation, 682 individuals were treated for gambling problems, and 14,355 received screening after showing warning signs, according to Ohio Department of Mental Health and

Addiction Services statistics.[20] In the previous three years combined, 184 people were treated and 5,898 were screened.[21]

Maryland is among the most densely packed casino markets, with six openings since 2010, but lawmakers did little to prepare for the fallout from high-volume gambling. Casino operators pay $425 per slot machine and $500 per table game each year into a state-administered fund to address problem gambling. In fiscal year ending June 30, 2015, that amounted to about $4 million—less than half of 1 percent of the casinos' annual revenue, according to a *Washington Post* calculation.[22] The money pays for programs such as a confidential toll-free help line and a voluntary exclusion list, both of which have seen increased demand. Unlike many other states, Maryland does not offer free counseling services.

In Iowa, lawmakers enacted a self-exclusion program for people in treatment for problem gambling. He or she signs a waiver agreeing to never gamble at a casino in the state. If the patron fails to follow the ban, the casino industry is released from any liability, meaning the casinos can keep any losses.[23] Terry Branstad, who was governor when Iowa legalized riverboat casinos in 1989, said in an interview in 2016 that he insisted from the start that a portion of casino money needed to fund gambling addiction services. "I think there's a big responsibility, especially if the state is in the business," said Branstad, who served as governor from 1983 to 1999 and returned to the office in 2011. "It's important to do what we can to help people who have gambling addictions."[24] He said he does not feel pressure to increase Iowa's revenue from the lottery and casinos, saying that he's never promoted gambling as a moneymaker for the state. "My focus is on economic development and bringing good jobs to Iowa, and I've seen the gaming industry play a role in helping with tourism, especially on our borders," he said.[25]

Neighboring Missouri also has a program in which thousands of people have voluntarily excluded themselves for life from the state's riverboat casinos. The compulsive gamblers are subject to arrest on a trespassing charge if they are discovered in one. Letters poured in to the

Missouri Gaming Commission pleading in vain to keep the lifetime ban. "My brother is a self-exiled bettor who lost everything he had at the casinos," one letter read. "Now you people are considering dangling a carrot in front [of] his nose."[26] In 2011 the state changed the rule and allowed the blacklisted gamblers to apply for re-entry after only five years. Critics called it a cynical maneuver by a cash-strapped state to exploit the biggest-spending casino customers.

Too often states are overly dependent on gambling revenue to scale back in consideration for those who are harmed. A city or town here and there may be successful in blocking a planned casino because of traffic or environmental reasons, but antigambling forces know that the war has long been lost. Casinos are here to stay, as are the lotteries. Online and sports betting will proceed as the barriers to legalization fall. Government watchdogs must question governors' rosy claims of gambling's economic salvation and hold politicians accountable for broken promises. Advocates need to redouble their efforts to ease the worst effects of omnipresent gambling. No one should expect much help from states because they have too much on the line to be dispassionate brokers. They, too, are hooked on gambling.

Acknowledgments

Researching a book of this scope would have been impossible without having unfettered access to the expansive holdings of the San Diego County and City of San Diego library systems. With a free library card, independent scholars and everyday readers also have broad access to the treasures within the region's college and university libraries. Hundreds of books and journals requested via computer magically appeared within days at my local branch library. For noncirculating materials, I received friendly guidance from librarians during my multiple visits to San Diego State University's Love Library and the University of California San Diego's Geisel Library, especially its Mandeville Special Collections Library.

During the six years I spent researching and writing this book, I had the good fortune to visit archival collections relating to gambling history. At the National Museum of Racing and Hall of Fame in Saratoga Springs, New York, historian Allan Carter guided me through the thick research files and rare books housed at the museum's John A. Morris Research Library. I enjoyed many productive hours at the Center for Gaming Research inside the Lied Library at the University of Nevada Las Vegas. Dr. David G. Schwartz, an author of several excellent books on the subject, is the director of the impressive center fittingly set in the heart of America's gambling capital. The staff members there responded with unfailing professionalism and good humor to my many requests. Many thanks to Special Collections, University of Nevada, Reno Libraries and

the Center on the American Governor at Rutgers University for granting me permission to use quotations from their outstanding oral history
interviews with important figures in gambling history.

I'm deeply appreciative to Terry Branstad, Pat Mahony, Dr. Richard J.
Rosenthal, and Keith Whyte for agreeing to be interviewed for this book
and for sharing their expertise with me. I also thank the handful of other
sources who chose to speak with me on background. My approach was
always to bring a journalist's sense of dispassion and a scholar's scrupulous
attention to detail to an often emotional and misunderstood topic.

I'm thankful to have found Anne G. Devlin of the Max Gartenberg Literary Agency, who believed in this book from practically our first email
exchange. She found a good home for it at Rutgers University Press. Marlie
Wasserman, the now-retired director of the press, championed the book,
as has her successor, Micah Kleit. I'm grateful to the press for taking a
chance on a first-time author. I also appreciate all of the employees there
for the care they brought to every stage of the project, particularly Elisa-
beth Maselli.

I benefited from the generosity of time and spirit of several people who
read early drafts of the manuscript. Mark Clary, Sheila Dougherty, and
David Franecki offered helpful comments and suggestions early on when
I needed it most. Marcia Rubin graciously edited sections more than once
and always brought her sharp eye and enthusiasm to the task. David Kamper, a professor in San Diego State University's American Indian Studies Department, read the chapter on tribal gaming and helped clarify my
thinking on the issue's legal and historical complexities. I thank Jay Posner,
sports editor at the *San Diego Union-Tribune*, for reviewing the chapter on
sports gambling.

Author Elizabeth Eulberg was the best possible resource and sound-
ing board for a newcomer to the world of book publishing. Author and
journalism instructor Kara Platoni helped with practical advice on how
to build an audience. Patrick Sammon went out of his way to provide
me with publishing contacts early on. Rachel Moore and Laura Redford
kept me honest about staying on task in the beginning stages and offered

well-timed words of encouragement. And at the *San Diego Union-Tribune*, managing editor Lora Cicalo provided unstinting support as I embarked on this project.

When people found out I was writing a book about gambling, I would jokingly add that it wasn't going to be a "how-to" manual. Though I'm not much use at the gaming tables, I've long been fascinated by the drama in casinos and other betting arenas. I have my parents, Donna and Hal Clary, to thank for kindling my interest in games of chance by taking me to race-tracks in New York state as a youngster and then to Las Vegas at age fifteen. My late father got a kick out of the craziness of Las Vegas and stored up a trove of stories gathered from his frequent visits that he never tired of sharing. I dearly wish he had been able to offer his suggestions on the book and read the finished product.

Finally, words fail me when I think of the sacrifices my wife, Jackie Clary, has made to allow me the time and space to write this book. On top of that, Jackie has been my biggest supporter and most incisive editor. With the bluntness one finds only in a truly honest marriage, she was unafraid to scrawl the word "boring" in the margins of slow-moving passages of prose. She was right, of course. Jackie and our children, Sammy and Elliott, are the lights of my life. To paraphrase an old R.E.M. song, they are my everything.

Notes

PROLOGUE

Epigraph from Christie's remarks on July 21, 2010. "Gov. Christie Pledges to Turn Atlantic City Casino District into 'Las Vegas East,'" *Newark Star-Ledger*, July 22, 2010.

1. Atlantic City casino statistics reported by David G. Schwartz, *Atlantic City Gaming Revenue: Statistics for Casino, Slot, and Table Win, 1978–2013* (Las Vegas: Center for Gaming Research, University Libraries, University of Nevada Las Vegas, 2014), http://gaming.unlv.edu/reports/ac_hist.pdf.

2. Ronda Kaysen, "Aided by New Jersey, Luxury Casino Nears Completion," *New York Times*, January 4, 2012.

3. David A. Fahrenthold, "Atlantic City's Mr. Fix-It," *Washington Post*, January 25, 2016.

4. Kaysen, "Aided by New Jersey."

5. Erin Carlyle, "Revel Without a Cause: The Spectacular Fall of Atlantic City's Biggest Casino," *Forbes*, December 1, 2014.

6. Christie at a March 28, 2012, news conference at Revel, https://www.youtube.com/watch?v=hfOgeAst65I.

7. Kaysen, "Aided by New Jersey."

8. The Revel brand became further tainted in 2014 with the release of a surveillance video showing NFL star Ray Rice assaulting his then-fiancée in a casino elevator.

9. *The World Count of Gaming Machines 2013*, report for the Gaming Technologies Association, March 2014, 7, http://www.gamingta.com/pdf/world_count_2014.pdf.

10. *When Gaming Grows, America Gains: How Gaming Benefits America*, 2014 report for the American Gaming Association, http://www.gettoknowgaming.org/sites/default/files/AGA_EI_Report_FINAL.pdf, 4.

11. The revenue figure includes such things as income taxes and Social Security taxes. Ibid., 3–5.

CHAPTER 1 — THE SPORT OF KINGS

Epigraph from Gardiner, *Canfield*, 291.

1. Bouyea, "Saratoga's Longest Shot," 13.

2. Asbury, *Sucker's Progress*, 363.

3. DeArment, *Knights of the Green Cloth*, 39–40.

4. Ibid., 40.

5. The film was based on the 1928 book *The Gangs of New York* by Herbert Asbury, the bard of the urban underworld.

6. Asbury, *Sucker's Progress*, 373.

7. Joe Drape, "At Saratoga, the People Are as Big a Draw as the Horses," *New York Times*, July 19, 2013.

8. Breen, "Horses and Gentlemen," 252.

9. Longrigg, *History of Horse Racing*, 105.

10. National Institute of Law Enforcement and Criminal Justice and Cornell University Law School, *The Development of the Law of Gambling: 1776–1976* (Washington, DC: Government Printing Office, 1977), 55.

11. Robertson, *History of Thoroughbred Racing*, 8.

12. Longrigg, *History of Horse Racing*, 223. The names of these financiers have long endured in history: Belmont's son built Belmont Park in Elmont, New York, home of the final leg of thoroughbred racing's Triple Crown; the Travers Stakes remains the highlight of the summer racing season at Saratoga Race Course; and one of Jerome's daughters married Lord Randolph Churchill and gave birth to a boy they named Winston.

13. Ibid.

14. Chafetz, *Play the Devil*, 285.

15. Theories abound that the club sandwich was invented at the Club House. The hearty sandwich was served to hungry clientele as a quick meal to keep them gambling at the tables.

16. Smith, *Bulls and Bears of Wall Street*, 180.

17. Gardiner, *Canfield*, 254.

18. Sasuly, *Bookies and Bettors*, 62.

19. Asbury, *Sucker's Progress*, 385.

20. Canfield was close friends with the painter James McNeill Whistler, who painted a portrait of the brooding gambler. By the end of his life, Canfield possessed the second-largest collection of Whistler's artwork in the nation. Asbury,

Sucker's Progress, 420; "R.A. Canfield Sells Whistler Pictures," *New York Times*, March 19, 1914.

21. Hotaling, *They're Off!*, 177.

22. Sasuly, *Bookies and Bettors*, 63–64.

23. Longrigg, *History of Horse Racing*, 229.

24. Parmer, *For Gold and Glory*, 113.

25. Biracree and Insinger, *Complete Book of Thoroughbred Horse Racing*, 142.

26. Longrigg, *History of Horse Racing*, 230.

27. Robertson, *History of Thoroughbred Racing*, 194.

28. Parmer, *For Gold and Glory*, 136.

29. Rosecrance, *Gambling without Guilt*, 25.

30. Schwartz, *Roll the Bones, Casino Edition*, 185–186.

31. Chafetz, *Play the Devil*, 267.

32. Bradley, *Such Was Saratoga*, 253.

33. Phil Maggitti, "The Winning Wagers of Pittsburgh Phil," *Spur*, September–October 1986, 24–25. His name is rendered as "Pittsburg Phil" in press accounts of the day.

34. Ibid., 27.

35. O'Brien, *Bad Bet*, 195.

36. Devereux, *Gambling and the Social Structure*, 436.

37. Biracree and Insinger, *Complete Book of Thoroughbred Horse Racing*, 143; and Hotaling, *They're Off!*, 158.

38. Biracree and Insinger, *Complete Book of Thoroughbred Horse Racing*, 143.

39. Robertson, *History of Thoroughbred Racing*, 196; and Parmer, *For Gold and Glory*, 170. Under pressure from racing interests, a state court in 1913 ruled that bets were permissible only if they were conducted orally. The convoluted system prevented the exchange of money or receipts at the time of the wager. By then Hughes had left the governor's mansion in Albany for a seat on the United States Supreme Court.

40. Chafetz, *Play the Devil*, 383.

41. Longrigg, *History of Horse Racing*, 230.

42. Robertson, *History of Thoroughbred Racing*, 96.

43. Winn, *Down the Stretch*, 71–72.

44. Ibid., 3.

45. For the 1949 Kentucky Derby, souvenir glasses were produced bearing a sketch of Winn and the phrase "He Has Seen Them All." The governor named Winn an honorary Kentucky colonel.

46. Biracree and Insinger, *Complete Book of Thoroughbred Horse Racing*, 144.

47. Winn, *Down the Stretch*, 70.

48. Ibid., 72–73.

49. Biracree and Insinger, *Complete Book of Thoroughbred Horse Racing*, 144.

50. Winn relentlessly promoted the Kentucky Derby and understood the importance of charming the press. He entertained out-of-town sportswriters and horse owners at his sprawling apartment at Churchill Downs and held court with influential columnists such as Damon Runyon and Grantland Rice at his off-season home at the Waldorf Astoria hotel in Manhattan.

51. Schmidt, *Win, Place, Show*, 99.

52. Rosecrance, *Gambling without Guilt*, 37.

53. Chafetz, *Play the Devil*, 376.

54. Davies and Abram, *Betting the Line*, 33.

55. Ibid., 34.

56. Ibid., 35.

57. *Gambling and Organized Crime: Hearings Before the Permanent Subcommittee on Investigations of the Committee on Government Operations, United States Senate*, 87th Cong., 1st Session (1961), 371, (testimony of former FBI Special Agent Downey Rice).

58. Cooney, *Annenbergs*, 69. Shields reported the intimidation to the FBI.

59. Ibid., 70.

60. Ibid., 69.

61. Schwartz, *Cutting the Wire*, 40; and Davies and Abram, *Betting the Line*, 37.

62. Sasuly, *Bookies and Bettors*, 114–115.

63. Cooney, *Annenbergs*, 65.

64. Sasuly, *Bookies and Bettors*, 119.

65. Schwartz, *Cutting the Wire*, 41.

66. Kefauver, *Crime in America*, 36.

67. *Report of the Special Senate Committee to Investigate Organized Crime in Interstate Commerce*, 82nd Cong., 1st Session (1951), 53.

68. Kefauver, *Crime in America*, 108.

69. Moore, *Kefauver Committee*, 94–95.

70. Kefauver, *Crime in America*, 47.

71. Interstate Wire Act of 1961, 18 U.S.C. §1084(a).

72. Interstate Transportation of Wagering Paraphernalia Act of 1961, 18 U.S.C. §1953.

73. Ernest W. Burgess, report to Governor Henry M. Horner, "The Next Step in the War on Crime—Legalize Gambling!" Chicago, 1935, 11.

74. Ibid.

75. Ibid., 12.

76. Ibid., 21.

77. Ibid., 21–22.

78. Peterson, "Gambling—Should It Be Legalized?" 298–299.

79. Ibid., 301.

80. Marx, *Gambling in America*, 175. O'Dwyer's proposal was addressed to legislative leaders in Albany on January 10, 1950.

81. Ibid.

82. Ibid., 176. Dewey's reply to O'Dwyer's proposal was issued to the legislature on January 16, 1950.

83. Ibid., 177.

84. Ibid., 179.

85. *The Case Against Legalizing and Taxing Off-Track Betting*, report by the Protestant Council of the City of New York, February 27, 1959, 5.

86. Davies and Abram, *Betting the Line*, 39.

87. Ibid.

88. Abt, Smith, and Christiansen, *Business of Risk*, 169.

89. Ibid., 171.

90. Michael Demarest, "Gambling Goes Legit," *Time*, December 6, 1976.

91. *Character of the OTB Bettor*, summary report prepared for the New York City Off-Track Betting Corporation, September 1971. Surveyors interviewed 1,100 customers at twelve OTB offices in New York City in July 1971.

92. Pat Mahony, interview with author, August 16, 2016.

93. Weinstein and Deitch, *Impact of Legalized Gambling*, 96; and Council of State Governments, *Gambling: A Source of State Revenue* (Lexington, KY: Council of State Governments, 1973), 22.

94. Mahony interview.

95. Ibid.

96. *Back in the Black: States' Gambling Revenues Rose in 2010*, Nelson A. Rockefeller Institute of Government, June 23, 2011, 18.

97. Mahony interview.

CHAPTER 2 — GOLDEN TICKET

1. Fabian, *Card Sharps*, 148.

2. *Old Aunt Dinah's Policy Dream Book*, New York, [1850?], 23.

3. Drake and Cayton, *Black Metropolis*, 475.

4. Ibid., 476.

5. Ibid., 476–477.

6. Ezell, *Fortune's Merry Wheel*, 53–54. By the start of the Revolutionary War, all colonies had had experience with lotteries. In his exhaustive work on early American lotteries, *Fortune's Merry Wheel*, historian John Samuel Ezell tallied 158 lotteries that received legal sanction in colonial America. The figure does not include

the many uncounted schemes with a "semilegal" status and private, unlicensed drawings.

7. Ministers who otherwise condemned gambling drew a distinction between lotteries that raised money for the public welfare and lotteries conducted for private purposes. Of course, churches stood to benefit from lottery proceeds, which no doubt shaped the softening attitudes.

8. Ezell, *Fortune's Merry Wheel*, 136.

9. Ibid., 140.

10. Ibid.

11. Aitken, "Yates and McIntyre," 37.

12. Ezell, *Fortune's Merry Wheel*, 123. The early 1800s are thick with examples of misbegotten lotteries. In 1811 Pennsylvania merged two canal companies into the Union Canal Company and granted it the authority to conduct a lottery to raise $340,000. Helped along by the multiplying numbers of lottery offices across the nation, the company sold twenty times more tickets than authorized. In 1832 a committee of the Pennsylvania House of Representatives reported the sale of $21,248,891 in tickets in a twenty-year period. However, the steep management fees, commissions, and payment of prizes meant that the company fell short of the amount it promised to raise. Committee of the Pennsylvania House of Representatives, *Hazard's Register of Pennsylvania* 9, no. 9 (March 3, 1832), 136.

13. New York State Assembly, *Report of the Select Committee to Whom Was Referred That Part of the Speech of His Excellency the Governor, Which Relates to Lotteries* (Albany, NY: Jesse Buel), April 6, 1819.

14. Tyson, *A Brief Survey*, 67–68.

15. Barnum, *Life of P. T. Barnum*, 75–77.

16. Ibid., 128.

17. From an advertisement for his lottery office published in the *Danbury Recorder*, April 13, 1831.

18. Kunhardt, Kunhardt, and Kunhardt, *P.T. Barnum*, 11.

19. Ezell, *Fortune's Merry Wheel*, 274.

20. *Phalen v. Virginia*, 49 U.S. 163 (1850), 168.

21. Howard and other lottery managers took great care in creating a positive public image of the company. Retired Confederate generals Jubal Early and P.G.T. Beauregard were handsomely paid to preside at the drawings to lend an air of credibility to the theatrical proceedings. Facsimiles of their signatures appeared in newspaper advertisements under a pledge that the drawings "are conducted with honesty, fairness and in good faith toward all parties." The Louisiana State Lottery Company typically paid multiple times the normal ad rate to ensure friendly press coverage. For an example of such an ad, see *Nashville Daily American*, June 27, 1885.

22. McGinty, "Louisiana Lottery Company," 337. The company spread its largesse across New Orleans as a calculated expression of goodwill. Howard family money built the church-like Confederate Memorial Hall, the company steered funds to the city to help raise levees, and lottery money flowed into churches, libraries, and other charities. However, Howard's tactics were not appreciated by the exclusive Metairie Jockey Club, which denied his membership application. When the Metairie Race Course fell into hardship, Howard purchased it, and according to local legend, turned it into a cemetery out of spite. Howard was laid to rest in an extravagant tomb at Metairie Cemetery in 1885. See Chafetz, *Play the Devil*, 302.

23. "It Is Discouraging," *Louisiana Capitolian*, May 1, 1880.

24. Estimates vary on how much money the Serpent was raking in, but a review of its financial documents offers a glimpse into its extraordinary performance. At the lottery's peak in 1889, stockholders received $3.4 million in dividends—a small portion of the company's net profits that year. A share of the company's stock jumped from $125 in 1880 to $1,350 in 1890. See Rogers, "Lottery in American History," 52.

25. Ezell, *Fortune's Merry Wheel*, 249–250.

26. Rogers, "Lottery in American History," 53.

27. McGinty, "Louisiana Lottery Company," 342.

28. Chafetz, *Play the Devil*, 306–307.

29. Bridges, *Bad Bet on the Bayou*, 12; and Ezell, *Fortune's Merry Wheel*, 251. Postmaster General John Wanamaker complained that the Louisiana State Lottery Company sent fifty thousand letters per month from its Washington office. Wanamaker noted that the lottery-related mail might be "safely counted by the ton." Each year, the company reportedly spent $120,000 on stamps to send 6 million pieces of mail. Ezell, *Fortune's Merry Wheel*, 262; and McGinty, "Louisiana Lottery Company," 341.

30. *Public Papers and Addresses of Benjamin Harrison* (Washington, DC: Government Printing Office, 1893), 166.

31. Ibid., 165.

32. McGinty, "Louisiana Lottery Company," 346. Many large newspapers circumvented this prohibition by publishing two editions, one without lottery ads and thus suitable for mailing and another edition with the ads for street sales.

33. Ezell, *Fortune's Merry Wheel*, 263–264.

34. *In re Rapier*, 143 U.S. 110 (1892).

35. McGinty, "Louisiana Lottery Company," 345.

36. Ezell, *Fortune's Merry Wheel*, 268–269.

37. *Champion v. Ames*, 188 U.S. 321 (1903).

38. Chafetz, *Play the Devil*, 298; and Sweeney, *Lottery Wars*, 41.

39. Broun and Leech, *Anthony Comstock*, 196.

40. Comstock, *Traps for the Young*, 67.

41. "Al Adams a Suicide, Following Misfortunes," *New York Times*, October 2, 1906. The unsavory aspects of Adams's character were included in his obituary.

42. Asbury, *Sucker's Progress*, 104.

43. Ibid., 101–103.

44. Chafetz, *Play the Devil*, 341.

45. Ibid., 342–343.

46. Morris, *Rise of Theodore Roosevelt*, 500.

47. Ibid., 499–500.

48. White et al., *Playing the Numbers*, 68.

49. Ibid., 66.

50. Whyte, *Street Corner Society*, 116–120.

51. Drake and Cayton, *Black Metropolis*, 482. The authors studied the numbers rackets in a neighborhood they called "Bronzeville," which was the South Side of Chicago.

52. Whyte, *Street Corner Society*, 123. Sociologist William Foote Whyte studied an Italian American slum he called "Cornerville," which was the North End of Boston.

53. Ibid., 124.

54. Ibid., 137.

55. Drake and Cayton, *Black Metropolis*, 488.

56. Ibid., 489.

57. Ibid., 493.

58. Ibid.

59. Fabian, *Card Sharps*, 142.

60. Sweeney, *Lottery Wars*, 73.

61. White et al., *Playing the Numbers*, 12–13.

62. Ibid., 18–19.

63. Ibid., 23.

64. Henry Lee Moon, "Policy Game Thrives in Spite of Attacks," *New York Times*, July 25, 1937.

65. Bender, *Tickets to Fortune*, 166.

66. Fred J. Cook, "Treasure Chest of the Underworld: Gambling, Inc.," *Nation*, October 22, 1960, 307.

67. *Gambling and Organized Crime: Hearings Before the Permanent Subcommittee on Investigations of the Committee on Government Operations, United States Senate*, 87th Cong., 1st Session (1961), 594.

68. Ibid., 595.

69. Davis, *Something for Nothing*, 48–49. The opponent of the sweepstakes was John Philip Lewis, publisher of the *Franklin (NH) Journal-Transcript*.

70. Daniel F. Ford, "Puritan Sweepstake," *New Republic*, April 25, 1964, 5.

71. 18 U.S.C. §1304.

72. Robert Cantwell, "Gambling for the Yankee Dollar," *Sports Illustrated*, March 30, 1964.

73. King, *Gambling and Organized Crime*, 160.

74. Clotfelter and Cook, *Selling Hope*, 144.

75. Ibid.

76. O'Brien, *Bad Bet*, 166.

77. National Institute of Law Enforcement and Criminal Justice and Cornell University Law School, *The Development of the Law of Gambling: 1776–1976* (Washington, DC: Government Printing Office, 1977), 612.

78. "Where Legal Gambling Doesn't Pay—Enough," *U.S. News & World Report*, August 28, 1967, 80.

79. *Law of Gambling*, 723.

80. Sweeney, *Lottery Wars*, 82.

81. "Winners and Losers," *Newsweek*, August 7, 1967, 35.

82. Sweeney, *Lottery Wars*, 82.

83. Murray Schumach, "Neighborhoods: Existing by the Numbers," *New York Times*, February 27, 1970.

84. David Burnham, "Legal 'Numbers' Urged for State to Reduce Crime," *New York Times*, November 26, 1972.

85. Sweeney, *Lottery Wars*, 83; and O'Brien, *Bad Bet*, 168.

86. "New Jersey Lottery Turns 40 with Record $2.6B in Revenue," *Newark Star-Ledger*, November 19, 2010.

87. Sweeney, *Lottery Wars*, 84.

88. *Law of Gambling*, 536.

89. O'Brien, *Bad Bet*, 168.

90. Charles Kaiser, "New York Lottery Tickets Selling Faster Than State Can Print Them," *New York Times*, September 17, 1976.

91. "8 Win Record U.S. Lottery Jackpot, $365 Million," Associated Press, February 23, 2006.

92. Tamara Lush, "Florida Lottery Winner's Hard-Luck Life," Associated Press, February 15, 2010.

93. Brent Kallestad, "84-Year-Old Florida Woman Winner of $590 Million Powerball Jackpot," Associated Press, June 5, 2013.

94. Fiscal 2012 figures from the North American Association of State and Provincial Lotteries.

95. Ron Stodghill, "Behind the Jackpot: The Lottery Industry's Own Powerball," *New York Times*, November 18, 2007.

96. Hoffer, *Jackpot Nation*, 203.

97. Dan Sweeney, John Maines, and Stephen Hobbes, "Lottery Expansion Entices Poor Families the Most," *Sun Sentinel*, August 5, 2016.

98. Sweeney, *Lottery Wars*, 85.

99. Thomas Zambito, "Lottery Killed Biz, Sez Numbers Guy," *New York Daily News*, May 24, 2006.

100. Sweeney, *Lottery Wars*, 85.

CHAPTER 3 — STATE OF PLAY

Epigraph from Land and Land, *Short History of Reno*, 43. Roberts campaigned on a pro-gambling platform and easily won reelection in 1931.

1. Skolnick, *House of Cards*, 104; and Burbank, *License to Steal*, 2.

2. McGrath, *Gunfighters*, 11–12.

3. Moody, "Nevada's Legalization," 84.

4. Ostrander, *Great Rotten Borough*, 206.

5. Skolnick, *House of Cards*, 108.

6. Land and Land, *Short History of Reno*, 43.

7. Elliott, *History of Nevada*, 281.

8. Turner, *Gamblers' Money*, 39–40.

9. Elliott, *History of Nevada*, 281–282.

10. Land and Land, *Short History of Reno*, 38–39.

11. Turner, *Gamblers' Money*, 39.

12. Elliott, *History of Nevada*, 281.

13. Evans, *They Made America*, 280.

14. Smith, *Quit Winners*, 160.

15. Ibid.

16. Kling, *Biggest Little City*, 61. Advertisement was published in the June 30, 1935, edition of the *Nevada State Journal*.

17. Smith, *Quit Winners*, 163–164.

18. Evans, *They Made America*, 281.

19. Smith, *Quit Winners*, 168.

20. Ibid., 169.

21. Lewis, *Sagebrush Casinos*, 139.

22. Kling, *Biggest Little City*, 64.

23. Smith, *Quit Winners*, 29.

24. Smith, *Quit Winners*, 29; and Lewis, *Sagebrush Casinos*, 157.

25. Ernest Havemann, "Gambler's Paradise Lost," *Life*, October 25, 1954, 67.

26. Evans, *They Made America*, 283.

27. Smith, *Quit Winners*, 215–216.

28. Kling, *Biggest Little City*, 69.

29. William F. Harrah, *Recollections of the Hotel-Casino Industry and as an Auto Collecting Enthusiast*, interview by Mary Ellen Glass, December 6, 1977, to June 7, 1978, University of Nevada Oral History Program, 24. Hereafter, Harrah interview. Quotations from this interview as well as others referenced from this oral history program are used with permission of Special Collections, University of Nevada, Reno Libraries.

30. Ibid., 25.

31. Ibid., 26.

32. Ibid., 32.

33. Incident recounted in Harrah interview, 45–47.

34. Mandel, *William Fisk Harrah*, 52.

35. Turner, *Gamblers' Money*, 124.

36. Ibid., 123.

37. Schwartz, *Roll the Bones*, 359.

38. Mandel, *William Fisk Harrah*, 105–106.

39. Most of the vehicles were sold off after Harrah's death in 1978. The remainder of his collection can be seen today as part of the National Automobile Museum in downtown Reno.

40. Mandel, *William Fisk Harrah*, 193.

41. Harrah interview, 313.

42. Hiltzik, *Colossus*, 349.

43. Elliott, *History of Nevada*, 280. See *Las Vegas Evening Review-Journal*, March 26, 1931.

44. Stocker's husband, Oscar, was a railroad worker and thus was not permitted to have his name on the license. Stocker Family Collection at the Center for Gaming Research, University of Nevada Las Vegas, box 1, folder 12.

45. Hiltzik, *Colossus*, 349.

46. Schwartz, *Roll the Bones*, 367.

47. *Las Vegas Review-Journal*, February 7, 1999.

48. Hess, *Viva Las Vegas*, 26.

49. Ibid.

50. Moehring, *Resort City*, 46.

CHAPTER 4 — MOB SCENE

Epigraph from Wiley and Gottlieb, *Empires in the Sun*, 194. The interview was conducted in early June 1947, just before his murder.

1. Wilkerson, *Man Who Invented Las Vegas*, 17–18. W. R. Wilkerson III, the author of *The Man Who Invented Las Vegas*, attempts to shed light on his father's largely

forgotten role as the Flamingo's true visionary. Wilkerson argues that his father was "the quintessential victim of myth" that gives all of the credit to Benjamin "Bugsy" Siegel. The book does not gloss over Wilkerson's faults and is especially unsparing in describing his destructive addiction to gambling.

2. Ibid., 12.

3. Ibid., 26.

4. Ibid., 39.

5. Ibid., 54.

6. Ibid., 61.

7. Burbank, *License to Steal*, 15.

8. Siegel conducted an illicit affair with actual royalty, Countess Dorothy di Frasso, an American heiress who had married an Italian count. In 1938 Siegel was visiting di Frasso's villa in Rome when he discovered that Nazi leaders Joseph Goebbels and Hermann Göring would also be there. The countess had to talk Siegel out of murdering them. See Gragg, *Bright Light City*, 56–57.

9. Eisenberg, Dan, and Landau, *Meyer Lansky*, 57.

10. Ibid., 56.

11. Lacey, *Little Man*, 30.

12. Eisenberg, Dan, and Landau, *Meyer Lansky*, 37.

13. Raab, *Five Families*, 87.

14. Okrent, *Last Call*, 273.

15. Raab, *Five Families*, 33.

16. Eisenberg, Dan, and Landau, *Meyer Lansky*, 149.

17. Lacey, *Little Man*, 108.

18. Eisenberg, Dan, and Landau, *Meyer Lansky*, 174. Details of the business arrangement between Lansky and Batista were revealed in an interview with Jewish syndicate leader Joseph "Doc" Stacher.

19. Gragg, *Bright Light City*, 43.

20. Lacey, *Little Man*, 152.

21. Ibid.

22. Ibid., 153.

23. Hess, *Viva Las Vegas*, 43.

24. Moehring, *Resort City*, 47.

25. Robbins E. Cahill, *Recollections of Work in State Politics, Government, Taxation, Gaming Control, Clark County Administration, and the Nevada Resort Administration*, interview by Mary Ellen Glass, November 1971 to August 1972, University of Nevada Oral History Program, 314. Hereafter, Cahill interview.

26. Hess, *Viva Las Vegas*, 41.

27. Ibid., 43.

28. Eisenberg, Dan, and Landau, *Meyer Lansky*, 235.

29. Ibid., 238.

30. Lacey, *Little Man*, 154.

31. Caldwell, *With All My Might*, 241.

32. Ibid., 242.

33. Eisenberg, Dan, and Landau, *Meyer Lansky*, 240.

34. Ibid., 266.

35. Barker and Britz, *Jokers Wild*, 33.

36. Smith, "Moe Dalitz and the Desert," 38.

37. Wiley and Gottlieb, *Empires in the Sun*, 195.

38. Cahill interview, 321–324.

39. Cooper, *Last Honest Place in America*, 30–31.

40. Clark to Truman, October 9, 1953. Wilbur and Toni Clark Collection, Center for Gaming Research, University of Nevada Las Vegas, 95–49, box 1, folder 4–5. Despite his penchant for private poker games, Truman was no fan of Nevada and its acceptance of legalized gambling. "I don't believe in it. Too many people have jumped out of windows because of Nevada. It is a fever. I don't mind a friendly game, but I don't go for legalized gambling," he said. See Wallace Turner, "Idaho Democrats Found Divided on Legalized Gaming for State," *New York Times*, September 30, 1962.

41. Johnson to Clark, November 1, 1956; Nixon to Clark, February 27, 1960. Wilbur and Toni Clark Collection.

42. Clark to John F. Kennedy, January 14, 1957. Ibid.

43. Jacqueline Kennedy to Clark, September 7, 1960. Ibid.

44. Cahill interview, 325.

45. McManus, *Cowboys Full*, 272.

46. Lester Ben "Benny" Binion, *Some Recollections of a Texas and Las Vegas Gaming Operator*, interview by Mary Ellen Glass, May 22–23, 1973, University of Nevada Oral History Program, 18.

47. Ibid., 9.

48. Ibid., 13.

49. Cahill interview, 317.

50. Johnston, *Temples of Chance*, 31.

51. Schwartz, *Roll the Bones, Casino Edition*, 249.

52. Alvarez, "Biggest Game in Town," 69.

53. McManus, *Cowboys Full*, 276; and Schwartz, *Roll the Bones, Casino Edition*, 250.

54. McManus, *Cowboys Full*, 276.

55. Alvarez, "Biggest Game in Town," 66.

56. McManus, *Cowboys Full*, 309.

57. Cahill interview, 111.

CHAPTER 5 — ENEMY WITHIN

Epigraph from Kefauver, *Crime in America*, 231.

1. Ibid., 15.

2. Lacey, *Little Man*, 203.

3. Raab, *Five Families*, 120.

4. Ibid., 233.

5. Burbank, *License to Steal*, 18.

6. Sergio Lalli, "A Peculiar Institution," in *The Players: The Men Who Made Las Vegas*, ed. Jack E. Sheehan (Reno: University of Nevada Press, 1997), 5.

7. Kefauver, *Crime in America*, 233; and Burbank, *License to Steal*, 19.

8. Burbank, *License to Steal*, 18.

9. *Report of the Special Senate Committee to Investigate Organized Crime in Interstate Commerce*, 82nd Cong., 1st Session (1951), 2. Hereafter, Kefauver Committee report.

10. Fontenay, *Estes Kefauver*, 180.

11. Newsreel cameras were not bound by the restriction. In a rare moment of levity, a committee member asked what good Costello had ever done as an American. He replied in a gravelly voice: "Paid my tax."

12. Gorman, *Kefauver*, 91.

13. Kefauver Committee report, 2.

14. Moore, *Kefauver Committee*, 212.

15. Ibid., 133.

16. Lacey, *Little Man*, 204–205.

17. Ibid., 205.

18. Lalli, "A Peculiar Institution," 7.

19. Glass, *Nevada's Turbulent '50s*, 34. Kefauver delivered the speech in 1956 when he was Democratic presidential nominee Adlai Stevenson's running mate.

20. Skolnick, *House of Cards*, 120.

21. Farrell and Case, *Black Book*, 4.

22. Skolnick, *House of Cards*, 123–124; and Farrell and Case, *Black Book*, 230.

23. Edward A. Olsen, *My Careers as a Journalist in Oregon, Idaho, and Nevada; in Nevada Gaming Control; and at the University of Nevada*, interview by Mary Ellen Glass, 1967 to 1969, University of Nevada Oral History Project, 93. Hereafter, Olsen interview.

24. Fred J. Cook, "Treasure Chest of the Underworld: Gambling, Inc.," *Nation*, October 22, 1960, 258.

25. Ibid., 259.

26. Thomas, *Robert Kennedy*, 82.

27. National Institute of Law Enforcement and Criminal Justice and Cornell University Law School, *The Development of the Law of Gambling: 1776–1976* (Washington, DC: Government Printing Office, 1977), 571.

28. Thomas, *Robert Kennedy*, 81.

29. Ibid.

30. Brill, *Teamsters*, 209.

31. Elliott, *History of Nevada*, 333.

32. Farrell and Case, *Black Book*, 28.

33. Quoted in Skolnick, *House of Cards*, 124.

34. Raab, *Five Families*, 153.

35. Grant Sawyer was interviewed by Gary E. Elliott for the University of Nevada Oral History Program during a nine-month period in 1991. R. T. King wrote a book narrative based on the lengthy oral history, published as *Hang Tough! Grant Sawyer: An Activist in the Governor's Mansion*, 91.

36. Alan Barth, "Lawless Lawmen," *New Republic*, July 30, 1966, 20.

37. Ibid.

38. King, *Hang Tough!*, 89.

39. Ibid., 93.

40. Thomas, *Robert Kennedy*, 256–257.

41. King, *Hang Tough!*, 92.

42. Barlett and Steele, *Howard Hughes*, 298.

43. Martin Griffith, "Sinatra's Old Tahoe Resort to Get Major Makeover," Associated Press, September 8, 2013.

44. Olsen recounted the Sinatra–Giancana incident in a memorandum dated September 4, 1963, to the Gaming Control Board. See King, *Hang Tough!*, 235.

45. Ibid., 236.

46. Ibid., 237.

47. Olsen interview, 165. Sinatra statement to the press on his withdrawal from Nevada gambling dated October 7, 1963.

48. Ibid., 166.

49. Edward F. Sherman, "Nevada: The End of the Casino Era," *Atlantic Monthly*, October 1966, 112–116.

50. Barlett and Steele, *Howard Hughes*, 291.

51. Nevada Gaming Commission report, September 1, 1966, 7.

52. Ibid., 3.

53. Skolnick, *House of Cards*, 132.

CHAPTER 6 — VEGAS, INC.

Epigraph from Gerri Hirshey, "Gambling Nation," *New York Times Magazine*, July 17, 1994.

1. Maheu and Hack, *Next to Hughes*, 4.

2. Barlett and Steele, *Howard Hughes*, 625.

3. Maheu and Hack, *Next to Hughes*, 153.

4. Barlett and Steele, *Howard Hughes*, 187.

5. Maheu and Hack, *Next to Hughes*, 155.

6. Ibid., 156.

7. Ed Koch and Mary Manning, "Greenspun, Hughes Changed Las Vegas," *Las Vegas Sun*, July 1, 2000. Earlier in his career, Greenspun worked for Bugsy Siegel as a publicist for the Flamingo.

8. Maheu and Hack, *Next to Hughes*, 158.

9. Ibid., 161.

10. Davenport and Eddy, *Hughes Papers*, 66.

11. Barlett and Steele, *Howard Hughes*, 292–293.

12. Ibid., 294.

13. Davenport and Eddy, *Hughes Papers*, 67.

14. Eisenberg, Dan, and Landau, *Meyer Lansky*, 268–269.

15. Barlett and Steele, *Howard Hughes*, 298.

16. Kenneth Auchincloss, "The Howard Hughes Puzzle," *Newsweek*, January 15, 1968, 27–30.

17. Barlett and Steele, *Howard Hughes*, 302.

18. Skolnick, *House of Cards*, 135.

19. Auchincloss, "Howard Hughes Puzzle," 27.

20. Barlett and Steele, *Howard Hughes*, 306–307.

21. Ibid., 312.

22. Ibid., 316.

23. Maheu and Hack, *Next to Hughes*, 3.

24. Barlett and Steele, *Howard Hughes*, 330; and Hughes memo to Maheu dated March 1968.

25. Ibid., 366.

26. Ibid., 367.

27. Maheu and Hack, *Next to Hughes*, 235.

28. Skolnick, *House of Cards*, 139.

29. Barlett and Steele, *Howard Hughes*, 451.

30. Turner, *Gamblers' Money*, 125.

31. Mandel, *William Fisk Harrah*, 166–167.

32. Schwartz, *Suburban Xanadu*, 39–40.

33. Keith Monroe, "The New Gambling King and the Social Scientists," *Harper's Magazine*, January 1962, 39.

34. Ibid.

35. William F. Harrah, *Recollections of the Hotel-Casino Industry and as an Auto Collecting Enthusiast*, interview by Mary Ellen Glass, December 6, 1977, to June 7, 1978, University of Nevada Oral History Program, 105.

36. Barlett and Steele, *Howard Hughes*, 309; and Hughes memo to Maheu dated February 10, 1968.

37. Skolnick, *House of Cards*, 142.

38. Ibid., 143–144.

39. Johnston, *Temples of Chance*, 42.

40. Mandel, *William Fisk Harrah*, 181.

41. Fey, *Slot Machines*, 182. As of 2016 the Las Vegas Hilton is the Westgate Las Vegas Resort & Casino and the Flamingo Hilton is the Flamingo Las Vegas, a unit of Caesars Entertainment.

42. Ibid.

43. Schwartz, *Nevada's Gaming Footprint.*

44. Schwartz, *Nevada Gaming Revenues.*

45. Brill, *Teamsters*, 210, 213.

46. Hopkins, "Jay Sarno," 98–99.

47. Thompson, *Fear and Loathing*, 46.

48. O'Brien, *Bad Bet*, 37.

49. Ibid., 38.

50. Hopkins, "Jay Sarno," 102.

51. Brill, *Teamsters*, 232.

52. Bruce Weber, "Lefty Rosenthal, Kingpin in Las Vegas, Dies at 79," *New York Times*, October 18, 2008.

53. Brill, *Teamsters*, 237.

54. Ibid., 241.

55. Lalli, "Peculiar Institution," 17.

56. Ibid., 18.

57. Commission of the Review of the National Policy Toward Gambling, *Gambling in America*, (Washington, DC: Government Printing Office, 1976), 78.

58. Elliott, *History of Nevada*, 335.

59. Ibid., 327.

60. Barlett and Steele, *Howard Hughes*, 318.

61. Torgerson, *Kerkorian*, 158–159.

62. Ibid., 160.

63. Ibid.

64. Ibid., 163.

65. Irwin Ross, "Kirk Kerkorian Doesn't Want All the Meat Off the Bone," *Fortune*, November 1969, 186.

66. Ibid., 201.

67. Ibid., 165.

68. Jonathan Kandell. "Kirk Kerkorian: Billionaire Investor in Film Studios and Casinos, Dies at 98," *New York Times*, June 16, 2015.

69. "Kerkorian's Cold Streak," *Time*, July 27, 1970, 65.

70. Ibid.

71. Torgerson, *Kerkorian*, 276.

72. Ross, "Kirk Kerkorian," 147.

73. Kerkorian remained the largest shareholder of MGM Resorts International until his death on June 15, 2015, at the age of ninety-eight.

74. Mark Seal, "Steve Wynn: King of Wow!" in *The Players: The Men Who Made Las Vegas*, ed. Jack E. Sheehan (Reno: University of Nevada Press, 1997), 175.

75. Ibid., 176.

76. TV host Merv Griffin, who always had an interest in casinos and later entered the business himself, interviewed Wynn for a *Merv Griffin Show* segment broadcast February 16, 1978. Wynn, who was then thirty-six years old, wore a Bugs Bunny sweatshirt during the interview, a surprisingly casual choice of attire for a man better known later for wearing sleek suits. Access to the video recording is courtesy of David Peck and Reelin' In The Years Productions, which represents the entire library of *The Merv Griffin Show*.

77. Schwartz, *Roll the Bones*, 482.

78. Seal, "Steve Wynn," 178.

79. Las Vegas Sands ranked at 241 and MGM Resorts International came in at 309. Caesars Entertainment and Wynn Resorts fell out of the Fortune 500 in 2016.

CHAPTER 7 — SIREN SONG

Epigraph from Bruce Springsteen, "Atlantic City," on *Nebraska*, Columbia Records, 1982.

1. Carey Winfrey, "Celebrity-Hunters, Plungers, $1 Bettors, Winners, Losers," *New York Times*, May 27, 1978.

2. Ibid.

3. Ibid.

4. Ibid.

5. James F. Clarity, "First Casino in Atlantic City Finds Gamblers Endure Initial Problems," *New York Times*, May 29, 1978.

6. James F. Clarity, "Crowds in Rest of Atlantic City Are Sparse, but Casino Is Packed," *New York Times*, May 28, 1978.

7. Mahon, *Bought the Boardwalk*, 164.

8. Clarity, "First Casino."

9. James F. Clarity, "Casino's Average $438,504 a Day," *New York Times*, June 6, 1978.

10. Donald Janson, "Casino Success Intensifies Rivalry for 2d Atlantic City Gaming Place," *New York Times*, May 30, 1978.

11. Atlantic City's permanent population soared from 13,037 in 1890 to 46,150 in 1910. Funnell, *By the Beautiful Sea*, 9.

12. Derek Harper, "80 Years Ago, the Mob Came to Atlantic City for a Little Strategic Planning," *Press of Atlantic City*, May 13, 2009. A frequently published photograph depicts Johnson escorting Capone along the Boardwalk, each wearing suits and bright smiles under the sun, but modern scholars have raised serious doubts about its authenticity.

13. "Enoch L. Johnson, Ex-Boss in Jersey," *New York Times*, December 10, 1968.

14. Johnson, *Boardwalk Empire*, 112.

15. O'Brien, *Bad Bet*, 67.

16. White, *Making of the President*, 276.

17. Funnell, *By the Beautiful Sea*, 142–143.

18. Ibid., 143. From the FBI's Uniform Crime Report released in August 1972.

19. Sternlieb and Hughes, *Atlantic City Gamble*, 37–38.

20. Ibid., 42. The poll was conducted for the New Jersey Tourism and Development Association.

21. Lehne, *Casino Policy*, 36.

22. Simon, *Boardwalk of Dreams*, 178.

23. Lehne, *Casino Policy*, 37.

24. Donald Janson, "Nongambling Casino Owner: James Morris Crosby," *New York Times*, May 29, 1978.

25. "Public Hearing Before New Jersey Assembly State Government, Federal and Interstate Relations Committee on Assembly Bill 2366 (Casino Control Act)," held December 15, 1976, in Assembly Chambers, 39.

26. Ibid., 51–52.

27. Mahon, *Bought the Boardwalk*, 136.

28. Lehne, *Casino Policy*, 128.

29. O'Brien, *Bad Bet*, 72.

30. Johnson, *Boardwalk Empire*, 202.

31. Lehne, *Casino Policy*, 92.

32. Ibid., 93.

33. Ibid., 94.

34. Byrne interviews conducted September 13, 2006, and August 11, 2009, for the Center on the American Governor at Rutgers University. Quotation used with permission from the center.

35. Janson, "Casino Success."

36. Schwartz, *Roll the Bones*, 432–433.

37. Simon, *Boardwalk of Dreams*, 185–186. Study was conducted by a Temple University law professor.

38. Johnson, *Boardwalk Empire*, 217.

39. O'Brien, *Bad Bet*, 85.

40. Johnson, *Boardwalk Empire*, 233.

41. Ibid., 234–235.

42. O'Brien, *Bad Bet*, 71.

43. Goertzel and Cosby, "Gambling on Jobs," 62.

44. Ibid.

45. Sternlieb and Hughes, *Atlantic City Gamble*, 83.

46. O'Brien, *Bad Bet*, 73.

47. Christie remarks at Margaritaville Resorts on May 23, 2013, https://www.youtube.com/watch?v=FeZIoeY6pYo.

48. Griffin, *Merv*, 144.

49. Ibid., 161.

50. Harriet Newburger, "Recent Study Examines Poverty in Atlantic City," Federal Reserve Bank of Philadelphia, http://www.philadelphiafed.org/community-development/publications/cascade/70/05_poverty-in-atlantic-city.cfm#footnotes.

51. Wayne Parry, "Atlantic City's Resorts Casino Tries Ambitious Overhaul," Associated Press, May 8, 2011.

52. David G. Schwartz, *Atlantic City Gaming Revenue: Statistics for Casino, Slot, and Table Win, 1978–2015*, Las Vegas: Center for Gaming Research, University Libraries, University of Nevada Las Vegas, 2016, http://gaming.unlv.edu/reports/ac_hist.pdf.

CHAPTER 8 — BETTING ON A BOOM

Epigraph from Jesse McKinley and Charles V. Bagli, "Albany Doubling Down as Casino Boom Fades," *New York Times*, August 10, 2014.

1. Twain, *Life on the Mississippi*, 197.

2. Saxon, *Father Mississippi*, 221.

3. Merrick, *Old Times*, 138.

4. Asbury, *French Quarter*, 200.

5. Asbury, *Sucker's Progress*, 205.

6. Chafetz, *Play the Devil*, 66.

7. Canada Bill anecdote related in Asbury, *French Quarter*, 209.

8. Hsu, *Legalized Casino Gaming*, 71.

9. Goodman, *Luck Business*, 97.

10. Terry Branstad, interview with author, October 6, 2016.

11. Ibid.

12. David Johnston, "Gamblers in Iowa Roll on the River," *Philadelphia Inquirer*, April 2, 1991.

13. O'Brien, *Bad Bet*, 110.

14. Ibid., 111. Poverty figures based on 1980 Census.

15. Nelson and Mason, *How the South Joined*, 22.

16. Ibid.

17. Goodman, *Luck Business*, 98.

18. Nelson and Mason, *How the South Joined*, 33.

19. Ibid., 22.

20. Stephanie N. Mehta, "Legalized Gambling Lifts a Depressed Town," *Fortune*, March 15, 2007.

21. Chico Harlan, "In the Deep South, an Opportunity Gamed Away," *Washington Post*, July 11, 2015.

22. Ibid.

23. Kevin McDermott, "Missouri's Casino Industry Turns 20: Is It a Winner?" *St. Louis Post-Dispatch*, May 25, 2014.

24. Ibid.

25. Holliday, *World Rushed In*, 364. Letter from William Swain to his mother and wife, dated April 15, 1850.

26. DeArment, *Knights of the Green Cloth*, 41.

27. Bennett, *Old Deadwood Days*, 139.

28. Ibid., 154–156.

29. Jensen and Blevins, *Last Gamble*, 15. South Dakota raised the betting limit to $100 and then to $1,000 in 2012 to boost revenue.

30. Ibid., 16.

31. Ibid., 90.

32. Stokowski, *Riches and Regrets*, 70.

33. Ibid., 113.

34. Von Herrmann, *Resorting to Casinos*, 44; and Jensen and Blevins, *Last Gamble*, 91.

35. Stokowski, *Riches and Regrets*, 124–125.

36. Jensen and Blevins, *Last Gamble*, 94.

37. Von Herrmann, *Resorting to Casinos*, 44.

38. Jensen and Blevins, *Last Gamble*, 191.

39. Asbury, *Sucker's Progress*, 110.

40. Bridges, *Bad Bet on the Bayou*, 7.

41. Asbury, *French Quarter*, 99–100.

42. The 1991 gubernatorial campaign in Louisiana was among the most bizarre in modern American history. Republican incumbent Buddy Roemer faced challenges from Edwards, a Democrat, and David Duke, a former grand wizard of the Ku Klux Klan running as a Republican. Roemer finished third in the open primary behind Edwards and Duke, who advanced to a runoff. Voters elected Edwards as the lesser of two evils. The race featured memorable slogans such as "Vote for the Lizard, not the Wizard" and "Vote for the Crook. It's Important."

43. Nelson and Mason, *How the South Joined*, 195.

44. Ibid., 198.

45. Bridges, *Bad Bet on the Bayou*, 219.

46. Ibid., 226.

47. Ibid., 229.

48. Eadington, "Contributions of Casino-Style Gambling," 63.

49. Casino revenue statistics from the Michigan Gaming Control Board.

50. Arthur Hirsch, "Dividing Up the Casino Winnings," *Baltimore Sun*, June 7, 2014.

51. Jonathan Starkey and Jon Offredo, "Dover Downs Casino: On the Brink," *Wilmington News Journal*, November 22, 2014.

52. Ibid.

53. Alan Johnson, "Ohio Casinos' Revenue Promises Haven't Panned Out," *Columbus Dispatch*, September 1, 2014.

54. Glenn Blain, "Resort World Casino Beats Its Own Revenue Record with $71.2 Million in March," *New York Daily News*, April 8, 2013.

55. Thomas Kaplan, "Expansion of Gambling in New York Is Approved," *New York Times*, November 5, 2013.

56. Governor Andrew Cuomo, State of the State Address, January 9, 2014, https://www.governor.ny.gov/news/transcript-governor-cuomos-2014-state-state-address.

CHAPTER 9 — RISE OF THE TRIBES

Epigraph from Duthu, *American Indians and the Law*, 117.

1. Benedict, *Without Reservation*, 32.

2. Taylor, *American Colonies*, 195.

3. Ibid.

4. Ibid., 196.

5. Fromson, *Hitting the Jackpot*, 10–13.

6. Benedict, *Without Reservation*, 64–65.

7. For a detailed look at Eliza George's tangled genealogy, see ibid., 144–149.

8. Ibid., 95.

9. Fromson, *Hitting the Jackpot*, 59–60.

10. Benedict, *Without Reservation*, 115–116.

11. Fromson, *Hitting the Jackpot*, 65–66.

12. Ronald Reagan, "Veto Message of the Mashantucket Pequot Indian Claims Settlement Act," April 5, 1983, Congressional Record.

13. Robert A. Hamilton, "Tribe's Bingo Lures Eager Crowds," *New York Times*, July 20, 1986.

14. Fromson, *Hitting the Jackpot*, 89.

15. Hamilton, "Tribe's Bingo."

16. Eisler, *Revenge of the Pequots*, 109.

17. Light and Rand, *Casino Compromise*, 29–30. The case in question was *Cherokee Nation v. Georgia*, 30 U.S. (1831).

18. Richard Nixon, "Special Message to the Congress on Indian Affairs," July 8, 1970, in Gerhard Peters and John T. Woolley, *The American Presidency Project*, http://www.presidency.ucsb.edu/ws/?pid=2573.

19. Light and Rand, *Casino Compromise*, 34.

20. Duthu, *American Indians and the Law*, 122.

21. Sandefur, "American Indian Reservations," 38–39.

22. A Gallup Poll in 1950 found that 57 percent of respondents played a game of chance in the previous year. They identified buying tickets in church or lodge raffles and playing bingo as the two most popular forms of gambling. George Gallup, "Gambling, Betting Popular with 57% in the U.S.," Public Opinion News Service, June 11, 1950.

23. Eisler, *Revenge of the Pequots*, 100.

24. Ibid.

25. See *Seminole Tribe v. Butterworth*, 658 F.2d (5th Cir. 1981).

26. Karmel, *Gambling on the American Dream*, 215; and Schwartz, *Roll the Bones*, 434–435.

27. See *California v. Cabazon Band of Mission Indians*, 480 U.S. 202. (1987).

28. Ibid.

29. Rossum, *Supreme Court and Tribal Gaming*, 139.

30. See *California v. Cabazon Band of Mission Indians*, footnote 21.

31. Rand and Light, *Indian Gaming Law and Policy*, 23.

32. Eisler, *Revenge of the Pequots*, 117.

33. Mason, *Indian Gaming*, 62.

34. Ibid.

35. Duthu, *American Indians and the Law*, 133.

36. O'Brien, *Bad Bet*, 138.

37. *Reservation-Based Gaming*, National Indian Policy Center at George Washington University, 1993. See Glen M. Feldman and O'Connor Cavanagh, "Survey of Public Opinion Regarding Indian Gaming," in ibid., 1.

38. Eisler, *Revenge of the Pequots*, 101.

39. Ibid., 102.

40. See *Seminole Tribe of Florida v. Florida*, 517 U.S. 44 (1996). The court ruled on the grounds that Congress did not have the power to strip the states of their sovereign immunity under the Eleventh Amendment.

41. Michael J. de la Merced, "Florida's Seminole Tribe Buys Hard Rock Cafes and Casinos," *New York Times*, December 8, 2006.

42. Rossum, *Supreme Court and Tribal Gaming*, 176–177.

43. Ibid., 170–171.

44. Light and Rand, *Casino Compromise*, 67.

45. Simmons, *California Tribal-State Gambling Compacts, 1999–2006*, 1.

46. Light and Rand, *Casino Compromise*, 68.

47. See *Rincon Band of Luiseno Mission Indians v. Schwarzenegger*, 602 F.3d 1019, 1026 n.8 (9th Cir. 2010), 5887. The US Supreme Court turned down the state's appeal in 2011, allowing the ruling to stand.

48. Jim Miller, "California's Share of Indian Gambling Money Dwindles," *Sacramento Bee*, September 6, 2015.

49. Ibid.

50. Jonathan Horn, "Getting Back in the Game," *San Diego Union-Tribune*, April 28, 2013.

51. Rob Hotakainen, "Tribes Push to Open Off-Reservation Casinos—and Face Stiff Resistance," McClatchy Newspapers, July 6, 2012.

52. National Indian Gaming Commission report on 2014 tribal gaming revenues, http://www.nigc.gov/images/uploads/reports/2014GGRbyGamingOperation RevenueRange.pdf

53. Ibid.

54. *2010 American Indian Population and Labor Force Report*, US Department of the Interior, Office of the Secretary Office of the Assistant Secretary—Indian Affairs, January 16, 2014, 33.

55. Ibid., 56.

56. Stephen Singer, "In a First for Indian Casinos, Revenue Has Fallen," Associated Press, March 8, 2011.

57. Benedict, *Without Reservation*, 187.

58. Fromson, *Hitting the Jackpot*, 121.

59. Benedict, *Without Reservation*, 221.

60. Fromson, *Hitting the Jackpot*, 132.

61. Benedict, *Without Reservation*, 245.

62. Fromson, *Hitting the Jackpot*, 137.

63. Benedict, *Without Reservation*, 246.

64. Kirk Johnson, "A Casino and a Crooner: They Did It Their Way; and for the Mashantucket Pequot Tribe in Connecticut, It Was a Very Good Year," *New York Times*, November 20, 1993.

65. Benedict, *Without Reservation*, 295.

66. To boost membership, the tribe waved any blood-quantum requirement. All a person had to do to join was show that he or she was related to someone listed as a Pequot on the 1900 or 1910 census. The tribe's population jumped from 194 adult members in 1990 to 383 in 1995. See Fromson, *Hitting the Jackpot*, 155; and Benedict, *Without Reservation*, 295.

67. Fromson, *Hitting the Jackpot*, 193.

68. Ibid., 244.

69. Karmel, *Gambling on the American Dream*, 222.

70. Fromson, *Hitting the Jackpot*, 203.

71. Ibid., 209–210.

72. David G. Schwartz, *Major Gaming Jurisdiction: Twelve-Year Comparison*, Las Vegas: Center for Gaming Research, University Libraries, University of Nevada Las Vegas, 2013. Tribes do not release full financial results.

73. Michael Sokolove, "Foxwoods Casino Is Fighting for Its Life," *New York Times Magazine*, March 14, 2012.

74. Matthew Sturdevant, "Foxwoods Report Details Revenue Erosion, Debt Details, Risks of Increased Competition," *Hartford Courant*, January 8, 2014.

75. Ibid.

76. *Mashantucket Pequot Gaming Enterprise Annual Report for the Fiscal Years Ending September 30, 2015, 2014 and 2013*, December 28, 2015. Accessed August 1, 2016, on Electronic Municipal Markets Access website, http://emma.msrb.org/ ES745646-ES584573-ES980439.pdf.

77. Timothy Williams, "$1 Million Each Year for All, as Long as Tribe's Luck Holds," *New York Times*, August 9, 2012.

78. Mohegan Tribal Gambling Authority news release dated July 22, 2015, http:// newsroom.mtga.com/wp-content/uploads/2015/07/FINAL-Press-Release-for -722151.pdf.

CHAPTER 10 — A TANGLED WEB

Epigraph from Oskar Garcia, "Online Gambling Fight Now About When, Who— Not If," Associated Press, January 3, 2012.

1. McManus, *Cowboys Full*, 366.

2. Ibid., 368.

3. Ibid., 285.

4. Jay Caspian King, "Online Poker's Big Winner," *New York Times Magazine*, March 25, 2011.

5. Ibid.

6. Ibid.

7. 18 U.S.C. §1084.

8. Schwartz, *Roll the Bones, Casino Edition*, 378.

9. "Shuffle Up and Deal," *Economist*, July 8, 2010.

10. Alexandra Berzon, "Poker Site Stacked Deck: U.S.," *Wall Street Journal*, September 21, 2011, 16.

11. Schwartz, *Roll the Bones, Casino Edition*, 380.

12. "Log on, Ante Up," *Economist*, July 8, 2010.

13. Text of the Unlawful Internet Gambling Enforcement Act of 2006.

14. McManus, *Cowboys Full*, 462.

15. Ibid., 458.

16. "At War with Luck," *Economist*, July 8, 2010.

17. McManus, *Cowboys Full*, 459.

18. Chris Parker, "Online Poker Kings Get Cashed Out," *Village Voice*, February 29, 2012.

19. Ibid. *Economist* cited an estimate by H2, a gambling consultant group.

20. Alexandra Berzon, "Online Poker Players Face Big Life Changes," *Wall Street Journal*, April 18, 2011.

21. Berzon, "Poker Site Stacked Deck: U.S."

22. Ibid.

23. Janet Morrissey, "Poker Inc. to Uncle Sam: Shut Up and Deal," *New York Times*, October 8, 2011.

24. Parker, "Online Poker Kings Get Cashed Out."

25. "Manhattan U.S. Attorney Announces $731 Million Settlement of Money Laundering and Forfeiture Complaint with PokerStars and Full Tilt Poker," July 31, 2012, news release on FBI website accessed August 1, 2016, https://www.fbi.gov/newyork/press-releases/2012/manhattan-u.s.-attorney-announces-731-million-settlement-of-money-laundering-and-forfeiture-complaint-with-pokerstars-and-full-tilt-poker.

26. "Ira Rubin Gets Three Years in Prison," Associated Press, July 26, 2012.

27. Leah McGrath Goodman, "How Washington Opened the Floodgates to Online Poker, Dealing Parents a Bad Hand," *Newsweek*, August 14, 2014.

28. Remko Rinkema, "Daniel 'Jungleman12' Cates: 'Online Poker Is Dying,'" iGaming.org, March 8, 2014, http://igaming.org/poker/interview/daniel-jungleman12-cates-online-poker-is-dying-/.

29. Alexandria Berzon, "Senators Push for Bill to Advance Online Poker," *Wall Street Journal*, December 5, 2012.

30. "Whether Proposals by Illinois and New York to Use the Internet and Out-of-State Transaction Processors to Sell Lottery Tickets to In-State Adults Violate the Wire Act," memorandum opinion for the assistant attorney general, criminal division, September 20, 2011, 1, http://www.antiguawto.com/wto/2011_09_2011_DOJ.pdf.

31. Goodman, "How Washington Opened the Floodgates."

32. Michael Muskal, "Nevada, Seeking a Big Jackpot, Legalizes Online Poker," *Los Angeles Times*, February 22, 2013.

33. Steve Green, "Online Poker: What You Need to Know About the Complex Industry," *VEGAS INC.*, November 19, 2012.

34. Hannah Dreier, "Online Poker Back: Legal Website Launches in Nev.," Associated Press, April 30, 2013.

35. Ibid.

36. David G. Schwartz, *United States Online Gaming*. Las Vegas: Center for Gaming Research, University Libraries, University of Nevada Las Vegas, 2015. Accessed August 1, 2016, http://gaming.unlv.edu/reports/US_online_gaming.pdf.

37. Howard Stutz, "Online Poker's Ultimate Gaming Folds After 19 Months," *Las Vegas Review-Journal*, November 14, 2014.

38. Ibid.

39. Garcia, "Online Gambling Fight."

40. New Jersey Division of Gaming Enforcement statistics.

41. Kate Zernike, "New Jersey Now Allows Gambling Via Internet," *New York Times*, November 26, 2013.

42. Adrienne Lu, "Online Gambling Revenues Fall Short," *Stateline*, June 24, 2014.

43. Green, "Online Poker."

44. Paul Merrion, "How the Illinois Lottery Is Fixing Its Online Ticket Sales Program," *Crain's Chicago Business*, September 15, 2012.

45. Celeste Bott, "Illinois Lottery Online Sales to Expire This Month," *Chicago Tribune*, March 3, 2016.

46. Moehring, *Resort City*, 123.

47. Connie Bruck, "The Brass Ring," *New Yorker*, June 30, 2008.

48. Ibid.

49. Peter Wallsten and Tom Hamburger, "Sheldon Adelson, Top 2012 Donor, Launching Campaign Against Internet Gambling," *Washington Post*, November 17, 2013.

50. Jon Ralston, "Sheldon Adelson's Internet Jihad," *Politico Magazine*, February 12, 2014.

51. Goodman, "How Washington Opened the Floodgates."

52. Kevin Freking, "Casino Execs to Make Pitch for Online Poker," Associated Press, May 11, 2011.

CHAPTER 11 — GAMES WITHOUT FRONTIERS

Epigraph from Ian Thomsen, "Weekly Countdown: Stern Open to Legalized Betting, Rule Changes," SI.com, December 11, 2009, http://www.si.com/more-sports/2009/12/11/weekly-countdown.

1. Jimmy Boyd, "How Much Is Bet on March Madness?" BoydBets.com, March 3, 2016, https://www.boydsbets.com/much-bet-march-madness/#infographic.

2. Ibid.

3. "March Madness Betting to Total $9.2 Billion This Year," American Gaming Association, March 14, 2016, https://www.americangaming.org/newsroom/press-releasess/march-madness-betting-total-92-billion-year.

4. Mike Fish, "A Life on the Line," *ESPN The Magazine*, February 16, 2015, 78.

5. Stuart Pfeifer, "Warren Buffett Offers $1 Billion For a Perfect March Madness Bracket," *Los Angeles Times*, January 21, 2014.

6. The deal is mild in comparison to Europe, where sports betting is legal in many countries. Marathon Bet and the online betting brand bwin have paid to have their names emblazoned across the jerseys of top football clubs in England and Spain. England's Premier League clubs have "official global betting" and "official social casino games" partners listed alongside their official suppliers of beer and athletic gear.

7. Ginsburg, *Fix Is In*, 5.

8. Ibid., 10.

9. Asinof, *Eight Men Out*, 11.

10. Ibid.

11. O'Brien, *Bad Bet*, 226.

12. Bill Pennington, "Whiff of Scandal," *New York Times*, May 15, 2011.

13. Lacey, *Little Man*, 48.

14. Katcher, *Big Bankroll*, 117.

15. Ginsburg, *Fix Is In*, 117–118.

16. O'Brien, *Bad Bet*, 230.

17. Asinof, *Eight Men Out*, 273.

18. F. Scott Fitzgerald, *The Great Gatsby*, New York: Scribner, 1925, 78.

19. McManus, *Cowboys Full*, 215.

20. Moldea, *Interference*, 48.

21. Ibid., 49.

22. Moldea, *Interference*, 48; and O'Brien, *Bad Bet*, 239.

23. Moldea, *Interference*, 71.

24. MacCambridge, *America's Game*, 48.

25. Ibid., 48–49.

26. Ibid., 49.

27. Maraniss, *When Pride Still Mattered*, 337.

28. MacCambridge, *America's Game*, 178–179.

29. John L. Smith, "Sportsman's Paradise," in *The Players: The Men Who Made Las Vegas*, ed. Jack E. Sheehan (Reno: University of Nevada Press, 1997), 72.

30. Ibid., 72–73.

31. Davies and Abram, *Betting the Line*, 127.

32. Ibid., 128.

33. Smith, "Sportsman's Paradise," 72–73.

34. David G. Schwartz, *Nevada Gaming Revenues: Long-Term Trends*. Las Vegas: Center for Gaming Research, University Libraries, University of Nevada Las Vegas, 2016, http://gaming.unlv.edu/reports/longterm_nvgaming.pdf.

35. Matt Youmans, "Nevada Set a Super Bowl Record Wagering Handle at $132.5 Million," *Las Vegas Review-Journal*, February 8, 2016. Total estimate based on AGA press release, "Americans to Bet $4.2 Billion on Super Bowl 50," January 27, 2016.

36. Hirsch, *Willie Mays*, 537.

37. Ibid., 536–537.

38. "The Pete Rose Inquiry: Excerpts from Report Submitted by Dowd to Commissioner Giamatti," *New York Times*, June 27, 1989. Testimony from hearing on April 5, 1989.

39. Davies and Abram, *Betting the Line*, 150–151.

40. Ginsburg, *Fix Is In*, 248–250.

41. Listings on peterose.com as of August 1, 2016.

42. "Decision of Commissioner Robert D. Manfred Jr. Concerning the Application of Rose for Removal from the Permanently Ineligible List," December 14, 2015, 3.

43. Kennedy, *Pete Rose*, 285.

44. Morse and Goss, *Governing Fortune*, 154.

45. Ibid., 155–156.

46. Schwartz, *Cutting the Wire*, 172–173. Delaware in 2009 introduced NFL "parlay" games involving betting on multiple contests with the cards available only at the state's racetrack casinos; Montana permits low-stakes fantasy sports; and Oregon eliminated sports gambling in 2007.

47. Professional and Amateur Sports Protection Act of 1992, 28 U.S.C., Ch. 178, §3701 et seq. It's called the Bradley Act after one of the law's sponsors, Sen. Bill Bradley of New Jersey, a former NBA star.

48. Ryan M. Rodenberg and L. Jon Wertheim, "Hedging Their Bets," *Sports Illustrated*, May 12, 2014, 53.

49. Ibid.

50. Schwartz, *Roll the Bones, Casino Edition*, 377.

51. Ibid., 380.

52. Unlawful Internet Gambling Enforcement Act of 2006, 31 U.S.C., Ch. 53, §5362.

53. Vindu Goel and Joe Drape, "Yahoo Will Enter Daily Fantasy Sports Market," *New York Times*, July 8, 2015.

54. Richard Sandomir, "Despite Industry Crisis, Fantasy Sports Leaders Pour On Ads," *New York Times*, October 16, 2015.

55. Brad Reagan, "A Fantasy Sports Wizard's Winning Formula," *Wall Street Journal*, June 4, 2014.

56. Ibid.

57. Joe Drape and Jacqueline Williams, "Scandal Erupts in Unregulated World of Fantasy Sports," *New York Times*, October 5, 2015.

58. Walt Bogdanich, Joe Drape, and Jacqueline Williams, "Attorney General Tells DraftKings and FanDuel to Stop Taking Bets in New York," *New York Times*, November 10, 2015.

59. "Governor Cuomo Signs Legislation to Legalize and Regulate Fantasy Sports in New York State," Office of the Governor press release, August 3, 2016, https://www.governor.ny.gov/news/governor-cuomo-signs-legislation-legalize-and-regulate-fantasy-sports-new-york-state.

60. Walt Bogdanich, James Glanz and Agustin Armendariz, "The Dark Reality of Sports Betting and Daily Fantasy Games," *New York Times*, October 16, 2015.

61. Steve Fainaru, Paula Lavigne, and David Purdum, "Betting on the Come: Leagues Strike Deal with Gambling-Related Firms," ESPN.com, January 28, 2016, http://www.espn.com/espn/otl/story/_/id/14660326/nba-nfl-mlb-nhl-striking-various-business-deals-gambling-related-firms.

62. Adam Silver, "Legalize and Regulate Sports Betting," *New York Times*, November 13, 2014.

EPILOGUE

Epigraph from Fyodor Dostoyevsky, *The Gambler and Other Stories*, trans. Constance Garnett (London: William Heinemann, 1914), 125.

1. Schüll, *Addiction by Design*, 55.

2. "Disgraced Former San Diego Mayor Maureen O'Connor: Brain Tumor Contributed to Gambling Addiction," CBS News, February 22, 2013.

3. Jennifer Medina, "San Diego Ex-Mayor Confronts $1 Billion Gambling Problem," *New York Times*, February 14, 2013.

4. Rosecrance, *Gambling Without Guilt*, 54.

5. Bergler, *Psychology of Gambling*, 240.

6. Custer and Milt, *When Luck Runs Out*, 40.

7. Rosecrance, *Gambling Without Guilt*, 111–112.

8. Keith Whyte, interview with author, August 19, 2016.

9. Joe Heim, "In Maryland, Gambling Addiction Is Growing, But Treatment Options Are Not," *Washington Post*, September 7, 2015.

10. Dr. Richard J. Rosenthal, interview with author, August 25, 2016.

11. Walt Bogdanich and Jacqueline Williams, "For Addicts, Fantasy Sites Can Lead to Ruinous Path," *New York Times*, November 22, 2015.

12. Ibid.

13. Jack Nicas and Alexandra Berzon, "States Rethink Gambling Limits," *Wall Street Journal*, December 7, 2011.

14. Stephen Singer, "Compulsive Gambling Funds Off Pace of New Casinos," Associated Press, May 4, 2013.

15. 2013 National Survey of Problem Gambling Services, 72.

16. Ibid., 79.

17. Whyte interview.

18. Rosenthal interview.

19. John Mangels, "Ohio Faces Obstacles, Conflicts in Regulating Casino Gambling," *Plain Dealer*, May 15, 2011.

20. Alan Johnson, "Ohio Casinos' Revenue Promises Haven't Panned Out," *Columbus Dispatch*, September 1, 2014.

21. Ibid.

22. Heim, "In Maryland."

23. Morse and Goss, *Governing Fortune*, 129–130.

24. Terry Branstad, interview with author, October 6, 2016.

25. Ibid.

26. Nicas and Berzon, "States Rethink Gambling Limits."

Bibliography

This list consists of books and scholarly articles consulted as research for this book. They are identified by the author's name when used as citations in the notes. Newspapers, popular magazines, interviews, and websites referenced are cited in full in the notes.

Abt, Vicki, James F. Smith, and Eugene Martin Christiansen. *The Business of Risk: Commercial Gambling in Mainstream America.* Lawrence: University Press of Kansas, 1985.

Aitken, Hugh G. J. "Yates and McIntyre: Lottery Managers." *Journal of Economic History* 13, no. 1 (Winter 1953): 36–57.

Alvarez, A. "The Biggest Game in Town." In *Literary Las Vegas: The Best Writing about America's Most Fabulous City*, edited by Mike Tronnes. New York: Henry Holt, 1995.

Asbury, Herbert. *The French Quarter: An Informal History of the New Orleans Underworld.* New York: Alfred A. Knopf, 1936. Reprint, New York: Thunder's Mouth Press, 2003.

———. *Sucker's Progress: An Informal History of Gambling in America from the Colonies to Canfield.* Dodd, Mead, 1938. Reprint, Montclair, NJ: Patterson Smith, 1969.

Asinof, Eliot. *Eight Men Out: The Black Sox and the 1919 World Series.* New York: Henry Holt, 1987. First published 1959.

Barker, Thomas, and Marjie Britz. *Jokers Wild: Legalized Gambling in the Twenty-first Century.* Westport, CT: Praeger, 2000.

Barlett, Donald L., and James B. Steele. *Howard Hughes: His Life and Madness.* New York: Norton, 1979.

Barnum, P. T. *The Life of P. T. Barnum, Written by Himself.* New York: Redfield, 1855.

Bender, Eric J. *Tickets to Fortune: The Story of Sweepstakes, Lotteries and Contests.* New York: Modern Age Books, 1938.

Benedict, Jeff. *Without Reservation: How a Controversial Indian Tribe Rose to Power and Built the World's Largest Casino*. New York: Perennial, 2001.

Benemann, William, ed. *A Year of Mud and Gold: San Francisco in Letters and Diaries, 1849–50*. Lincoln: University of Nebraska Press, 1999.

Bennett, Estelline. *Old Deadwood Days*. New York: Charles Scribner's Sons, 1935.

Bergler, Edmund. *The Psychology of Gambling*. New York: Hill and Wang, 1957.

Binkley, Christina. *Winner Takes All: Steve Wynn, Kirk Kerkorian, Gary Loveman, and the Race to Own Las Vegas*. New York: Hyperion, 2008.

Biracree, Tom, and Wendy Insinger. *The Complete Book of Thoroughbred Horse Racing*. Garden City, NY: Dolphin Books, 1982.

Bobbitt, Randy. *Lottery Wars: Case Studies in Bible Belt Politics, 1986–2005*. Lanham, MD: Lexington Books, 2007.

Borg, Mary O., Paul M. Mason, and Stephen L. Shapiro. *The Economic Consequences of State Lotteries*. Westport, CT: Praeger, 1991.

Bouyea, Brien. "Saratoga's Longest Shot." In *Official Guide to the National Museum of Racing and Hall of Fame, 2013–14 edition*. Saratoga Springs, NY: National Museum of Racing and Hall of Fame, 2014.

Bradley, Hugh. *Such Was Saratoga*. New York: Doubleday, Doran, 1940.

Breen, T. H. "Horses and Gentlemen: The Cultural Significance of Gambling among the Gentry of Virginia." *William & Mary Quarterly* 34, no. 2 (April 1977): 239–257.

Bridges, Tyler. *Bad Bet on the Bayou: The Rise of Gambling in Louisiana and the Fall of Governor Edwin Edwards*. New York: Farrar, Straus and Giroux, 2001.

Brill, Steven. *The Teamsters*. New York: Simon and Schuster, 1978.

Broun, Heywood, and Margaret Leech. *Anthony Comstock, Roundsman of the Lord*. New York: Literary Guild of America, 1927.

Burbank, Jeff. *License to Steal: Nevada's Gaming Control System in the Megaresort Age*. Reno: University of Nevada Press, 2000.

Caldwell, Erskine. *With All My Might*. Atlanta: Peachtree Publishers, 1987.

Cattelino, Jessica R. *High Stakes: Florida Seminole Gaming and Sovereignty*. Durham, NC: Duke University Press, 2008.

Chafetz, Henry. *Play the Devil: A History of Gambling in the United States from 1492 to 1955*. New York: Bonanza Books, 1960.

Christiansen, Eugene M., and Michael D. Shagan. "The New York Off-Track Betting Law: An Exercise in Selective Decriminalization." *Connecticut Law Review* 12, no. 4 (Summer 1980): 854–869.

Clotfelter, Charles T., and Philip J. Cook. *Selling Hope: State Lotteries in America*. Cambridge, MA: Harvard University Press, 1989.

Collins, Peter. *Gambling and the Public Interest*. Westport, CT: Praeger, 2003.

Comstock, Anthony. *Traps for the Young*. New York: Funk & Wagnalls, 1883. Reprint, Robert Bremner, ed. Cambridge, MA: Belknap Press of Harvard University Press, 1967.

Cook, Kevin. *Titanic Thompson: The Man Who Bet on Everything*. New York: W. W. Norton, 2011.

Cooney, John. *The Annenbergs*. New York: Simon and Schuster, 1982.

Cooper, Marc. *The Last Honest Place in America: Paradise and Perdition in the New Las Vegas*. New York: Nation Books, 2004.

Cressley, Donald R. *Theft of the Nation: The Structure and Operations of Organized Crime in America*. New York: Harper and Row, 1969.

Custer, Robert, and Harry Milt. *When Luck Runs Out*. New York: Facts on File Publications, 1985.

Dasgupta, Anisha S. "Public Finance and the Fortunes of the Early American Lottery." *Quinnipiac Law Review* 24, no. 2 (2006): 227–264.

Davenport, Elaine, and Paul Eddy. *The Hughes Papers*, with Hark Hurwitz. London: Andre Deutsch, 1977.

Davies, Richard O., and Richard G. Abram. *Betting the Line: Sports Wagering in American Life*. Columbus: Ohio State University Press, 2001.

Davis, Clyde Brion. *Something for Nothing*. Philadelphia: J. B. Lippincott, 1956.

DeArment, Robert K. *Knights of the Green Cloth: The Saga of the Frontier Gamblers*. Norman: University of Oklahoma Press, 1982.

Demaris, Ovid. *The Boardwalk Jungle*. New York: Bantam Books, 1986.

Denton, Sally, and Roger Morris. *The Money and the Power: The Making of Las Vegas and Its Hold on America, 1947–2000*. New York: Knopf, 2001.

Devereux, Edward C., Jr. *Gambling and the Social Structure: A Sociological Study of Lotteries and Horse Racing in Contemporary America*. New York: Arno Press, 1980. Originally presented as a doctoral dissertation at Harvard University, 1949.

Drake, St. Clair, and Horace R. Cayton. *Black Metropolis: A Study of Negro Life in a Northern City*. New York: Harcourt, Brace, 1945.

Duthu, N. Bruce. *American Indians and the Law*. New York: Penguin Books, 2009.

Eadington, William R., ed. "Contributions of Casino-Style Gambling to Local Economies." *Annals of the American Academy of Political and Social Science* 556 (March 1998): 53–65.

———. "The Economics of Casino Gambling." *Journal of Economic Perspectives* 13, no. 3 (Summer 1999): 173–192.

———. *Gambling and Society: Interdisciplinary Studies on the Subject of Gambling*. Springfield, IL: Charles C. Thomas, 1976.

Eisenberg, Dennis, Uri Dan, and Eli Landau. *Meyer Lansky: Mogul of the Mob*. New York: Paddington Press, 1979.

Eisinger, Peter K. *The Rise of the Entrepreneurial State: State and Local Economic Development Policy in the United States*. Madison: University of Wisconsin Press, 1988.

Eisler, Kim Isaac. *Revenge of the Pequots: How a Small Native American Tribe Created the World's Most Profitable Casino*. New York: Simon and Schuster, 2001.

Elliott, Russell R. *History of Nevada*. Lincoln: University of Nebraska Press, 1987.

Evans, Harold. *They Made America: Two Centuries of Innovators from the Steam Engine to the Search Engine*. New York: Little, Brown, 2004.

Ezell, John Samuel. *Fortune's Merry Wheel: The Lottery in America*. Cambridge, MA: Harvard University Press, 1960.

Fabian, Ann. *Card Sharps, Dream Books & Bucket Shops: Gambling in 19th-Century America*. Ithaca, NY: Cornell University Press, 1990.

Farrar, Edgar Howard. "The Louisiana Lottery: Its History." *Charities Review: A Journal of Practical Sociology* 1, no. 4 (February 1892): 143–151.

Farrell, Ronald A., and Carole Case. *The Black Book and the Mob: The Untold Story of the Control of Nevada's Casinos*. Madison: University of Wisconsin Press, 1995.

Fey, Marshall. *Slot Machines: An Illustrated History of America's Most Popular Coin-Operated Gaming Device*. Las Vegas: Nevada Publications, 1983.

Findlay, John M. *People of Chance: Gambling in American Society from Jamestown to Las Vegas*. New York: Oxford University Press, 1986.

Fischer, Steve. *When the Mob Ran Vegas: Stories of Money, Mayhem and Murder*. New York: MJF Books, 2007.

Fitzgerald, F. Scott. *The Great Gatsby*. New York: Scribner, 1925.

Fontenay, Charles L. *Estes Kefauver: A Biography*. Knoxville: University of Tennessee Press, 1980.

Fromson, Brett D. *Hitting the Jackpot: The Inside Story of the Richest Indian Tribe in History*. New York: Grove Press, 2003.

Funnell, Charles E. *By the Beautiful Sea: The Rise and High Times of That Great American Resort, Atlantic City*. New Brunswick, NJ: Rutgers University Press, 1983.

Gardiner, Alexander. *Canfield: The True Story of the Greatest Gambler*. Garden City, NY: Doubleday, Doran, 1930.

Ginsburg, Daniel E. *The Fix Is In: A History of Baseball Gambling and Game Fixing Scandals*. Jefferson, NC: McFarland, 1995.

Glass, Mary Ellen. *Nevada's Turbulent '50s: Decade of Political and Economic Change*. Reno: University of Nevada Press, 1981.

Goertzel, Ted G., and John W. Cosby. "Gambling on Jobs and Welfare in Atlantic City." *Society* 34, no. 4 (May/June 1997): 62–66.

Goodman, Robert. *The Luck Business: The Devastating Consequences and Broken Promises of America's Gambling Explosion*. New York: Free Press, 1995.

Gorman, Joseph Bruce. *Kefauver: A Political Biography*. New York: Oxford University Press, 1971.

Gragg, Larry. *Bright Light City: Las Vegas in Popular Culture*. Lawrence: University Press of Kansas, 2013.

Griffin, Merv. *Merv: Making the Good Life Last*. New York: Pocket Books, 2007.

Grinols, Earl L. *Gambling in America: Costs and Benefits*. New York: Cambridge University Press, 2004.

Halberstam, David. *The Fifties*. New York: Villard Books, 1993.

Haller, Mark H. "The Changing Structure of American Gambling in the Twentieth Century." *Journal of Social Issues* 35, no. 3 (Summer 1979): 87–114.

Hansen, Kenneth N., and Tracy A. Skopek, eds. *The New Politics of Indian Gaming: The Rise of Reservation Interest Groups*. Reno: University of Nevada Press, 2011.

Hauptman, Laurence M., and James D. Wherry, eds. *The Pequots in Southern New England: The Fall and Rise of an American Indian Nation*. Norman: University of Oklahoma Press, 1990.

Herman, Robert D., ed. *Gambling*. New York: Harper and Row, 1967.

———. *Gamblers and Gambling: Motives, Institutions and Controls*. Lexington, MA: Lexington Books, 1976.

Hess, Alan. *Viva Las Vegas: After-Hours Architecture*. San Francisco: Chronicle Books, 1993.

Hiltzik, Michael. *Colossus: Hoover Dam and the Making of the American Century*. New York: Free Press, 2010.

Hirsch, James S. *Willie Mays: The Life, The Legend*. New York, Scribner, 2010.

Hoffer, Richard. *Jackpot Nation: Rambling and Gambling Across Our Landscape of Luck*. New York: HarperCollins, 2007.

Holliday, J. S. *Rush for Riches: Gold Fever and the Making of California*. Berkeley: Oakland Museum of California and the University of California Press. 1999.

———. *The World Rushed In: The California Gold Rush Experience*. New York: Simon and Schuster, 1981.

Hopkins, A. D. "Jay Sarno: He Came to Play." In *The Players: The Men Who Made Las Vegas*, edited by Jack E. Sheehan. Reno: University of Nevada Press, 1997.

Hotaling, Edward. *They're Off! Horse Racing at Saratoga*. Syracuse, NY: Syracuse University Press, 1995.

Hsu, Cathy H.C., ed. *Legalized Casino Gaming in the United States: The Economic and Social Impact*. New York: Haworth Hospitality Press, 1999.

Hulse, James W. *The Nevada Adventure: A History*. Reno: University of Nevada Press, 1990.

Jensen, Katherine, and Audie Blevins. *The Last Gamble: Betting on the Future in Four Rocky Mountain Mining Towns*. Tucson: University of Arizona Press, 1998.

Johnson, Nelson. *Boardwalk Empire: The Birth, High Times, and Corruption of Atlantic City*. Medford, NJ: Plexus, 2002.

Johnston, David. *Temples of Chance: How America Inc. Bought Out Murder Inc. to Win Control of the Casino Business*. New York: Doubleday, 1992.

Karmel, James R. *Gambling on the American Dream: Atlantic City and the Casino Era*. London: Pickering and Chatto, 2007.

Katcher, Leo. *The Big Bankroll: The Life and Times of Arnold Rothstein*. New York: Harper and Brothers, 1959.

Kefauver, Estes. *Crime in America*. Garden City, NY: Doubleday, 1951.

Kennedy, Kostya. *Pete Rose: An American Dilemma*. New York: Sports Illustrated Books, 2014.

Kennedy, Robert F. *The Enemy Within*. New York: Harper and Brothers, 1960.

King, R. T. *Hang Tough! Grant Sawyer: An Activist in the Governor's Mansion*. Reno: University of Nevada Oral History Program, 1993.

King, Rufus. *Gambling and Organized Crime*. Washington, DC: Public Affairs Press, 1969.

Kling, Dwayne. *The Rise of the Biggest Little City: An Encyclopedic History of Reno Gaming, 1931–1981*. Reno: University of Nevada Press, 2000.

Kunhardt Jr., Philip B., Philip B. Kunhardt III, and Peter W. Kunhardt. *P.T. Barnum: America's Greatest Showman*. New York: Alfred A. Knopf, 1995.

Lacey, Robert. *Little Man: Meyer Lansky and the Gangster Life*. Boston: Little, Brown, 1991.

Lalli, Sergio. "A Peculiar Institution." In *The Players: The Men Who Made Las Vegas*, edited by Jack E. Sheehan. Reno: University of Nevada Press, 1997.

Land, Barbara, and Myrick Land. *A Short History of Las Vegas*. Las Vegas: University of Nevada Press, 2004.

———. *A Short History of Reno*. Las Vegas: University of Nevada Press, 1995.

Lane, Ambrose I., Sr. *Return of the Buffalo: The Story Behind America's Indian Gaming Explosion*. Westport, CT: Bergin and Garvey, 1995.

Lears, Jackson. *Something for Nothing: Luck in America*. New York: Viking, 2003.

Lehne, Richard. *Casino Policy*. New Brunswick, NJ: Rutgers University Press, 1986.

Lewis, Oscar. *Sagebrush Casinos: The Story of Legal Gambling in Nevada*. Garden City, NY: Doubleday, 1953.

Light, Steven Andrew, and Kathryn R. L. Rand. *Indian Gaming & Tribal Sovereignty: The Casino Compromise*. Lawrence: University Press of Kansas, 2005.

Longrigg, Roger. *The History of Horse Racing*. London: Macmillan, 1972.

Longstreet, Stephen. *Win or Lose: A Social History of Gambling in America*. Indianapolis: Bobbs-Merrill Company, 1977.

MacCambridge, Michael. *America's Game: The Epic Story of How Pro Football Captured a Nation.* New York: Anchor Books, 2005.

Maheu, Robert, and Richard Hack. *Next to Hughes: Behind the Power and Tragic Downfall of Howard Hughes by His Closest Adviser.* New York: HarperCollins, 1992.

Mahon, Gigi. *The Company That Bought the Boardwalk: A Reporter's Story of How Resorts International Came to Atlantic City.* New York: Random House, 1980.

Mandel, Leon. *William Fisk Harrah: The Life and Times of a Gambling Magnate.* Garden City, NY: Doubleday, 1982.

Maraniss, David. *When Pride Still Mattered: A Life of Vince Lombardi.* New York: Simon and Schuster, 1999.

Martinéz, Andres. *24/7: Living It Up and Doubling Down in the New Las Vegas.* New York: Villard, 1999.

Marx, Herbert L., Jr., ed. *Gambling in America.* New York: H. W. Wilson, 1952.

Mason, John Lyman, and Michael Nelson. *Governing Gambling.* New York: Century Foundation Press, 2001.

Mason, W. Dale. *Indian Gaming: Trial Sovereignty and American Politics.* Norman: University of Oklahoma Press, 2000.

McGinty, G.W. "The Louisiana Lottery Company." *Southwestern Social Science Quarterly* 20, no. 4 (March 1940): 329–348.

McGowan, Richard. *Government and the Transformation of the Gaming Industry.* Northampton, MA: Edward Elgar, 2001.

———. *State Lotteries and Legalized Gambling: Painless Revenue or Painful Mirage?* Westport, CT: Praeger, 1994.

McGrath, Roger D. *Gunfighters, Highwaymen & Vigilantes: Violence on the Frontier.* Berkeley: University of California Press, 1984.

McManus, James. *Cowboys Full: The Story of Poker.* New York: Picador, 2009.

Merrick, George Byron. *Old Times on the Upper Mississippi: Recollections of a Steamboat Pilot from 1854 to 1863.* Cleveland: Arthur H. Clark, 1909. Reprint, Minneapolis: University of Minnesota Press, 2001.

Moehring, Eugene P. *Resort City in the Sunbelt: Las Vegas, 1930–2000.* Reno: University of Nevada Press, 2000.

Moldea, Dan E. *Interference: How Organized Crime Influences Professional Football.* New York: William Morrow, 1989.

Moody, Eric N. "Nevada's Legalization of Casino Gambling in 1931: Purely a Business Proposition." *Nevada Historical Society Quarterly*, Summer 1994, 79–100.

Moore, William Howard. *The Kefauver Committee and the Politics of Crime, 1950–1952.* Columbia: University of Missouri Press, 1974.

Morris, Edmund. *The Rise of Theodore Roosevelt.* New York: Modern Library, 1979.

Morse, Edward A., and Ernest P. Goss. *Governing Fortune: Casino Gambling in America*. Ann Arbor: University of Michigan Press, 2007.

Mullis, Angela, and David Kamper, eds. *Indian Gaming: Who Wins?* Los Angeles: UCLA American Indian Studies Center, 2001.

Nelson, Michael, and John Lyman Mason. *How the South Joined the Gambling Nation: The Politics of State Policy Innovation*. Baton Rouge: Louisiana State University Press, 2007.

Nibert, David. *Hitting the Lottery Jackpot: State Governments and the Taxing of Dreams*. New York: Monthly Review Press, 2000.

O'Brien, Timothy L. *Bad Bet: The Inside Story of the Glamour, Glitz, and Danger of America's Gambling Industry*. New York: Times Business, 1998.

Okrent, Daniel. *Last Call: The Rise and Fall of Prohibition*. New York: Scribner, 2010.

Ostrander, Gilman M. *Nevada: The Great Rotten Borough, 1859–1964*. New York: Alfred A. Knopf, 1966.

Patterson, Benton Rain. *The Great American Steamboat Race: The Natchez and the Robert E. Lee and the Climax of an Era*. Jefferson, NC: McFarland, 2009.

Parmer, Charles B. *For Gold and Glory: The Story of Thoroughbred Racing in America*. New York: Carrick and Evans, 1939.

Peterson, Virgil W. "Gambling—Should It Be Legalized?" *Journal of Criminal Law and Criminology* 40, no. 3 (September–October 1949): 259–329.

Phelan, James. *Howard Hughes: The Hidden Years*. New York: Random House, 1976.

Pierce, Patrick A., and Donald E. Miller. *Gambling Politics: State Government and the Business of Betting*. Boulder, CO: Lynne Rienner, 2004.

Raab, Selwyn. *Five Families: The Rise, Decline, and Resurgence of America's Most Powerful Mafia Empires*. New York: Thomas Dunne Books, 2005.

Rader, Benjamin G. *American Sports: From the Folk Games to the Age of Televised Sports*. Upper Saddle River, NJ: Prentice Hall, 2004.

Rand, Kathryn R. L., and Steven Andrew Light. *Indian Gaming Law and Policy*. Durham, NC: Carolina Academic Press, 2006.

Reid, Ed, and Ovid Demaris. *The Green Felt Jungle*. New York: Trident Press, 1963.

Robertson, William H. P. *A History of Thoroughbred Racing in America*. Englewood Cliffs, NJ: Prentice-Hall, 1964.

Roemer, William F., Jr. *War of the Godfathers: The Bloody Confrontation Between the Chicago and New York Families for Control of Las Vegas*. New York: Donald I. Fine, 1990.

Rogers, Howard O. "The Lottery in American History." *Americana Illustrated* 13, no. 1 (January 1919): 40–54.

Rose, I. Nelson. *Gambling and the Law*. Hollywood, CA: Gambling Times, 1986.

Rosecrance, John. *Gambling without Guilt: The Legitimation of an American Pastime*. Pacific Grove, CA: Brooks/Cole, 1988.

Rossum, Ralph A. *The Supreme Court and Tribal Gaming: California v. Cabazon Band of Mission Indians*. Lawrence: University Press of Kansas, 2011.

Sandefur, Gary D. "American Indian Reservations: The First Underclass Areas?" *Focus* 12, no. 1 (1989): 37–41.

Sasuly, Richard. *Bookies and Bettors: Two Hundred Years of Gambling*. New York: Holt, Rinehart and Winston, 1982.

Saxon, Lyle. *Father Mississippi*. New York: Century, 1927.

Scarne, John. *Scarne's New Complete Guide to Gambling*. New York: Simon and Schuster, 1974.

Schatzberg, Rufus. *Black Organized Crime in Harlem: 1920–1930*. New York: Garland, 1993.

Schmidt, John C. *Win, Place, Show: A Biography of Harry Straus: The Man Who Gave America the Tote*. Baltimore: G.W.C. Whiting School of Engineering, Johns Hopkins University, 1989.

Schüll, Natasha Dow. *Addiction by Design: Machine Gambling in Las Vegas*. Princeton, NJ: Princeton University Press, 2012.

Schwartz, David G. *Cutting the Wire: Gambling Prohibition and the Internet*. Reno: University of Nevada Press, 2005.

———. *Nevada's Gaming Footprint, 1963–2014: Total Licenses, Games, Tables, and Slots*. Las Vegas: Center for Gaming Research, University Libraries, University of Nevada Las Vegas, 2015.

———. *Nevada Gaming Revenues 1984–2014: Calendar Year Results for Selected Reporting Areas*. Las Vegas: Center for Gaming Research, University Libraries, University of Nevada Las Vegas, 2015.

———. *Roll the Bones: The History of Gambling*. New York: Gotham, 2006.

———. *Roll the Bones: The History of Gambling, Casino Edition*. Las Vegas: Winchester Books, 2013.

———. *Suburban Xanadu: The Casino Resort on the Las Vegas Strip and Beyond*. New York: Routledge, 2003.

Sheehan, Jack E., ed. *The Players: The Men Who Made Las Vegas*. Reno: University of Nevada Press, 1997.

Simmons, Charlene Wear. *California Tribal-State Gambling Compacts, 1999–2006* (Sacramento: California State Library, California Research Bureau, February 2007).

Simon, Bryant. *Boardwalk of Dreams: Atlantic City and the Fate of Urban America*. New York: Oxford University Press, 2004.

Skolnick, Jerome H. *House of Cards: The Legalization and Control of Casino Gambling*. Boston: Little, Brown, 1978.

Skolnik, Ben. *High Stakes: The Rising Cost of America's Gambling Addiction*. Boston: Beacon Press, 2011.

Smith, Harold S., Sr. *I Want to Quit Winners*, with John Wesley Noble. Englewood Cliffs, NJ: Prentice-Hall, 1961.

Smith, John L. "Moe Dalitz and the Desert." In *The Players: The Men Who Made Las Vegas*, edited by Jack E. Sheehan. Reno: University of Nevada Press, 1997.

———. *Sharks in the Desert: The Founding Fathers and Current Kings of Las Vegas*. Fort Lee, NJ: Barricade Books, 2005.

Smith, Matthew Hale. *Twenty Years Among the Bulls and Bears of Wall Street*. Hartford, CT: J. B. Burr, 1871.

Sternlieb, George, and James W. Hughes. *The Atlantic City Gamble*. Cambridge, MA: Harvard University Press, 1983.

Stiles, T. J. *The First Tycoon: The Epic Life of Cornelius Vanderbilt*. New York: Alfred A. Knopf, 2009.

Stokowski, Patricia A. *Riches and Regrets: Betting on Gambling in Two Colorado Mountain Towns*. Niwot, CO: University Press of Colorado, 1996.

Sullivan, George. *By Chance a Winner: The History of Lotteries*. New York: Dodd, Mead, 1972.

Sweeney, Matthew. *The Lottery Wars: Long Odds, Fast Money, and the Battle Over an American Institution*. New York: Bloomsbury, 2009.

Taylor, Alan. *American Colonies*. New York: Viking, 2001.

Thomas, Evan. *Robert Kennedy: His Life*. New York: Simon and Schuster, 2000.

Thompson, Hunter S. *Fear and Loathing in Las Vegas: A Savage Journey to the Heart of the American Dream*. New York: Vintage Books, 1972, 1998.

Thompson, William N. *Gambling in America: An Encyclopedia of History, Issues, and Society*. Santa Barbara: ABC-CLIO, 2001.

———. *Legalized Gambling*. Santa Barbara: ABC-CLIO, 1997.

Torgerson, Dial. *Kerkorian: An American Success Story*. New York: Dial Press, 1974.

Tronnes, Mike, ed. *Literary Las Vegas: The Best Writing About America's Most Fabulous City*. New York: Henry Holt, 1995.

Turner, Wallace. *Gamblers' Money: The New Force in American Life*. Boston: Houghton Mifflin, 1965.

Twain, Mark. *Life on the Mississippi*. Boston: James R. Osgood, 1883.

Tyson, Job R. *A Brief Survey of the Great Extent and Evil Tendencies of the Lottery System as Existing in the United States*. Philadelphia: William Brown, 1833.

Valley, David J., with Diana Lindsay. *Jackpot Trail: Indian Gaming in Southern California*. San Diego: Sunbelt Publications, 2003.

Venturi, Robert, and Denise Scott Brown and Steven Izenour. *Learning from Las Vegas*. Cambridge, MA: MIT Press, 1972.

Von Herrmann, Denise. *The Big Gamble: The Politics of Lottery and Casino Expansion*. Westport, CT: Praeger, 2002.

———, ed. *Resorting to Casinos: The Mississippi Gambling Industry*. Jackson: University Press of Mississippi, 2006.

Weeks, Lyman Horace, ed. *The American Turf: An Historical Account of Racing in the United States*. New York: Historical Company, 1898.

Weinstein, David, and Lillian Deitch. *The Impact of Legalized Gambling: The Socioeconomic Consequences of Lotteries and Off-Track Betting*. New York: Praeger, 1974.

Wiley, Peter, and Robert Gottlieb. *Empires in the Sun: The Rise of the New American West*. New York: G.P. Putnam's Sons, 1982.

Wilkerson, W. R., III. *The Man Who Invented Las Vegas*. Ciro's Books, 2000.

Winn, Matt J. *Down the Stretch: The Story of Colonel Matt J. Winn as told to Frank G. Menke*. New York: Smith and Durrell, 1945.

White, Shane, and Stephen Garton, Stephen Robinson, Graham White. *Playing the Numbers: Gambling in Harlem Between the Wars*. Cambridge, MA: Harvard University Press, 2010.

White, Theodore H. *The Making of the President—1964*. New York: Atheneum Publishers, 1965.

Whyte, William Foote. *Street Corner Society: The Social Structure of an Italian Slum*. Chicago: University of Chicago Press, 1981.

Wolfe, Tom. *The Kandy-Kolored Tangerine-Flake Streamline Baby*. New York: Bantam Books, 1999.

Index

About the Author

DAVID CLARY is a news editor at the *San Diego Union-Tribune* and has been a journalist for more than twenty years. He previously worked at the *Plain Dealer* in Cleveland and is a graduate of Syracuse University. This is his first book.